Soul of a Lifter

Author: Gino Arcaro
email: gino@ginoarcaro.com
Website: www.ginoarcaro.com

Copyright © Jordan Publications Inc. 2014

Jordan Publications Inc.
Canada

Editor: Janice Augustine
Cover Design: Shelley Palomba
Design: Jessica Ingram
Design Consultant: Luciana Millone
Logistics Manager: Jordan Mammoliti
Technical Support: Leeann King

Arcaro, Gino, 1957
ISBN 978-1-927851-06-7
http://www.ginoarcaro.com
Printed in Canada

SOUL OF A LIFTER

∞

Forward ... and Backward

Here's what this book is about ... and is not about.

This book is about how odds were beaten. It's a theory about what happens when you listen to your soul and when you don't. I believe that our soul is our connection to our physical, intellectual, emotional and spiritual health – potential, and destiny. We have the choice of strengthening our soul or killing it.

This book is a personal philosophy – developed through insights and lessons learned from countless connections with remarkable people.

This book is about addictions.

First and foremost, I am addicted to working out. One of the worst workout addictions in the history of wo/mankind. A seven-day iron-sweat-and-pain addict. I can't take one day off without heavy withdrawal symptoms.

Every morsel of food I eat has one purpose – the next workout. Every song on my iPod has one purpose – how it affects my next set. When I go out of town, the first priority is Googling "gyms." Where is the nearest 24-hour gym? Does it have enough free weights? Does it have heavy bags and speed bags? And where can I run? How can I eat enough protein? Packing priorities – workout clothes, iPod and charger. My addiction led to starting a business – a 24-hour gym. X Fitness Welland Inc.

I am addicted to not talking about anything related to working out. And addicted to ensuring no one confuses me with a bodybuilder, powerlifter or anyone remotely associated with the fitness industry. Example. X Fitness recently sponsored a bodybuilder. The gym manager convinced me to attend the contest – a daughter knows how to manipulate her father. After sitting only minutes in the deepest, darkest recess of the auditorium, I left through a side entrance to avoid talking about biceps, pecs and posing. The question, *"How do you build your arms?"* has the same appeal to me as bee-stings and viewing autopsies.

I am addicted to coaching football. Sometimes two teams per year – unpaid. Spring/Summer. Then Fall – just in case the withdrawal symptoms threaten to get out of control. During football season, I forget which body parts I've washed during my shower. Water on, water off, on, off, on, off. Did I shampoo? Did I rinse? Back out of the driveway, stop the car, run back in the house to brush my teeth and gargle because trying to diagram pass plays in my head knocked out any memory of whether I took care of basic personal hygiene.

The addiction teams up with other addictions – addiction to being unconventional and the addiction for more and more challenges – like how to personally fund Canada's only collegiate-level football team that plays in the United States. A match up that is the equivalent of David meeting Goliath without five smooth stones. Getting pounded by Goliath over and over until David makes a choice – flee ... or find bigger stones.

I am addicted to avoiding any conversation whatsoever about professional football. *"Saints or Colts?"* is the verbal equivalent of fingernails on a chalkboard. *"Do you want Bills tickets?"* another classic, is like getting punched in the gut during a panic attack. Talk radio debating the virtues of a four-three defense feels like a jackhammer attacking my mind.

I was addicted to policing. First I was a street addict – addicted to uniform patrol. Then like a vampire, addicted to midnight shifts because that's when the "big" stuff happens. Any call that didn't start with "9-1-1" was an emotional letdown. Only the heavy calls were a quick fix – disturbance, domestic violence, death. Destruction out of my district was an outrage. Not because of senseless pain and suffering ... only because I couldn't be there. Addicted to "backing-up" ... having to be there. Addicted to going-in-first. Getting shit from the platoon boss for crossing districts was worth it – conflict mismanagement. When a major crime happened while I was off-duty – inconsolable. The audacity of criminals killing and hurting people when I wasn't working! Day shift brought on darkness.

Minor fender bender – no injuries, was a direct insult. If weapons weren't involved – frustration.

Addicted to being on the SWAT team. White-knuckle anticipation. Fingers tightly crossed hoping that some mad gunman would take hostages while I was working. Finally, addicted to being a detective. Addicted to getting informants – not just a few, a network bigger than Facebook. And not just the local degenerates. The big-leaguers. The most information, the craziest informants, and the best information. *"I know who stole a car stereo,"* was like offering coffee to an alcoholic – no buzz, small stuff ... not a big enough fix. Severely addicted to getting confessions – from anyone. Friends, family ... didn't matter. Any confession was a quick fix. *"Bullshit. Tell me the truth!"* became my signature statement – everywhere. My only motivation to go to Confession was the thought of getting one from the Priest. To an addict, a rush trumps redemption.

Then I got addicted to avoiding any talk whatsoever about policing. Ex-colleague lunches became a pain-in-the-ass ... *"Didyahear Regis got booted out of the detective office?"* brought on symptoms similar to constipation. *"Didyahear about the break-in?"* prompted involuntary anti-social responses – leaving the room, hanging up the phone, "block sender" on email. To this day, acid reflux, gas and bloating are still more pleasurable than watching cop movies.

I was addicted to college law-enforcement teaching. Ordinary lesson plans weren't enough. Nope. A curriculum overhaul was the answer to the problem – the one invented by my addiction – soft curriculum, soft minds. Solution: Advanced investigative concepts taught to 19-year-olds – the same teenagers who were posting self-portraits of debauchery on Facebook. Advanced homicide investigation to hung-over kids who couldn't muster enough energy to get a driver's license or find a part-time job.

But I didn't stop there. I got severely addicted to coordinating and growing two college law-enforcement programs. A program with only 150 students wasn't enough. Neither was 300, 450 or 600. For my cause, I started more academic street fights than anyone in the history of post-secondary education. Cries of, *"quality of education!"* consumed meeting after meeting with administrators – the same ones who I'm sure were recalling that the sign at the campus entrance was "Community College" not "Harvard."

Then I got addicted to writing. Publish or perish – literally. Not one textbook, not two … 19 editions of six different policing textbooks and 200 case law articles – written long after I became addicted to not talking about policing. Finally, my addiction spread to writing about another addiction – football. Describing systems that advocated suffocating pressure and Formula-1 racing speed. Unheard-of concepts. Warp-speed no-huddle, no punting, no kicking. And **3-D** Offense – go **Deep**, go **Deeper**, go **Deepest**. *"That crazy sonuvabitch!"* – flattery unmatched by even a Hallmark card.

I am addicted to earning university degrees. I want enough initials after my name to fill a two-sided business card. And while working toward those degrees, I'm addicted to being the class pain-in-the-ass, refuting everything taught by academics.

I am addicted to being different. No, not just different – addicted to Culture Shock. Raised eyebrows isn't enough. Speechless isn't enough. I am addicted to thinking so far outside the box that the box disappears. I am deeply committed to not doing things by the book – while writing my own book … books. My addiction has spread to how I write books. Chapter numbers, structure, content. I have trouble with conventional anything. Like numbering chapters in order starting at "1." I am addicted to being a mystery and writing mysteries – forcing readers to figure out the message. The "enigma" paradox – simultaneously revealing and concealing everything about myself.

I am addicted to coffee. The intravenous kind. Because it helps fuel my life-long addiction – working out.

Then there are the serious addictions – addiction to the rush, addiction to risk, addiction to making the biggest impact humanly possible on as many lives as humanly possible. My greatest fear in life is being bored straight to death and boring others straight to death. It's not an ordinary fear, it's hell. It's connected to an intense aversion to ordinary, routine, mundane, IQ-dropping mind-numbingness. *"Hey, did you hear the one about?"* scares the shit out of me worse than, *"How 'bout that cold?"*

The fear of boredom is worse than my other dread – the intense fear of wasting my life, the only life that's been given to me. The fear of spending eternity regretting the trashing of the potential I've been blessed with. The intense fear of replacing destiny with mediocrity. Being asked,

"You work out after midnight?" is scarier than seeing a ghost but nowhere near as horrifying as THE living-dead question, *"How long 'til you can retire?"* Legislation is needed to criminalize any communication of the R-word. The government should ban it.

But my worst addiction, the one I'm most proud of, is wanting to put up ladders for every soul who asks for help. It's the worst because it leads to another addiction – saying, *"Yes, no problem, follow me."*

My wife says I have the **E-Gene**. Extreme. I deny it. Won't confess. I'm not sure if addictions are part of DNA. Our three daughters haven't revealed any of the above symptoms – yet.

This book has several messages that correspond with my **3-M** Beliefs. I believe in **M**iracles, **M**essages and **M**isery-busting. They're connected.

I believe that miracles didn't stop happening 2,000 years ago. They happen every day. Seeing just one would have been an honor but I have had the great fortune to have witnessed countless miracles. It's tough to rank them but the top three have been the birth of my three daughters. Childbirth is mindboggling. It's impossible not to believe in God after witnessing a child enter planet Earth. And I have been an eyewitness to many, many more modern-day miracles. Like seeing the desperate, untalented, forgotten or discarded – all members of the St. Jude Club for the hopeless – reach higher and higher and higher. Back-of-the-packers pushing and shoving to the front of the line. I have been privileged to coach thousands of student-athletes on the football field, in the weight room and in lecture halls. Infinite blessings in teaching the science of survival to young warriors and wannabe cops at the lowest levels. The bottom of the ladder. No actually, to those standing at the bottom of the wall without a ladder.

There is no greater rush than telling a group of student-athletes (formerly classified as assholes) to, *"Go out in this world and make an impact!"* – and witnessing them taking it seriously. Feeling it sink in. Especially when it happens on a plot of grass after a loss or in a lecture auditorium late on a Friday afternoon when no one gives a shit about anything except which bar they're going to later that night. The epic thrill and chill of making an impact. Makes the skin bubble. Watching potential unexpectedly unleash from a hiding spot, buried deep inside kids who have been beaten down with self-doubt and negativity, has given me a front-row seat to a world of infinite miracles. And fuel for my addictions.

I believe in good and evil – and that they fight hard for our attention. I believe both send messages that are eerily similar. Evil is a copycat – good with a twist. I believe that we are bombarded by unconventional text messaging – the mysterious kind – that need to be figured out, analyzed. I believe we receive omens – signs telling us what to do and what not to do. The problem is recognizing the signs, translating the messages and trying to figure out who sent them because good and evil both work extremely hard to recruit to their team. It's up to us to see the message, interpret it and make the call.

I believe in connections. Nothing just happens. Nothing just happens automatically and nothing happens randomly. All events are connected. We have to work extremely hard to make things happen.

I believe in free will. We are blessed with decision-making – the freedom to make the call. Total control in choosing how to respond to everything that happens so that we can make more good things happen.

I firmly believe that every human was created for one purpose – to reach full potential so we can fulfill our individual calling or callings. I believe that we have a built-in need to grow. To change. Not simply to re-invent ourselves but to keep adding-on. I believe that we have a natural need to keep building. And ignoring that need leads to misery.

I believe that miracles are gifts waiting to happen every day if we let them, see them, recognize them because every miracle has a natural struggle – it's easy to get tired, quit, or simply not realize a miracle is happening. I believe we have to fight through the natural struggle to make things happen so we can receive our gifts. No shortcuts. I believe that the secret to witnessing miracles is facing misery, busting it up before it busts you up ... using your tag-team partner – your soul.

This book is about how to change what you don't like about yourself. About overcoming obstacles that stop you from becoming what you want to become – that stop you from doing what you need to do ... what you're called to do. It's also a cautionary tale – it's easy to get sidetracked. This book is about how to get on track and stay on track.

This book was written for many reasons – somewhere between 254,400 and 1,766,550. The estimated number of requests for free advice about:

- How to lose fat.
- How to make big muscles.
- How to get/survive a police job.
- How to get/survive a college teaching job.
- How to get/survive a coaching job.
- How to get a scholarship.
- How to write a book.
- How to start a business.
- How to change/get a better job.
- How to cope with and change rebellious or underachieving teenagers.
- How to be escape the misery of a dead-end job.
- How to achieve more.
- How to pass a job interview.
- How to deal with a bad relationship.
- How to find your calling.
- How to be fearless enough to follow that calling.

And, what to tell the curious … *"How do you find the time to do everything? How do you do it?"* I'm repeatedly asked how to make things happen.

I got addicted to writing the answers to every question I've ever been asked. The addiction of saying, *"yes"* to every single request for help. The "yes addiction" gave me a vision – to write a record-breaking number of books … the most books written by one human. *Soul of a Lifter* is only the first.

This book is not specifically about making big muscles or losing fat. But it will explain what I firmly believe is the secret – the basics. The essentials. This book is not about crime-fighting, coaching football, college teaching, business, or playing sports, but it does give insights about how to overcome the toughest, fiercest opponent we will ever meet, in anything we do in life – fear.

This book explains a different perspective about working out – its connection to life performance – making things happen, getting things done. Unique, life-altering lessons. This book guarantees to motivate you. And to inspire you to achieve more. To hold on to every dream and never, ever let go.

I believe I am not the only addict. I believe I am not the only person who hasn't figured out "what to do when I grow up." But I know that I don't want rehab. I don't need an intervention. I intend to workout hard for the rest of my life. I'll be lifting heavy at 102. Supersets. Dropsets. Megasets.

I remain addicted to creating opportunities for anyone who wants to reach their full potential. I remain addicted to the belief that the greatest reward is putting up ladders for others, looking outside ourselves and developing as many people as humanly possible. I remain addicted to enjoying the success of protegés, those willing to take full advantage of opportunities to grow.

I remain addicted to lifetime learning – to reading everything I can, going to school, piling up degrees … to never stop learning, even when I think I have learned enough. I am addicted to learning as much as possible because I believe knowledge is more than power – it's internal peace.

Chapter 20
Unnatural Causes

The unchallenged body softens.

The unchallenged mind weakens.

The unchallenged soul rots.

40 years. 2,080 weeks. Over 10,000 workouts.

No stage, no judges, no medals, no trophies, no posing, no photo shoots, no endorsements. No anabolic steroids. Forty years of continuous lifting without a conventional purpose. Heavy weight, heavy metal, heavy lifting – between 200,000 and 400,000 sets … two-million to four-million reps. Day after day. Six, sometimes seven days a week. Completely natural. Drug-free. No audience, no applause, no glory. On the surface, no apparent reason fueling a four-decade drive to tear down and rebuild the body for the slightest improvement.

There's a blurry line between obsession and passion. They share the same DNA. They look the same, talk the same language, drive at the same break-neck speed and … no "off" switch. Just a jammed "on" switch. And neither obsession nor passion just happen. Nothing just happens. The key is to go deep. Then go deeper … and deepest.

A 40-year heavy-lifting career is unnatural. But it makes a deep impact.

$$\infty$$

When we open our mouths, we can either be mind-numbing mumblers or memory-makers. Like, "Say No to Drugs" speeches. They are either more mind-numbing than actual drugs, or memorable – depends on the impact. I used to tell my football players and wannabe-cop college students that steroids are for cowards and chickenshits unwilling and incapable of working hard to achieve a goal. And that anything worth achieving involves a natural struggle. And that avoiding the natural struggle is not only a hideous form of laziness, but also an enormous disadvantage intellectually because you miss out on all the valuable insights and lessons learned from the natural struggle. And that bypassing the natural struggle keeps you in the dark. Unenlightened. And that the results of steroids are artificial, superficial and unofficial.

Their faces showed tension … but not real attention. So I changed the speech.

"Here's why you don't want to do steroids. The last death I investigated is the best reason not to do steroids or jam anything into your arm or into your nostrils or into your lungs."

2:00 a.m., a uniform officer arrives at a dark, dingy house in response to an "unknown problem" – a message just like we get in real-life over and over again. "Unknown problem" can paralyze you with fear if you let it because it's made up of the two most terrifying elements known to wo/mankind – uncertainty and risk. "Unknown problem" forces you to fight through it or run from it. One makes you stronger, the other makes you weaker until you shrivel up and crumble.

The officer knocks. Silence. No one answers the door. No clue about what's inside, but walks in anyway. Into the darkness and starts searching, with one hand on a flashlight and the other on his holster. Room to room – nothing. Until he goes downstairs, deep in the basement and sees him. The unclothed body of a man, slumped over, perched on a toilet in the bathroom. Bent-over like he had been beaten down. Lifeless. No pulse. Rigor mortis has set in, just like that stiff feeling after a brutal workout, except this kind of stiffness leads to decomposition instead of recovery.

I arrive next. The lead detective. I'm surrounded by people old enough to be my parents. It's my job is to determine what happened. Like arriving at the end of a movie. Or opening a book filled with blank pages, except the last page that reads, "The End." I have to write the rest of the book – the beginning and the middle – tell a story without having witnessed it. And it has to be a true story, not fiction. Even if it becomes a horror story, it has to be the truth, the whole truth and nothing but the truth. I can't make up parts of the story to entertain the reader.

Everything in the house sends a message, telling parts of the story. I search the house, in case someone – something – was missed. Nothing, no one. No other human to help tell the story. I have to look for clues – signs. But here's the key. It's impossible for anything to happen without there being signs left all over the place – a trail of clues. All I have to do is find them and figure out what they mean.

The house is unkempt – filthy. And it stinks. A nauseating stench that builds up with stillness – immobility. Non-movement. I walk downstairs into the washroom, look at the dead guy's face … and have a flashback, 15 years.

I'm an 18-year-old rookie cop working out in the basement of the hardest of hardcore gyms. No socializing. No cell phones. No tight shirts. No mindless chatter. Just the symphony of heavy metal. Two streams of it, mixing together. One from the radio, the other from the plates.

From my position at the squat racks, I see a guy casually walk to the main powerlifting bench. Jed. We nod to each other. An unwritten rule from the "Hardcore Gym Code of Conduct:" Non-verbal communication only. Talking is limited to essentials. **SUAL – S**hut **U**p **A**nd **L**ift.

Jed's ritual starts. He takes ownership of the bench, even when he's not using it, until he's finished, violating another unwritten rule: Don't hog the bench. Violators get tagged with the "punk" label. A pain-in-the-ass. An asshole. But in a place with zero tolerance for punk behavior, no one bothers Jed. He has earned the right to be a bench hog. Not through entitlement – earned. Bigger, scarier lifters give him implied consent – go ahead, hog the bench. Performance counted.

Six days before this workout, I had encountered Jed at a call at a bar where he worked as a bouncer. The bar was a drug-infested assembly of sociopaths, a community of violent social misfits. Jed was a 27-year-old factory worker, moonlighting as a bouncer. His T-shirt was two sizes too small. Layers of clothes removed to show layers of another kind – vein-popping, fat-free, magazine-cover mass of muscle. *I wonder what his workout program is? I wonder what his diet is?* The gullibility of an 18-year-old rookie cop has no limits.

Three fighters were arrested at the disturbance. Jed never got involved. He never moved a muscle. Standing near the bar casually looking on, playing with his mustache, Jed looked bored. Like he always did. Like he did now, sitting on the bench with no shirt on, committing counts #3 and #4: Must wear a shirt, and, Shirt must be baggy.

Jed is in no hurry to start the first set. No intensity, no sense of urgency as he commits count #5: Grooming in the mirror. Staring at the guy in the glass without lifting a weight. Self-admiration. Like strong paper towels, self-absorption. I'm wondering if he is preparing to go on a date or getting ready to lift. *Ripped, lean, massive, eight-pack … and doesn't even work out hard! Must be genetics!* Losing gullibility doesn't just happen. It doesn't leave automatically or mysteriously. It happens with experience – reps.

Jed is not a giant. Only 5'10". But he casts a big shadow because of what he's done in the past and is about to do now. His first bench press set has two 45-pound plates on each side of the Olympic bar. Twelve reps. A warm-up set. 225 pounds for 12 reps – strictly, slowly, effortlessly. No bouncing. He doesn't use his chest like a trampoline. No primal screaming. And nowhere near failure. The miracle of **M**aximum **M**uscular **F**ailure (**MMF**) is one of the secrets to making big muscles. But Jed doesn't care. He leaves at least 15-20 reps hidden inside. Plenty left in the tank. He wastes a glorious opportunity – a growth opportunity. 225 pounds is a heavy weight. It's the bench press testing standard used by university and pro football coaches to measure the strength of world-class athletes. Yet, here is a part-time bouncer using it as a warm-up set – effortlessly. And lazily. Does less than half of what he could, should do.

For set #2, Jed slides another 45-pound plate on each side for a total of 315 pounds. After a mini-vacation rest, he casually completes 10 reps. Again, strictly, slowly, effortlessly with plenty left in the tank ... leaving unused reps inside. Hiding them. Locking them up with the rest of his potential he keeps packed away. Afraid to go to failure. Fear of busting through limits – not even getting close to the edge. And, most of all, fear of pain. Scared of the thought of discomfort. The needle on the tank barely budges after two sets. Hidden reps, concealed potential, buried treasure, wasted growth opportunities – the road to misery.

He adds one more 45-pound plate to each side– 405 pounds. Set #3 has almost doubled in weight from the first set. Jed sits down on the bench like he's waiting for a bus. No rush. A few more glances in the mirror, another straightening of the hair, one more smoothing of his mustache. And silence.

"He'll wait forever to do the next set. Fuckin' asshole pisses me off." A guy I would arrest three years later whispers the outrage shared by the entire gym. The hog is in no rush. The dual sacrilege of too much rest between sets ... and of not going to failure. But no one bothers Jed. No one challenges him. Jed gets a free pass. Left alone, he becomes a victim ... of enabling.

Spectating is prohibited – Code rule #6: No gawking – at women or men. Staring is reserved for tourists. So the best one can do is watch using peripheral vision while trying to look busy. *There's no way he can bench 405.* The naiveté of an 18-year-old is infinite.

There is one exception to the SUAL rule.

"Can you spot me?"

"Sure."

But I forget to ask when he intends to lift.

"I'll let you know when I'm ready."

After another long-weekend type of rest, Jed casually announces, *"Ready. Don't touch the bar unless I tell you. Just stand there."*

I'm not a spotter. I'm an eyewitness. Proof. Evidence of performance. People use a 400-pound bench press as the benchmark for fabricated glory days.[1] Like fiction novelists, they re-write the past – insert false realities – to entertain the present: *"I used to bench four plates until* (insert an ailment or a misfortune)." But, like information cops receive from a confidential informant, there is no way to prove a claim of a 400-pound bench press. It could be the truth. Or it could be bullshit. A heavy pile of bullshit.

Fictional bench press stories share three elements – no witnesses, no video and, a vague narrative … no evidence and an abstract story – the red flags of deception.

"When did you lift four plates?"

"Oh it was awhile ago."

"Where?"

"Errr, a bunch of places."

Credibility depends on how the story is told. Abstract narratives are suspicious – inspired by some true events, but most likely out-right lies. Science fiction. Only concrete stories have substance.

Witnessing a 400-pound bench press for the first time is Culture Shock. Like a perfect game in baseball, it rarely happens. The odds are staggering. So when you see it, it's memorable. Especially memorable because Jed never asked for any help to take the bar off the racks, lift it, or put the bar back onto the racks. And especially memorable since it was obvious he could have lifted it again. More hidden reps, more concealed potential. More waste.

One isolated, single rep at 405 pounds. And … plenty left in the tank.

∞

---

1   A tribute to a masterpiece, *Glory Days*. By Bruce Springsteen.

Witnessing incredible performance makes an impact. Huge impact. First, you face the realization of how far you have to go – what your competition is doing … and what you're not. Secondly, it causes you to re-define "personal best." Mine was 85% of Jed's. An insult. A disgrace. A sign to get better. No, a loud message: You're not as good as you think you are. That being "good" at something is contextual. Third, seeing a remarkable performance plants the seed of passion – or obsession. A goal that becomes a basic survival need. Turning your goal into a survival need will help you build the most important muscle of all – mindset. Iron-will mindset.

Without iron-will mindset, it's impossible to break barriers – impossible to reach higher – reach your goal. Mental strength is the secret to all achievement. It is connected to physical strength yet it precedes physical strength. And it is made stronger by physical strength. The spiral effect. The mind gives out way before the body. Training the mind trains the body.

15% improvement. 15% more weight. 15% more strength. At age 18, it had taken me only six years to reach 85% of 400. According to the math, only 15% of six years would be needed to break the barrier – smash the limit. And then pass it. Far beyond it. Every pound would be added every workout – 401, 402, 403 pounds. And after 100 workouts, the 500-pound barrier, gone.

How can any of us know that the first time we see something will be the last? Never saw it happen again, in person. From any position – not behind the bar, not under the bar. Never witnessed a live performance of a 400-pound bench press again.

∞

"The Coroner said he's on the way."

Blood all over the place and on the crumpled body of a young man – Jed was only 42. Homicide. Theory #1 – the starting point. Always think dirty – then work backwards.

Searching a crime scene where a dead person is lying, is like walking through Culture Shock waves. Start near the body and widen the search. The search tells the story. An office near the bathroom. A desk and filing cabinet with business records. A cheap journal with bad handwriting – customer's names with product orders: "Meth" … "Coke" … "Decadurabolin" … "Winstrol" … "Testosterone." Probably a **3-D** homicide – **D**rugs, **D**ebt or **D**omestic. Unresolved conflict is the cause of all evil – no exceptions. The unresolved inner and outer conflict created by trying to fill a need, causes extreme behavior … unpredictable, outside-the-box behavior.

"Look here … post-mortem-lividity on the back of the legs but nowhere else. The body wasn't moved. Time of death was over eight hours ago." All that from a deep purple stain that develops after death, on an area of the body that touches a surface. Story-telling through purple haze.[2]

"The body is fully engulfed in rigor mortis, indicating time of death was 12-24 hours ago."

∞

An autopsy site is a morbid classroom, void of emotion. *"No injuries from violence. No self-inflicted injuries. No overdose."* Everything is cut, measured, analyzed. Body parts sliced, scaled, bagged. Free PhD in forensics at the expense of a dead person.

"Hey, how do you write 'bleeding outta his ass' in professional medical terms for the police report?" Forensic guys have a warped sense of humor. It's hard to tell when they're kidding.

"He was bleeding out of his ass, his balls were shriveled up, his liver was shot and his heart failed. The acne on his back is one of the worst I've ever seen. A 42-year-old with the insides of an 80-year-old. That's what heavy, long-term use of anabolic steroids will do to you." Coroners speak/teach in simple language. No confusion about the message. No trying to impress with trainwreck vocabulary.

Every "sudden death" investigation needs one of four conclusions, representing "THE END" – homicide, suicide, accident, or natural causes. Jed's death didn't fit any of the conventional four causes. His death invented a new conclusion. Death by "unnatural causes." An unnatural death in exchange for a 400-pound bench press.

∞

---

2 A tribute to a masterpiece, *Purple Haze*. By Jimi Hendrix.

"It's the lazy, cowardly way to avoid the natural struggle. It's the foolish way to bypass natural growth opportunities, natural lessons-learned, natural insights. The natural struggle is not only intended to separate the strong from the weak, it gives the weak chances to get up and try again. And a chance for the strong to get stronger. Avoiding the natural struggle results in extinction. It's impossible to survive without fighting through the natural struggle. Shortcuts keep you weak and weaker. Using steroids is the equivalent of cheating on exams, cheating at sports, cheating at business, cheating at work, cheating in any relationship. All the rationalization in the world will not cancel the fact that sticking a needle in your ass is the chickenshit way out of a challenge, the coward's way out of working hard. And it's degrading – admitting you can't handle the natural struggle. The natural struggle is where you grow balls. Steroids shrivel them up.

Using steroids is an admission of defeat – it tells the whole world you can't handle pressure. It sends a bad message – scared shitless of an inanimate object, like a bar and some metal plates. Using steroids sends a message: Can't count on the steroid guy for backup in an alley because … no balls."

Every "Say No to Drugs" speech needs a backup – just in case the first was mind-numbing. A supplement. Another rep.

"One more thing about steroids and drugs. In case you think the first speech was bullshit, think of this. The two sickest criminals I ever dealt with were addicted to drugs. Enzo and Greg. Both had tons of potential – smart, strong … but they wasted it. Threw it in the trash with their used syringes. Enzo was a meth addict who jacked every kind of anabolic steroid into his ass. His favorite was testosterone. Got wired up on meth, lost tons of weight, then built himself back up by injecting testosterone. A walking pharmaceutical laboratory. Endless cycles of down, down deeper, and up. And, he couldn't shut up. Motor-mouth.

Greg snorted, swallowed and injected every substance ever invented. Same thing – cycles of thinness and thickness, skinny and jacked. Both became violent sociopaths. They did unconscionable things that hurt many people. In and out of jail for violent crimes. And neither one gave a shit about the mess they caused in victim's lives. Both were cowards, picking on defenseless people. And they didn't even argue when it was pointed out to them that they were chickenshit cowards who terrorized senior citizens, women and anyone less than half their size. Psychopathic bullies. Why? Because their brains were scrambled – toasted, mush. And they needed tons of money because they could not control their addiction. Shriveled brains and shriveled balls."

Here's the point. Both came from normal Beaver Cleaver-like families. Both had decent hard-working parents. Drugs destroyed them and their families. They became toxic – radioactive **P-Force** – **P**oison **F**orce. Poisoned inside, poisoned outside. Laid waste to everyone around them. Both admitted to me that drugs caused this mess. Addictions. Incurable addictions. Drugs made them crazy – hard drugs and anabolic steroids. Both tried to clean up but they kept failing. Round after round, kept getting knocked down. Eventually, they lost the fight – by knockout. Greg is dead – died at a young age. Enzo is walking dead – technically alive but has never lived.

Steroids are like Enzo and Greg – home invaders – stealing, plundering, pillaging and wreaking havoc. Like violent thieves, steroids steal health and life but they also rob another valuable – the natural struggle, the chemical-free, substance-free battle to reach higher, get to the next level and fulfill God-given potential. The natural struggle is the most important part of working out. The lessons learned from any natural struggle represent the highest form of learning – a PhD in street smarts. Reality IQ. Nothing is more enlightening than the insights learned from the natural struggle.

Avoiding the natural struggle is the equivalent of wealth without work – one of Ghandi's "seven deadly sins" against humanity. Like insider trading, steroids dramatically increase gains by circumventing the natural course of growth. A false reality is built. A deadly one. A tilted playing field that is no longer competitive. A short-cut for the weak-minded. Missing out on the natural struggle keeps you mired in the darkness of an artificial, insular world. A brutal form of isolation, where self-absorption disconnects the self-immersed from the best mentor that money cannot buy – natural struggle.

Natural struggle paves the way to natural growth – physically, intellectually, emotionally, spiritually. The bad news is that natural growth takes a long time. A very long time. The good news is that natural growth gives you lifelong learning – new material every day. It should never get boring. But, like cutting classes, you learn nothing from cutting the natural struggle from working out. Falsehoods are learned from false realities. Nothing of any value is learned from a false reality.

Muscles built by jamming needles in your ass is fraud. False pretenses. Bullshit muscles. Using steroids is the equivalent of a criminal's confession of guilt: Can't handle the pressure of working out. Scared of the heavy metal. Engulfed in fear of lifting an inanimate object. Using steroids is an admission that the bar won – the bar beat you. And if an inanimate object, a piece of metal can scare the shit out of you, imagine what a human opponent can do.

"There is no logical way to rationalize ramming a needle up your ass to get muscles. None. And if you try to find even one justification, that search itself is evidence of a deeper, growing mental and emotional problem. Who in their right mind would chemically engineer themselves to get puss-infected acne, shriveled balls, falling out hair, a Goliath-sized skull, smoker's voice and rotted internal organs? Who would intentionally transform into a semi-evolved Neanderthal? Every time you jam the syringe, you're signing a confession – one that says, 'Incapable of doing something the right way' … scared of hard work."

There is a direct correlation between attendance and performance. Show up and you have a chance to get better. Show up and bust your ass while you're there and you dramatically improve the chance to dramatically improve. But, "fail to appear" is a robbery-in-progress – it steals growth opportunities. Missing the natural struggle is the kind of skipping-out that can't be made up. Steroid use is an artificial makeover – a superficial layer that masks a deeper issue.

∞

There's a crooked line that separates obsession, and passion for the perfect body. The soul of a lifter is not obsessed with a perfect body. The passion is for the perfect connection. And it's fueled by the intense fear of being mediocre. Substandard. The soul of a lifter is attracted to risk. High risk. The kind of risk that causes separation. The kind of risk that beats down the monotony and the drudgery of existing instead of living. The kind of risk that fights the quiet fight – the regret of wasted potential.

Unfulfilled potential torments the soul. The gym is one place where you have total control of your potential. A place where every call you make shapes your destiny. A place where you exercise your free will to the fullest.

Chapter 51
Ladders

Mind meets metal – the road to the big leagues.[3]

The term "Big Leagues" is not reserved for major sports. The big leagues is any place where you can get your ass kicked real hard. It's any alley where you have to meet Goliath – without a slingshot. The soul of a lifter has met enough metal to know that when young minds meet metal, they are on track to the big leagues – an uphill track that makes any load the heaviest to push and pull.

The greatest impact is getting someone else called up to the big leagues. Helping someone reach higher ... putting up ladders at just the right angle for them to climb. The impact is not made in the weight you lift, it's in the weight you make others lift.

The gym knows how to flip the switch, unleash the rush and harness the full potential needed to get to the next level and the next. And the next. But, the climb isn't easy. No cakewalk. Climbing any ladder needs repetition – boring reps. The gym teaches the secret of escaping the stagnating effects of boredom – you have to work in boredom to escape it. Boring reps are the key to escaping the grips of boredom.

The gym teaches the miracle of programming through infinite repetition. Tens of thousands of reps, productive reps that challenge mind, body and soul are needed to move ahead, to release the locked-up potential, to connect with the rest of the world in order to make an impact.

The gym is the product of love-hate relationships created by either attraction or detraction. It can attract with grassroots charm and charisma or repulse with the horrors of extreme, unreasonable expectations. The gym has infinite capacity to build memorable moments that make an eternal impact, or to drive crowds away with the force of a SWAT team. The strength of the iron-will attraction is determined by the quality and quantity of your workout – every rep and every set – what gets built – strength or weakness. It determines how long you work out or how often you quit. Whether you even get in the game.

---

3   A tribute to a masterpiece, *Big Leagues*. By Tom Cochrane, an underrated Canadian artist – globally ... everyone dreams of making in the big leagues.

The gym is a place that guarantees a life-altering experience each time – if you choose it. Without shouting, it screams the same message – the same life-changing golden rule over and over again: Get off your ass, then bust your ass! The two-step secret to success, by whatever definition of success. Move, then work.

But, the gym will not make anything happen without your expressed consent. Without your permission, without your commitment. The gym expects full cooperation. Holding up your end of the bargain is non-negotiable. The gym will not do your work for you ... will not push you up the ladder. The gym is a magical place where the miracle of transformation happens before your eyes, day after day – if you make the call. If you make the decision to make it happen. If you are attracted to it.

All "attractions" are not created equal. There are short-term attractions and long-term attractions. One is superficial, the other is deep. One is style, the other is style with substance. Short-term attractions are diversions – amusements ... temporary respite from drudgery. But the long-term kind grabs hold, sinks its claws way deep inside ... touches your soul. Captures it. Holds on and will ... not ... let ... go ... ever. No matter what. Sticking to anything needs deep attraction.

The gym has the rare ability to make us both survive and thrive. Teaches us hope and how to cope. Anything that helps us cope and gives us hope is attractive. And, if it helps us survive and then thrive, it's deeply attractive.

The gym teaches that you have to learn how to hone your craft in isolation to separate from the rest. The soul of a lifter preaches, *"Be a mystery – the solvable mystery."* The soul of a lifter does the impossible – reveal and conceal at the same time. Never hide who you are but make people wonder. Build a wall – with doors, windows that open ... and seal shut. Opened and closed. Entrances with strict-access regulations. The ambiguously obvious. Show it, expose it, but be a head-scratcher. The isolated connection – the connected isolation. The secret to long-term attraction.

The gym knows that isolation leads to separation ... leading to connection.

The soul of a lifter doesn't want or take center-stage. The soul of a lifter wants to be an enigma. The soul of a lifter puts up ladders behind the scenes then teaches exactly how to climb each step … but will not climb the ladder for you.

∞

The gym never fails to teach us and never teaches us to fail. No days off. It won't cancel a class, take a vacation, blow a sick day, use up a mental health day … or just mail it in.

Chapter 40.5
U-Force

The soul of a lifter is a mystery. And a mystery writer.

The need to work out to the brink of exhaustion every single day is a mystery. So is the mystery of needing to feel muscles expanding to the point of skin-bursting. So is the mystery of wanting to feel stiff and sore the next day, and the next day. A big mystery is doing somewhere between 150,000 and 300,000 gut-wrenching lifetime sets without the slightest desire for even one shiny trophy. A tough case to crack. A lifting career not just outside the box – no box at all.

But the deeper soul-searching mystery is the fear of taking even one day off. Statutory holidays, birthdays, anniversaries, weddings … no event is big enough to kill the fear even for one day. And no amount of scientific evidence can defend a day off … not in the mind of an iron addict. Iron deficiency shouldn't set in after only 24 hours, there should be a grace period. Just one day away from iron shouldn't bring on nasty withdrawal symptoms. But it does … a price is paid – guilt, remorse, self-doubt, self-loathing. What a waste of a day. *How do people cope with never working out?* Distraction, darkness. Flashbacks of bouncing blubber, the inner voice narrating the visual: *"You lazy sonofabitch. Can't handle it?"*

A dialogue crueler than throwing stones at a chained dog.

Running endless miles over pavement is a cheap thrill – an ordinary rush but not the real thing.

Pounding the bags keeps the light flickering – temporarily. But iron is the only real fix. Only heavy metal feeds the addiction. It's a basic survival need – like breathing and eating.

There's no rehab for the soul of a lifter. Missing one workout shuts off the lights. Not just dusk – sunset. Two days off – a total eclipse. Three days? Tortured soul.

The difference between working out forever and quitting is the strength of the need. How bad we need it determines how long we do it. When we need it bad – real bad – there are no limits. "Needs" are not created equal. An ordinary need is a weak need. It doesn't have super-magnetic pull – the type of force that doesn't just attract – the type that unwillingly latches on, attaches to us with an iron-clad death grip, and drags. Ordinary need has some attraction but not the kind that gets hard-wired into machine-like efficiency, proficiency and insistency. We can take it or leave it. Escape is easy. The doors are unlocked and wide open. Free to leave – commitment is optional. The ordinary-need desire is not drilled into our blood, not welded to our brain, not melted onto our heart, and certainly not branded on our soul.

The secret to becoming good at anything, really good, is to turn it into a basic survival need. Basic survival needs build the most important weapon for the gym, for the field, for the job, for the biggest stage – the one called "Real Life." Iron-will mindset. Makes you fight for it, stops you from backing down, stops you from turning and running … and running. With iron-will mindset, the battle against excuse-making, half-assed effort, indifference, mediocrity, laziness, the temptation to not show up – to go through the motions … and the temptation to quit, is won. Without that level of willpower, it's impossible to endure, to fight through, to last … to survive at anything you dream of doing. To achieve beyond the ordinary … to do what your soul is burning to do.

Here's the problem – we are born with a desire for only a few basic survival needs. Air, food, shelter – the essentials. If you want to reach a level of unshakable commitment to working out, or anything that will make living on planet Earth better, it has to be added to the "Basic Survival Needs" list. Making iron an essential element in your diet makes you crave it – turns you into a machine – a force. Thirst makes you yearn for it. Hunger makes you go after it … hunt it down. An appetite sharpens your survival skills.

But adding it to the list doesn't just happen. It's not automatic. Won't happen on its own.

Basic survival needs remove choice. What you need to survive becomes non-negotiable. No substitutes. No decision. No-brainer. And there's plenty of help – the miracle of the brain going into survival mode. Flip the switch and the brain figures out a way to make survival happen – tapping into the greatest source, the strongest workout partner – the soul of a lifter – who teaches you how to lift the heavy weight that life stacks on the bar. The kind of weight that tries to crush you. The kind that needs strict form, endless reps to unleash the **U-Force** – the **U**nstoppable **F**orce buried deep inside … to survive.

Basic survival needs build passion ... and obsession. The "basic survival need" paradox – the same ingredient for both a positive and a negative. A gas pedal without a brake pedal. A stick-shift stuck on overdrive with no low gear, no neutral and no reverse. The high-octane blend that fuels high performance ... and the inability to stop. Or slow down. A basic survival need is a powerful motivator – a U-Force – a relentless drive. It is the key that unlocks what's been hidden inside. And ... it can break the "off" switch.

The mystery writer's dictionary has a unique definition of "athlete." The title is not reserved for grossly over-paid jillionaire professional game-players. An athlete is anyone whose very survival depends on working out. Anyone who stays in the game long after everyone leaves, a game where the training is the actual competition, a game carried on without the approval of an audience, a game where the opponent is the meanest bastard, a ruthless sonuvabitch who stops at nothing to beat you – self. The insider. The litmus test for the title "athlete," is getting off your ass and busting your ass when no one is watching. No one except the soul of a lifter.

A team with one heartbeat. The soul of a lifter doesn't attract strong souls. It doesn't recruit the fit – leaving the unchallenged soul to rot. To fulfill the soul of a lifter's purpose, like doesn't attract like. Opposites attract. The soul of a lifter seeks out weak souls – the fragile souls that need to grow. Recruiting them is easy. Changing them into athletes isn't.

The soul of a lifter's unique language doesn't include: casual, half-assed, laid-back, mellow, apathetic, low-key, coast, just-maintaining. "Hobby" has been struck from its reference book and replaced with "career." Working out is not a hobby. A hobby is an uncommitted, disposable activity. Not a basic survival need. A pastime. Something you don't give a shit about. If you care about it and are committed to it, it's a career. Never write "fitness" under the title "hobby" on a resume – unless it really is just a hobby.

Like any career, working out develops transferable skills. To lift heavy weight, go deep, find the hidden strength, turn on the switch and lift the weight. When the weight gets too heavy, let a spotter help you build U-Force with forced reps – shared strength. Assisted reps. Strength debit – borrowing strength from a spotter until your strength account fills back up.

Training hard-wires strength, skill and iron will. Dedicated training builds a machine – a fearless machine that switches to automatic pilot. The soul of a lifter will never let down – not the bar, not a heavy weight, not an insurmountable challenge. U-Force is the secret weapon that meets the challenge and defeats it.

U-Force. Training without an audience.

U-Force doesn't just happen.

Friday nights, weekends, midnights. Working out becomes a marathon without a finish line. A 40-year uninterrupted odyssey, addicted to the most powerful anabolic agent of all – the rush. The rush from lifting heavy weight. Streaks develop – consecutive days working out without a day off … 50, 60. My personal best is 156. A silent record, for eyes of the lifter's soul only. Eyes that witness it being done the hardest way possible. Not just the long road, the bumpy one – the one with the biggest pot holes. 100% natural. Steroid-free. Not one boost from a performance-enhancing drug. Never even held a pill or a syringe … except when seizing them with a search warrant.

U-Force. Addicted to the stage of real-life.

$$\infty$$

The gym is a place where free will gets vigorous exercise, where intense exercise turns free will into iron will, where the judges are not human, where the critics don't matter, where you go outside yourself, outside the box – where there is no box. No approval junkies, just adrenaline junkies, the only drug that matters.

Chapter Zero
Culture Shock

Culture Shock goes deep. Too deep.

My father's suffering was my blessing. I lucked out – I am an immigrant's son. I learned lessons growing up that can't be taught in any school, by any teacher, by any coach, by any human mentor. I never knew my father when he was 20, or 35, or 40. The first time I formally met him, he was 44 years old. I didn't actually see his nightmarish journey called "life." Didn't experience it first-hand, but I saw the outcome. The product of depression, despair and poverty. The result of misery and misfortune. A survivor.

A father old enough to be a grandfather is unnatural but the gravity of it can be a force of nature … and nurture. I don't believe we are put on the Earth to do less than previous generations. We're supposed to do more. Not let the sacrifice and struggle of those who came before us go to waste. But no matter how hard I try, I can't outdo my father.

∞

Imagine.

Imagine growing up without any education – not even finishing elementary school. Imagine working in the fields instead of playing on the field, raising four siblings as a teenager in a village stuck somewhere between Medieval Times and the Dark Ages. Living through the Great Depression, forced into a military led by a madman, getting sent into a world war without any choice and without even knowing why, dodging bullets and bombs for the first three years, then caged in a POW camp for the last three. Freed only to be plunged deeper into post-war poverty during which time your spouse dies leaving you to raise two daughters alone, broke, without any shred of real hope. Getting loaded onto a cattle boat to sail across the ocean to a foreign place – illiterate and penniless … and alone, leaving your children behind until you make enough money to rescue them. Age 40, trying to make it in the foreign land where you can't read even a road sign in the new language, your old language, or any language, except the one with the arrow on it, pointing to a one-way career path – a road to hard manual labor. Eight hours a day, five days a week, and no real choice about overtime because of the 1950's management style that included the motivational speech called "**DP**" – the constant reminder and threat that a **D**isplaced **P**erson could become a **D**eported **P**erson and have their ass dragged back across the ocean where they came from. Then, getting re-married by proxy, to someone you barely know on the other side of the planet, bringing her and your two daughters to the new land where they can't read and write either, having a third child in the foreign land, still unable to understand a newspaper, TV, radio that you can't afford anyway, or your neighbor who doesn't really trust "Dagos." Top it all off with no prospect of moving up the work ladder. Heavy manual labor for the next 25 years. No early retirement, no high hopes, no dreams, just survival. Isolation, separation, frustration. No hope of connection.

Imagine over a decade passing in the foreign land, turning 52 years old, and being only half-way through a back-breaking career in the Flour Mill, carrying 140-pound flour bags like a human beast of burden, eight hours a day, five to six days a week. The greatest workout program ever. The ultimate supersets ... megasets, with absolutely no concern about rest, recovery, lactic acid, mirrors, posing, whining, crying, bitching, moaning, hair-fixing, socializing, talking on cell phones between sets, sticking needles in your ass, energy drinks, supplements, implants, bad equipment, old equipment, new equipment, six-packs, symmetry, or sympathy. No excuses about over-training, peaking too soon, peaking too late, not enough bicep peak. Just an iron will to survive ... an iron will built from strength and built by strength. Thousands of heavy reps – intense forced reps – lifted during a 40-52 hour workweek, 50 weeks per year ... for minimum wage. The ultimate fat loss program – carrying a heavy load back and forth across the inside of a boat or train, piling up bag after 140-pound bag of flour. Isolated reps. Heavy load plus motion. Powerlifting and cardio rolled up in one set. The real-life version of "go heavy or go home."

A new meaning of the word "adversity," or maybe the true meaning ... the intended meaning. Before the post-modern age butchered the definition by replacing, "inconceivable, mountainous obstacles," and "exhausting struggles that shape one-of-a-kind cast-iron character," with basic routine inconveniences and nuisances of daily life – the type that are broadcast on the cyber-airwaves of social networks. A true reality survivors' series, not a 21st century false-reality show that entertains the new-age couch-sitting emptiness. The heavyweight mindset. No need for inspirational quotes, motivational speeches, team-building retreats, self-esteem-building seminars. No time for mind-numbing, soul-rotting workplace drama, gossip and every other form of toxic waste that decomposes workplace environment. No need for gyms, cardio, or roadwork. No need for low-carb diets.

Deprivation of one's fundamental needs builds a burning hunger – a force of nature and nurture – partners that cause the hunger to become hard-wired. Programmed. Deep hunger loads the barrel. The fear of the certain past and fear of the uncertain future pulls the trigger. DNA loads the bar, nurture lifts it.

The conventional immigrant story – the unconventional struggle. The natural struggle … the foreign struggle. Culture Shock. The kind that builds a deep hunger. Makes a deep impact.

$$\infty$$

Fear of the father, fear of the son, and fear of the un-holy ghosts. Anticipating fear is worse than experiencing the real thing. Depression breeds depression. Some escape it, some don't. Simple life ideology. Emotionless, mechanical workdays – bust your ass to exhaustion … and never show it. Never show you're tired, never show incompetence and, above all, never complain. And grow up. Don't be an asshole. The bar raised at its highest … you'll-get-your-ass-kicked-bad-if-you-do-anything-stupid … don't-come-back-home-if-you-embarrass-the-family … performance demands. No multiple choices, no discretion, no discussions … demands.

The more you fear the harder you'll train.

No time for weakness. Anything that detracted from work – extreme hard work – was weakness, an affliction that made life not worth living. Weakness was a foreigner. A trespasser. Unwelcomed guest – no room in the house. Weakness was a symptom of something deeper, something too embarrassing to handle. A zero-tolerance policy was the only proactive measure and remedy. Performance demands served a dual-purpose – prevention and cure for the dreaded social plague called "weakness."

Antonio loathed sports. Sports were for those who were allowed to be children. Sports didn't put food on the table. No throwing the ball around. No camping trips, no fishing, no golfing. No vacations, no restaurants … just get ready for the next depression. Be prepared to fight the next depression because the next one will be "The Big One." Focus, concentrate … expect the worse and never take your eyes off the worst. History is bound to repeat itself – if history is all we know. It's constantly chasing and haunting … running after us, forcing us to twist and turn our head to look over our shoulder. If the past is a ghost, then the future scares the shit out of us even more. So, train hard – real hard – and beat the next depression. Survive it. Antonio's world was different.

The story of Antonio's struggle – an unnatural life – though never spoken, was louder than any motivational speech I have ever heard, more powerful than any motivational book I have ever read, and more moving than any inspirational movie I have ever seen. The greatest mentor is one who has endured the struggle – the product of unimaginable misery. The survivor.

Rest in peace, Dad.

Chapter 1-12
The Darkest Enemy

"What's the nutrition secret, Coach? Share with us the secret to staying lean and mean? Right after the break, Coach will tell the audience the key nutrition advice for losing fat and staying in shape. But first a message from our sponsor."

Magic Fat Loss Pill is the magic fat loss way to magically lose fat. I take Magic Fat Loss Pill every day. I started taking Magic Fat Loss Pill one month ago and I lost fifty-two pounds, like magic! Magic Fat Loss Pill has made me more attractive, leaner and meaner. Magic Fat Loss Pill is the secret fat loss formula. Call now, operators are standing by. And if you call in the next thirty minutes, we'll send you a free sample of Magic Fat Loss Drink. But wait. There's more. If you order two, you get the Super Magic Fat Loss Powder.

"We're back! Coach Arcaro, what's the secret?"

"Food as fuel. That's the mindset. Change your attitude toward food. Consider food as fuel for your next workout and it's impossible to fail."

"Food as fuel folks. You heard it here first."

∞

Fat is a tough enemy to lose.

I have been blessed to have coached countless athletes who have let me share their countless wins – come-from-behind wins, close wins, runaway wins, upset wins, Goliath-sized wins. Even the wins that the scoreboard didn't officially recognize. But no win was as big as the biggest loss of my life – fat loss. Mounds of lost childhood blubber – the thrill of losing, the agony of gaining. And the fear of ghosts – those that haunt an obese child forever.

∞

Imagine.

Imagine being a fat child. So fat that you can't do up your pants, can't button your shirt, can't run, can't skate – can't function. Imagine looking down at your gut and seeing flabs – rows of bumps … fat bumps rippling along your stomach, hiding your abs with mounds of blubber. Imagine thinking that you start high school in one year.

Fat is a heavyweight opponent for adults, but for a child, fat is an evil mismatch. It's a fight that should never be sanctioned. It's not a fair fight because fat attracts a team – mob mentality. It's never a one-on-one fight. The fight versus fat needs serious training, the kind that children are not adult enough to handle.

Childhood obesity makes a deep impact.

Childhood dysfunctionalism and fat are connected.

Imagine being a child who has no idea "how to be" – how to be a child, how be "in place." Imagine not being able to make eye contact with 98.6% of humans, not able to communicate. Imagine hearing all the misguided diagnoses from self-professed experts, those whose advice your parents followed blindly – the powerful effects of conformity. Imagine being engulfed in fear, overwhelmed with anxiety, incapable of forming any normal relationships. Paralyzed, immobilized and terrorized by fear – before even becoming a teenager. Imagine "not being" – and being "out-of-place."

Then imagine no conventional escape plan.

Fear is a super-heavyweight opponent for adults to fight, but for a child, fear is an evil mismatch. It's a bloodsport that should be outlawed. It's not a fair fight because a child's fear attracts a gang – a mob mentality. Always out-numbered by crowds of cowards. The fight versus fear needs intense training, the kind that needs a special coach – a fearless leader.

Childhood dysfunctionalism made a deep impact. It was the driving force for extreme fat loss. Self-initiated, self-imposed, self-disciplined … at the age of 12. The secret that motivated my fat loss was not an ad for a magic pill, or master motivator, or fitness expert. It was need. Deep-rooted need. Intense self-disgust brought on by the brutal inner conflict of not being what I wanted to be and being what I didn't want to be. I was sick of being fat. Tired of being obese. Had enough.

I don't believe a 12-year-old can make a life-altering decision alone – a mentor is needed. A mentor connected to the protégé 365/24/7 – the soul of who we are and what we will become.

∞

The harder you train, the less you fear.

The enemy is not the bar that has to be lifted, not the opponent that has to be fought – it's the work that has to be done and the temptation to avoid it. The opponent lined up across from you is not the enemy – the enemy is the unwillingness, inability and fear of working hard to train and prepare.

Beating the real enemy beats the opponent.

The secret to working out for a lifetime starts at the top – mindset. Iron-will mindset. Not the type of workout program, not supplements, not the state-of-the-art exercise machines, not fancy gyms, not secret diets – iron-will mindset. Balls of steel.

Free will is connected to iron will. We all have a choice to turn free will into iron will but there's a price attached. The conversion is costly. Expensive. Free will doesn't turn into iron will automatically or by chance. Nothing just happens. Free will needs an exercise program to put the nuts and bolts together to lift it, to transform it into an iron will. And iron will is a work-in-progress. One nut, one bolt at a time. And without a guarantee that they'll stay in place. It's easy to lose some nuts and bolts along the way, no matter how big they are, no matter how tight they're twisted in.

∞

When dreams and reality don't connect, a nightmare starts. Unfulfilled potential causes conflict, an ugly fight that spreads inside out until the battlefield grows to the size of the universe. Left unchecked, the fight becomes bigger and bloodier than the mightiest of warriors can handle alone. A face-to-face meeting of the actual self and the intended self brings on a stare-down. But when they have to cohabitate, the bell sounds. Punches fly. No dancing, no bobbing, no weaving. Just toe-to-toe bombs.

The gym is the alley where the two can settle their differences ... iron out their problems.

The gym is not a "house of pain." The word "pain" is derived from the Latin word "poena" meaning, "a fine, a penalty." The dictionary defines "pain" as: An unpleasant sensation occurring in varying degrees of severity as a consequence of physical injury, disease, or emotional disorder.

The gym does not intend to punish – it strives to reward. The gym's goal is not to inflict physical pain. The objective is to eliminate pain by fighting pain, beating pain to the ground. The gym was invented to cure all pains – the pain of being physically and emotionally unfit. The gym is a place of pain conversion, pain transformation, where pain melts away like excess fat.

The gym is not a dysfunctional place. The gym's purpose is not to cause emotional suffering or mental distress. The gym doesn't exist to cause emotional disorders, but to build emotional order.

The gym is unforgiving[4]. The gym doesn't reward laziness, it won't enable pretenders – it exposes them. The gym will not hide incompetence, will not reward ineptitude and will not conceal deep-rooted fear of hard work. The gym exposes imposters, reveals weaknesses … and strengths. The gym is a forum to test what you've got, show what you've got and find out exactly what you haven't got and what you need to get.

The gym is the place where the size of the impact matches the strength of the impact. Nothing is out of whack. What you can't handle crashes down … who you lift up, reaches higher.

The gym is a place where you become what you repeatedly do, where you can change what you don't like, where you can build what you dream, where failure is temporary, where second chances – unlimited chances – let you pick up whatever pieces you drop on the floor, where you practice what you preach, where it's impossible to perform at a higher level than you train for, where the strong thrive and the weak get a chance to survive, where you cannot disrespect the game.

We won't know who we are until we face pressure – the relentless kind that won't back down, go away, bend, or break on its own. The kind that has to be faced, fought and beaten down.

---

4 A tribute to a masterpiece, *The Unforgiven*. By Metallica. Heavy   metal lifters owe a debt of gratitude to Metallica's heavy metal. Despite all the geniuses who have given us amazing gym music, no one does it better than Metallica.

Chapter 40
Destiny

Every workout has an individual destiny. "Workout destinies" are not created equal. Failed destinies, missed destinies, under-achieved destinies, rich/poor destinies, exciting/boing destinies. Negative. Positive.

Workout destinies are sculpted, not reached. Shaped, not attended. Produced, not imposed. Workout destinies are works-in-progress. They are built, one set at a time, one rep at a time – one call at a time. Workout destiny doesn't just happen. Nothing just happens. Nothing happens by chance – automatically. We don't get lazy by chance. We are not driven by chance. Accomplishments don't just happen. Neither do failures. Wins don't just happen. Neither do losses.

The destiny of every single workout is reached by fulfilling its purpose of making the impact it was intended to make – on self and on others. When the soul of a lifter meets heavy metal, an impact happens. The strength of the impact is tied to the strength of its purpose. Strengthening both mind and body makes an impact inside – then outside. There is no such thing as being strong for the sake of being strong. The strength we build in ourselves is purposeless until it reaches its potential by being lifted beyond ourselves. Beyond the triceps, biceps, traps and pecs. Beyond the lats, shoulders, abs. Beyond the quads and calves. And way beyond the posing, beyond trophies, beyond ribbons.

Destiny stays concealed until purpose is revealed.

$$\infty$$

The #1 police crime-solving theory is: When two items meet, a traceable change happens. Each connection causes a change – even slight – that leaves a trail of evidence. It's impossible for a connection to happen without an impact happening. A small impact or big impact … an impact is guaranteed. When two lifter's souls meet the impact causes strength and weakness to transfer according to the "exchange rate." An unbalanced exchange rate makes one stronger and one weaker – one spirit drains while the other fills. But, if the exchange rate is balanced, both get stronger.

The soul of a lifter is never fully conflict-free. Sometimes, it's a war zone. Sometimes it's a demilitarized zone. But the troops never withdraw. Whether its collateral damage, residual damage, or combustible material, any spark can ignite the soul of a lifter, plugging the force of iron will into the spiritual source – intuition, and creating **I-Force** – the twin engine Intuition and Iron will. Intuition makes the tough calls, iron will is the mindset that puts them in motion.

I-Force is the most potent survival mechanism against the enemy – in and out of the gym. It is the communications director for the soul of a lifter. I-Force builds armor – bulletproof but not soundproof. The inner voice can't be heard if it's being shouted down or pushed aside.

Intuition is the force of nature that compels us to make the right call. Street smarts. Reality IQ. It is the muscle that exercises free will – a practical wisdom centre, a place of higher learning – built, developed and shaped by doing it – being in the game, not spectating in the stands. It is the tuition-free education – the school of insights and lessons-learned through sweat, blood and dirt ... then stored on the inner hard drive. The miracle of intuition – processing more data than any computer, under intense pressure ... in the blink of an eye.

Intuition is the secret to designing a workout program. Intuition training connects workouts. Knowing the past creates the present. It's impossible to make the right call during a workout without knowing the recent and distant past. The best way to know the past is to keep extensive notes – record every workout. Not during the workout – after. Two reasons. Writing notes during a workout is among the worst distractions that block the potential of a workout. Broken focus is the leading cause of failure. It's impossible to plug yourself in carrying around a pad and pen. Second, memorizing a workout is the best way to build the burning type of concentration needed to reach full workout potential – what you focus on grows.

Possessing an iron will makes you work tirelessly to make an impact. What we can't do today is preparation for what we can do tomorrow. A lesson, full of insights that teaches us "can't do" is part of the natural struggle and "won't do" is the outcome of avoiding it. Caving into the pressure and demands of the natural struggle. "Iron will" means: No capacity to abandon, neglect or harm. Iron will try to kill you only if you let it – if you give it permission. Without consent, iron will never cause pain. Iron will is a tough, mean bastard with an unbending will.

Without I-Force, we're on our own, winging it with seat-of-the-pants bumper-car journeys that become the commercials for Friday night demolition derbies.

The ultimate destiny of a workout is not an isolated place. It's connected to the journey – the past, present and future – set after set, rep after rep, and every person influenced along the way. Sets and reps don't work out in isolation. They have to join together to lead somewhere.[5] The place where working out leads depends on how the individual destinies of each workout connect. The chain of workouts. Iron links joined together, solidly attached ... or detached under pressure. It's impossible to work out completely disconnected from yesterday's workout, last week's workout, or last year's workout. Every workout meshes. Otherwise, nothing happens ... and you'll quit working out.

No workout routine, by itself, will ever reach deep down inside to release the passion and the intensity needed to realize a workout's destiny. No "secret workout."

DON'T QUIT.

The secret to reaching workout destiny is not the new "special program" that claims to transform in a few short weeks.

That's not enough weight. One more plate!

The secret to reaching a workout's full potential?

LIFT!!!

The secret is not a cheerleader.

EMPTY THE TANK!!!!

The secret is not a high-powered supplement.

You're not done. It's not over!!

---

5   A mega-tribute to a mega-masterpiece, *Somewhere*. By Barbra Streisand. Recorded in 1985, we can hear what God sounds like. But *Somewhere* is only one of the many voices of God, alongside Andrea Bocelli (*Canto Della Terra and Con Te Partirò*) Geoffrey Tate of Queensryche (*Silent Lucidity*) and countless others who have contributed to the eclectic workout iPod. The secret to workout longevity includes the proper music, sounds that vary with the tastes of each Soul of a Lifter. An eclectic iPod is the key – situational music. Fit the mood, fit the circumstances.

The secret is not a timely energy drink.

Lazy sonofabitch … LIFT!!!

The secret is a relentless, merciless taskmaster – a bastard.

More sets.

The secret is a non-conformist. An original. A one-of-a-kind who can't be dragged down the traditional path that someone cut and everyone followed.

MORE REPS.

The secret is a tyrant who is never satisfied. A tireless, workmanlike, I-Force. Unforgiving. A kick-your-ass-but-make-you-feel-important, shockingly-blunt leader – a fearless leader.

You have two choices – be the same or be different … YOUR CHOICE!!!

The secret appears to be a mystery. An enigma. But it's not. The secret to workout destiny is the soul of a lifter.

Chapter Zero
Italian Battalion

There are no movies about Leonardo da Vinci, Michelangelo, Galileo, or Marconi.

"Dumb Italian" attracts. "Dumb, tough, violent Italian" attracts more. "Dumb, tough, violent and morally-bankrupt Italian" is the most attractive. The Academy Awards[6] love them. The *Godfather* trilogy endeared us to the Corleone family as Vito, Sonny and Michael shot their way to a bullet-ridden Oscar. In *Raging Bull,* Jake and Joey Lamotta re-defined family dysfunctionalism as they savagely littered the screen with knockouts, knockdowns and beat-downs, earning Robert De Niro a blood-soaked Oscar. The lovable Rocky Balboa became a cultural icon with his single-digit IQ and scud-missile fists. Television carried on the tradition as Tony Soprano, Christopher Moltisanti and the rest of an organization of madmen entertained us with weekly hedonistic bloodbaths. *Jersey Shore* made sure the cultural connection remained strong, ensuring that the 21st century didn't miss out on Italian muscle and mindlessness. Four decades of Italian psychopaths – iron-fisted, uneducated, uncivilized, mentally unstable, barbarians. IQs slightly above plant life. Box office hits. T-shirts, posters, bumper stickers … endless.

No one wants to be a "smart Italian." "Intellectual Italian" is surely an oxymoron. "Deranged" and "Dumb Italian" are sexy and glamorous – even a career goal – except to those who take exception to being labeled. Labels that blend and assimilate, bunch and cram into a … mob. Except those who don't fear their own personal identity. Except those who don't need a stereotype to masquerade their unwillingness and incapacity to break the mold and escape the box.

"Are your parents from the north or south of Italy?"

The "Law of Fascination" meets the "Law of Repulsion." Southern Italian immigration was considered one notch above the spread of a

---

6   Tribute to a masterpiece, *Taxi Driver*. Robert De Niro's portrayal of dysfunctional characters make him the greatest actor of our all-time. Michael in the *Deer Hunter*, Travis Bickle in *Taxi Driver*, the young Vito Corleone in the *Godfather,* and Jake Lamotta in *Raging Bull* separate De Niro from the rest of Hollywood. And his grandparents and my parents all came from Campobasso, Italy.

plague. "Europe is vomiting. She is pouring her scum on the American shore," is just one example of the 20th-century anti-Italian public sentiment.[7] The 1960s and '70s were not the Enlightened Era.

Residual effects of dark ages still linger in the 21st century. In 2008, Rocco Mediate was battling it out with Tiger Woods in the final round of the U.S. Open. During an NBC broadcast, NBC's lead golf analyst, Johnny Miller said, *"Mediate looks like the guy who cleans Tiger's swimming pool,"* and *"Guys with the name of Rocco don't get on the trophy, do they?"* Bias broadcast spreads.

Bias is a powerful motivator – inspiring mindlessness and ignorance, unifying those who share nothing in common except the desire to manufacture indelible labels – the kind with the super-glue adhesive on the back. *"You Dumb Wop!" "You Dumb Dago!"* Not "Nerd" Wop or "Bookworm" Dago. Dumb Wop and Dumb Dago. Brothers. Everybody in the family gets the same first name – an Italian tradition.

Bias makes an elementary school principal entertain Grade 5 kids with a one-man skit – mocking my father using an original one-liner, *"Bigga boss"* – childish minds know exactly how to gain the approval of a childish audience.

Bias makes strangers, converted to family by law, comfortably announce, *"You're the only Italian I can stand."* Bias makes a police veteran, who managed to repeat the exact same one-year career 30 times, welcome a rookie with, *"So … you're the third fucking Italian they hired!"*

∞

The **E-Gene** is a paradox. It's essential … needed to fuel the drive. Without the **E**mbarrassment gene, it's impossible to improve. But too much is a heavy weight to carry. The **EE-Gene** is rocket fuel. The **E**xtreme **E-G**ene has a launch switch that can ignite with major combustion and explode.

The **L-words** – **Lazy, Low-life, Loser, Liar** – lasting labels that can be lived up to – or … left behind. The attempted attaching of a label is not a curse – it's a blessing … training. Teaches you how to make the tough calls in life. Learn from your coach, don't shy away from reps, make the call and burn the image. Remember how the call was made. Never forget the lesson learned from an impact moment.

---

7 O'Brien, Michael (1987). Vince: a personal biography of Vince Lombardi. Quill. William Morrow, New York.

The soul of a lifter guarantees impact moments – **REPS** – **R**epeatedly **E**xperiencing **P**ersonal **S**lights makes an impact. **REPS** teaches important lessons. How not to behave or judge based on irrelevant information. Instead, how to evaluate based on evidence – hard evidence. How to make the call – how to exercise free will. Accept a label – or change it. Embrace a label – or tear it off. Wear someone else's label – or make your own. Assimilate into the mob – or separate from the rest.

Don't complain about what you tolerate. What is tolerated grows. Tolerating a wrong is an anabolic agent – it packs on size. If you accept it, you own it – you become it – grow into it. Ignoring **REPS** is running … sprinting from the problem.

∞

The gym encourages you to build your own path and follow it without fear of being a freak … feeling like a freak because of the audacity to differ from the pack. The audacity to be original instead of stuck in a pile of Xeroxed, carbon-copy humans waiting to be shredded and discarded into a recycling box.

The gym will not judge you, brainwash you, try to run your life, turn you into a lemming blindly following those who do not have your best interests at heart … or any interests at heart, except self-interest.

The gym does not discriminate. No jealousy, no envy, no bias, no prejudice. Equal opportunity. The gym does not play favorites. Admission is not conditional, it's guaranteed. No exclusion. No admission standards. A special place, where you make it on your own or you break on your own, where you can't ride coattails and no one can ride yours.

The gym is not a micromanaging megalomaniac. It doesn't restrict you, will never limit you, chain you to a desk, belittle you, overlook you, put you down, keep you down, block your growth, bend your will, or try to break your will.

The gym has no sympathy. The gym is a great listener but it has lousy shoulders to cry on. The gym shuts out chronic complaining – the whining, bitching, moaning, groaning, blaming, excuse-making, finger-pointing of sympathy-seekers. The gym has a strict accountability system. It does not recognize martyrs.

Chapter 40.2
Rush

The Oxford English Dictionary has 171,476 words currently in play and 47,156 obsolete words.[8] But none defines the "iron rush."

Working out is a relationship. First with yourself – with your mind, body, and soul. Second, it's a relationship with others. What you accomplish with a workout matters. Who else benefits, who improves, whose life becomes better ... other than your own, depends on the relationship built.

The first relationship tries to solve the impossible, never-ending battle of building a whole person. A complete, balanced human. Working out accomplishes this – temporarily. A glimpse at Utopia. The miracle of the iron rush – the natural rush. A brief flood of natural chemicals that fills the incurable narcissism – the need for big muscles, big brain ... and big connection to the source that can answer the mystery of the universe. For a few moments, the body, mind and soul are working in harmony. The perfect workplace. Aligned and unmaligned. Pumped muscles, pumped veins, pumped brain ... and pumped soul. The miracle of the pain exchange – self-inflicted pain in exchange for a pain-free body, pain-free mind and pain-free soul.

The second relationship makes the biggest impact – putting up iron ladders. Coaching others to fight the good fight.[9] The influence of teaching and mentoring is infinite – a spiral effect without limits.

Working out makes everything rise – muscle fiber, IQ, clarity of thought. Fleeting moments of personal inflation – expanded body, expanded mind, expanded soul. And a provisional truce. Not a full peace accord, not armistice. Just knowing exactly what to do and when to do it. The feeling of being "in place" – plugged in to a source – inner and outer. A lost soul momentarily finds peace in doing what not many can or are willing to do – push body, mind and soul past what it thought couldn't be done. Until the iron rush stands still.[10]

---

8   http://www.oxforddictionaries.com/page/howmanywords.
9   A tribute to a masterpiece, "Fight the good fight of faith." 1 Timothy 6:12.
10   A tribute to a masterpiece, *Time Stands Still*. By Rush, a great but underrated Canadian band.

The iron rush is a financial investment – saves on beer, hard liquor, prescription drugs, recreation drugs and performance enhancing drugs. Saves money and brain cells. And, a two-for-one bargain. Alongside the miracle of the rush is the miracle of the 20-minute window of opportunity. A 1,200-second post-workout time clock. A growth opportunity. Physical prosperity. All that's needed is the right fuel to fill the tank. A simple protein shake with glutamine does the trick. A guaranteed reward for intense work.

The gym doesn't just teach how to hope and cope. It doesn't teach just how to get by. How to merely survive another workout. No, the gym teaches how to stand up, fight, overcome, overwhelm, win … and win big. Repeatedly. Not just once in awhile – every day. The gym does not just teach positive thinking – it teaches exactly how to bust your ass to get something done. Something big – out of the ordinary. Something that most people can't do and won't even try. Something that goes beyond – way beyond – what and where the average person is willing and capable of doing … and going. The gym solves the mystery of hard work – extreme hard work. Debilitating work. It solves the mystery through the greatest teacher – first-hand experience. Facing, then breaking the fear that scares, terrifies and immobilizes many people – extreme hard work. The gym teaches that extreme hard labor will not break, devastate, or incapacitate.

The gym teaches the secret to building an iron-will mindset – convert pain to pleasure. Transform grief to gratification. Feel the rush instead of fear. Face fear with a fight, not a warp-speed flight. Changing the focus changes the outcome.The gym sets the stage for an attitude adjustment – with no guarantees. The gym won't make you fearless – it will only provide the resistance.

Addiction is connected to fear. And avoiding it. Fear of boredom, of the ordinary, of rushless days. Fear of mediocrity. Fear of the mundane, unfulfilled potential, unreached destiny, of meaninglessness. Fear of the automaton existence.

Fear of the broken ladder. Of going back to living with fear, darkness. Fear of fat. Fear of decomposing while still alive. Avoiding what is feared is more than a motivator – it becomes a passion. Or obsession.

The soul of a lifter fears waste – toxic waste.

∞

An iron-rich diet is one of the keys to fat-loss, anti-aging, depression and every other stress-inducer that attacks the mind, body and soul. The cure for feeling old is working out with 21st-century coddled athletes or spoiled wannabe cops, all younger than your workout clothes – and watching them quit, vomit, or vice-versa … and never return. Showing them up and/or them never showing up again when faced with the fear of extreme hard work, is not an ego-boost. It's survival – for both parties. Saves on mid-life crisis expenses for one side; saves the cost of a reality check for the other. Participating in a reality show is more painful than sinking in a couch and watching one. Role reversal – 52 is the new 22. Twenty-two qualifies for discounts at the pharmacy and the barber.

No rush? The side effects of keyboard overdose – the artificial insular world of Facebook, Twitter and YouTube has softened bodies, minds and souls.

The gym operates on the perfect exchange rate. It's a place where you get back exactly what you put in, where you take in what you put out, where work exactly matches results. It's impossible to get ripped off in a gym. The gym never lets hard work go unrewarded. What hard work expects, hard work gets. Hard work never results in failure and failure always happens without hard work. The gym is a place where success is guaranteed … if the price is paid. No freebies. The gym will not give away value. No hypocrisy, no contradictions. The gym is not paradoxical. No contradictions. No mixed signals.

The gym has a compelling purpose, a deep meaning, and is a relentless attraction. The gym is a magnetic force. It's a place where you totally control potential and destiny, where destiny does not control you. The gym is a place where you can learn to be, a place where the out-of-place can be in-place.

The gym is a place where you can let the miracle of the rush happen.

Chapter 40.3
Last Rep

The soul of a lifter holds the "last rep" in contempt.

The lifting impact goes deep. There is no meter that measures the impact of a soul-shaking workout. Every workout has the potential to make an explosive impact, just like a bullet smashing through a pane of glass, sending shock waves outward from the center, hitting places that have never been touched, reaching deep inside. But the biggest impact happens when the shock waves connect outside ... with your team, your protégé – whoever was put in your way to fix, to mend, to shape, to lift, to paste back together and send back into the game.

Constant change and growth is the key to defending against insanity – to not losing your mind. Physical, intellectual, emotional and spiritual prosperity fights off madness. Not re-invention. Not re-engineering what we are but adding on to what is – adding on to the past. Building onto the existing structure. Good or bad, the foundation doesn't get vanquished. A wrecking ball cannot tear down where we came from – what we did, what we learned, what we absorbed. The myth of "re-inventing" – we don't re-invent ourselves ... we build. A "work-in-progress." But when the work stops progressing, everything regresses back to ground level. An empty basement.

Impacts add up. Ten-thousand impacts over a 40-year workout career stretch beyond the years ... to infinity. The impact of spill-your-guts workouts add layers of armor. Like a second bullet hole through a pane of glass, a second-workout impact connects to the first, spreading its shock waves far beyond the original impact, reaching out to a new level just waiting to connect with the next impact. And, the next. And, the next.

Impacts become addictive. The deeper the impact, the deeper the need. The deeper the need, the deeper the hunger. And, out of deeper hunger,[11] a drive. An intense drive fueled by a growing tank that gets harder to empty and even harder to fill.

"Impacts" are not created equal. Some barely scratch the surface. Some go deep. Eventually, the soul of a lifter expects deeper impacts. Demands

---

11   A tribute to a masterpiece, *Out of a Deeper I   *y Lawrence Gowan, a great but underrated Canadian artist.

them. The soul of a lifter hard-wires the heart, mind and muscle to expect extreme impacts, those that pack a heavier punch with each lift. The infinite supply and demand economy. An intolerance for supply deficit that starts the endless search for heavier weight to lift. The hunt for bar-bending weight to challenge the will, to set the stage for the main event – "Mind versus Metal."

The total impact of ten thousand workouts builds a complicated network of connections that run too deep for the human eye to see. The full impact can't be measured. Only the soul of a lifter has the vision to see the score – and only if "Mind" is winning.

"Workouts" are not created equal. Every single workout is a connection of sets and reps – a chain of sets and reps with no guarantee that the chain will be strong. The quality and quantity of sets and reps defines each workout – hiding or revealing potential. Shaping or distorting the destiny of every individual workout.

Every set has potential – the potential to be ordinary, extraordinary, average, mediocre or not-in-the-game at all. It depends on where, when, how and why the last rep happens. Every set has a last rep, the equivalent of the finish line in a short foot race. Ordinary sprints have fixed finished lines. Extraordinary sprints have finish lines that keep getting pushed back, extended farther and farther, all the way to another level. Pushing back the finish line forces you to keep going deeper and deeper. And deeper.

The myth of "scripted workouts." In reality, they are limiting. A script that reads "set of eight reps" paints a fixed finish line. If the finish line is too close, you breeze past it effortlessly – unchallenged. An unchallenged test is an oxymoron. It's not a test at all. It's a formality.

It's impossible to paint a finish line when you can't read the needle on the tank. There's no sense in making a short finish line when the tank is full. Or a long finish line when the tank is empty. The finish line and the tank have to correspond – they have to connect so that the muscle goes to complete failure while recruiting as many fibers as possible to do its work. The twin miracles of **MMF** and **MMFR** – **M**aximum **M**uscular **F**ailure and **M**aximum **M**uscle-**F**iber **R**ecruitment. In the gym, failure is a goal, not a disgrace. The closer you get to failure the more success you achieve.

When the game gets tough, more players get off the bench. All for one purpose – to fight for the real last rep ... not the suspected last rep.

The last rep is the inner battlefield that both tortures the soul of a lifter and fuels it. Yet, the soul of a lifter refuses to define "last rep," refuses to acknowledge it, ignoring the looming presence of the last rep, and, fights to delay it. When the last rep is in sight, the soul of a lifter throws a flurry of punches – heavy bombs. Because if the last rep arrives too soon, hell visits the soul of a lifter. The inferno called unfulfilled potential – hidden reps – buried gifts. Dropping the weight before the real last rep is a cardinal sin, a unforgivable sin that haunts the soul of a lifter because the easy last rep is evidence – hard evidence of laziness, softness … no balls.

Eventually, the soul of a lifter views the last rep with contempt – deep contempt.

One more rep …

Two more reps – DON'T QUIT.

The last rep is the enemy. Fighting the last rep becomes the unwinnable war because neither the soul of a lifter nor "Mind" will accept defeat.

Chapter 12
Fat Fatigue – Fat Chance

Fat is fatiguing. Fat is deceiving – it looks like a soft enemy but it's a hard-as-rock, animalistic, tough-as-nails, vicious opponent. Sagging, bouncing, jiggling, protruding – fat is a heavy weight to carry around. Fat wears you down physically and mentally. Fat disconnects the inside from the inside, the inside from the outside, and the outside from the inside.

Fat versus an adult is a tough fight to watch. For mature audiences only. Not for the squeamish. Fat versus a 12-year-old is barbaric. It's enough for adults to turn their eyes away – or close them. Or simply get up and leave. Fat is strong enough to break the will of grown women and men. Fat can kill the spirit – unless you fight back. And fight hard.

But no one is born a fighter. No one is born with survival skills. Fighters are developed. Survivors are made – one rep at a time. The soul of a 12-year-old is not a fighting soul. It's a soul-in-training. And it's impossible for a 12-year-old to train alone and fight alone. If not guided, the child will become misguided.

The soul of a lifter doesn't bother giving reasons to a 12-year-old but there is a method to the madness. No sense explaining why … it's better to simply show how. Practice before theory. The soul of a lifter believes in scenario-based teaching, real-life case studies with simulated tests, street-survival tests. The soul of a lifter puts an unusual demand on nature and nurture in order to build strength, deep strength … unlimited strength. And the meaning behind it all is for later, much later. Can't go too deep with a 12-year-old.

A driving force can come in different shapes and sizes. Some are human, some are inhuman. And others are inhumane. Humans can send messages – simple, clear messages using the power of words. Humans have the capacity to make an impact, as many as they want, as often as they want, if they happen to be around. If they are interested. If they are called. Humans can teach, inspire, mentor … if the call gets through. Humans can coach and make a soul-rattling impact, if the call is accepted.

Substitute teachers can also be effective messengers. Inhuman forces can make as big an impact as human forces, or bigger. Like dysfunctionalism.

Childhood dysfunctionalism makes an impact. Thunderous, repeated impacts. Soul-jarring impacts. Impact reps – unrepaired Culture Shocks. Starting with one single shock that leads to another and another, stacked up until the shock waves crack the pile. Rubble, debris, shattered[12] pieces, messes frantically cleaned up hopefully before the next wave hits, fracturing the structure, followed by re-building, more tumbling, more piling ... until the mess is simply scattered around in the hopes that things will stick on their own.

"Culture Shocks" are not created equal. There are mild Culture Shocks, seismic Culture Shocks, tsunami Culture Shocks. None are isolated. All Culture Shocks are connected to each other, to the aftermaths, to the rest between that fills the tank. Shock, aftermath, rest. Shock, aftermath, rest. Set after set, rep after rep, forming a chain of Culture Shocks, all different.

Childhood dysfunctionalism comes in all shapes and sizes, packaged with the same ignored warning: Fragile – Handle with Care. Each one has its own personality – or lack of one. There is no universal, predictable set of symptoms. Each one has its own DNA, its own personal brand and its own personal narrative. And each one is connected to isolation and the Law of Detraction ... the insider is isolated from outsiders and outsiders are not attracted to the insider.

Isolation leads to separation. Disconnected. Unplugged. The inner circle shrinks to the size of a halo, a small confined radius, incapable of stretching or spreading on its own, wound-up tighter than yellow tape with "DO NOT CROSS" painted in bold letters, wrapped around the child – the crime scene. Inner-circle management becomes a life-long trial-and-error circus. Winging it – carnival-like inner circle where people step right up, take their prize, then pull up stakes and move on. The isolation of childhood dysfunctionalism is not a place – it's being "out-of-place." It's not knowing "how to be." Searching for a place, any place, simply to be and to be "in place."

"What's wrong with him?"

"I suppose it could be worse."

"Does he ever talk?"

---

12   Tribute to a research masterpiece by Dr. Carl Rogers who warned us about the shattered personality, the disastrous meltdown that happens when the gap gets too big and becomes recognized.

"Your son is mentally retarded. He might not finish Grade 3."

"What an embarrassment. What do Antonio's relatives think?"

"Have you talked to your priest?"

"Number 26 is a chickenshit. That's why he can't block."

The frustrations of childhood dysfunctionalism lead to conflict – in every direction. Toward, away from, inside-out, outside-in, upside-down, backside to frontside. Things get heated. Everything starts to miss – misdiagnosis, misfit, misled, misinterpretation, mistakes – all leading to medieval practices. Exorcisms of sorts – beat the demons out of the child, scare the shit out of the demons by screaming and cursing, or simply insult the demons – call them names hoping they'll pick up and leave when they've had enough and can't take it anymore.

Childhood dysfunctionalism attracts dysfunctional adults … people who fell through the cracks, making more cracks. Teachers, coaches, doctors, boat loads of professionals who achieved a title without becoming fully-functional adults. "Expert in dysfunctionalism" is an oxymoron – an amateur posing on a stage with professionals. Like inept criminals, "experts" who treat dysfunctionalism leave a trail of shocking evidence – spewing from their mouths. Statement after incriminating statement, stemming from a compulsion to voice absurdities.

And so, when the attempts of "loved-ones" fail, experts take their turn using the same play from the same playbook, over and over again. The play called, "public humiliation." Calling the same play, at warp-speed, no-huddle pace. Hit after hit, sack after sack.

But the impacts don't work. They can't knock the dysfunctionalism out – yet.

Repeated Exposure to Pressure – REPS, can be the strongest cure for childhood dysfunctionalism – if the pressure is heavy enough to cause a crack. If the pressure is properly supervised. If the soul of a lifter is coaching the child.

The causes of childhood dysfunctionalism go deep. Too deep. But there's one certainty – the Force of the Environment builds mindset. **E-Force** makes an impact. Positive or negative, mindset hard-wires attitude. DNA is the raw material – genetics install the "on" switch. Nature lines up the formation, nurture throws the bomb. But E-Force pushes the button.

The mystery of the "off" switch – missing from birth or broken through time? Nature or nurture ... the broken switch leads to extremes ... addictions. Addicted to the rush, addicted to the pain of the natural struggle ... addicted to being different.

A child's environment is simple – inner circle, the perimeter, outer circle. A three-layer network that surrounds the core. Generally, children have no choice about the occupants, no choice about who moves in and who moves out of each circle – each circle is fairly constant. Some new visitors and a few tourists, but mostly the same faces, same places. Like Saturn, a child is stuck inside the rings. Unlike Saturn, not all the rings are solid, shiny and bright.

Adult networks are much more complicated. The rings around an adult bend, twist, warp, sink, shake and sometimes break. The lines of demarcation get blurred. One ring blends into the other. Eventually, there's confusion about who's in which circle. Free roaming blends together invited guests, trespassers, intruders, invaders ... and occupants. Eventually, you can't tell them apart – who belongs, who doesn't. Who's a pain-in-the-ass, who isn't. An adult's environment becomes an unpredictable complex mess that changes daily, hourly, even momentarily. Like a seven-day weather forecast, E-Force changes with the wind, mixing sunlight with darkness, calm with storm ... and always making an impact.

A child's inner circle is like the first set of a workout. It sets the mood, the tone. It can stretch, flip the switch and start the rush of exhilaration, or it can go through the motions ... go too heavy and pull something, piss you off, frustrate you and double the struggle of the rest of the workout. Or triple it. An unnatural start makes the natural struggle harder than it should be. One cloudy day can darken the brightest of moods. Two days without sun turns down the dimmer switch a few notches. But constant darkened skies can blow a fuse and shut off the lights. "Gloom and doom" is impenetrable – nothing gets in, nothing gets out. The evil twins. Bringing on the worst darkness, keeping you in the dark without a single ray of light or hope.

"Gloom and doom" is both the product of, and the producer of family dysfunctionalism. Dysfunctional families are not formed, they're inherited. They cross oceans, span generations. My family's perpetual darkness started with reverse Culture Shock. An impact taking a wrong turn. A blackout caused by the wrong wires touching and the right wires not touching. Extremely foreign experiences that not only blew a fuse, but knocked the sockets out. Unplugged and unwired but connected to the past – tied to it, chained to it. Soon the past became cemented in the present and the future.

Rage, sadness, frustration, sadness, anger, sadness, impatience, sadness, volatility, sadness, hostility. More sadness. Isolation. Nothing touches the dysfunctional family and the dysfunctional family touches nothing. Slamming and smashing ... but no touching. Gloom and doom, no longer part of a forecast, becomes an expectation.

Fat violates the Laws of Nature. And nurture. Statues teach us that the human body was not intended to be fat. Elementary schools (the schoolyard, not the curriculum) teach us that children are never supposed to be fat. Fat has no place to hide. Fat has no benefit. Zero advantage. Fat is the weight of disadvantage carried around to exhaustion. Fat is always on your mind. Fat gets in the way. There's no way around fat. People stare at fat. Fat adults are treated differently. You don't see fat news anchors on TV. Fat is soft, mushy ... unstable, flopping around, trying to be held together. You can't just drop fat. Can't shake it like a cold. There's no vaccine. No one can be immunized against fat. There is no overnight magical remedy. And unlike drugs and alcohol for adults, there is no pill to swallow to ease the pain of being a fat kid.

"Fat" is not created equal. Fat believes in disproportionate distribution – easy to appear, hard to disappear. Fat disfigures, distorts, distends, disturbs, disrupts, but it just won't disappear.

Fat won't let you forget. Fat is a visible reminder of something gone wrong. And in a child's network, he is reminded often. Not his inner circle, not his perimeter circle, not even his outer circle will let him forget that something is wrong ... with him.

Fat is a speed demon. It builds up at warp-speed. All it took was one summer of lying on my back with a broken leg. Four months of sedentary isolation with a Goliath-sized cast, fueled by the three Italian-immigrant food groups – carbs, sugar and grease.

∞

In 1970, there was another place of isolation, one that inspired motivation, stimulation, exhilaration, concentration, separation, fascination ... The Library. In addition to wisdom on demand, there were librarians. Fitness models, before legwork became fashionable. An era when women in pants was considered unfashionable.

Twelve-year-old boys did not simply walk through the front entrance to The Library. Instead, covert operations, alternate routes and any disguise to prevent the dread of facial recognition. The extra legwork paid off. Stack upon stack, cover after cover. Full immersion. Every page became a vision board. But a price had to be paid. Research plus reading equals reject. The library whisperers: *"He spends hours in The Library ... READING!"*

But the soul of a lifter is an intolerant, skin-thickening message center. The soul of a lifter will not accept missed readings ... builds layers of armor and floods the minds of writers to guarantee viral messaging.

Books are both a offense and an defense mechanism for a dysfunctional child. Books can stop it from going deep while making the child go deep. Books position themselves in the child's inner circle. The E-Force supplement. Page after page, line after line, word after word. Books teach, coach, inspire, motivate, mentor, guide, brighten, build dreams, make dreams happen ... and, start the dream process over and over and over again. Written messages have a purpose – to make an impact, to stretch, to spread ... to make connections so that more impacts can be connected and spread. Impact distribution.

But, reading happens in isolation – deep isolation. The dysfunctional child was wrong. He wrongly accused the soul of a lifter of gross negligence, abandonment, incompetence and cowardice – not realizing the soul of a lifter was busy coaching. Training the lifter with set after set, rep after rep of "Reality 101" – not a beginner's program, but an advanced program – unconventional training. Opening the playbook, throwing everything – forced reps, supersets, dropsets, megasets ... all with no rest in between. Teaching survival skills. Unknowingly combating gloom and doom – negative E-Force.

∞

The soul of a lifter guarantees quality education, higher education – street smarts and book smarts. Credibility is earned, not awarded. Titles do not entitle instant credibility.

No one gets a free pass. No exemptions granted. No automatic belief in competence. S/he who asserts must prove. Everyone is questioned.

Chapter 40.6
Workout Partner

The greatest force in the gym is the release of hidden reps – reps concealed during years of underachieving. Hidden reps accumulate. They pile up until the weight of unfulfilled potential is too heavy to lift alne. The key to releasing concealed reps is a team effort, led by a coach – someone who can unlock the force that was intentionally packed away when the mind couldn't last a few more seconds … couldn't handle pain a little longer. Lost focus for just a few seconds and paid the steep price of underachieving. The untrained mind didn't want to go to the next level because the pain barrier seemed insurmountable. The untrained mind is a fierce opponent. The trained mind is the strongest ally. Training the mind trains the body. And vice-versa.

The myth of the "workout partner." A partner is an equal – a friend. A best friend who comforts and coddles like a cheerleader. A workout partner keeps company, prevents the pain of isolation and yells the obligatory, *"No pain, no gain!"* But one workout partner can't unlock the other's hidden reps. Workout partners are not escape artists, they're accomplices. They don't help the real lifter break out; they keep the real lifter caged in.

The soul of a lifter is not a workout partner. The soul of a lifter is a coach. A mentor with a master key that can unlock the sturdiest cage. A teacher who instructs and finds and pushes the "on" switch. The soul of a lifter is a multi-tasker – communications director, power source, internal GPS, moral compass, emotional paramedic, reserve tank, calculator, smoke detector, lie-detector, emotional pulse, spiritual pulse, evangelist, psychiatrist, coach, guardian angel, homeland security, beat cop, unit-to-back, informant, anabolic agent, mentor, sparring partner … but not a workout partner.

FMI … **For My** Information, how long will it take? The soul of a lifter never lies. There are no shortcuts. The soul of a lifter has the hardest product to sell – hard work. Extreme hard work. The soul of a lifter is not a snake-oil salesperson peddling short-term miracles. You can choose to ignore the soul – lower the volume, try to turn away, try to walk away, selectively translate the soul's messages, hear what you want to hear, discard what you don't, argue, be contemptuous and impetuous – but the soul of a lifter will not lie.

Unlike witnesses and suspects, the soul of a lifter always tells you the truth, the whole truth and nothing but the truth. No credibility issues. No need to waste energy on adding up the facts. No need to dissect, analyze, process and judge. The soul of a lifter is solid, like a rock. You can question, interrogate, cross-examine, but the soul of a lifter won't crack. You can choose to hate the truth ... be scornful, impulsive, impatient, disdainful, even view the truth with contempt, but the soul of a lifter will not lie. The natural struggle has bridges to cross but no bypasses.

The soul of a lifter cannot be left behind. Won't leave you, abandon you, desert you, ignore you, mock you, back-stab you, turn its back on you, fail to block for you.

∞

The "bench" paradox. The gym is the only place where first-stringers are on the bench and the only place where the bench is the playing field. Outside the gym, the bench is a place of inactivity. Non-participation. The place where the "reserves" sit. Bench-warmers. Second-stringers. And third-stringers. Watching the game play out instead of playing in the game. Watching the first-stringers live their dreams – dream on.[13] Inside the gym, the bench is the playing field – the place where the action happens. The place where dreams turn to reality – the ultimate change agent. The place where the inactive become active, the weak become strong, the poor become rich. The place where the switch turns on the light. And where you learn not to blink.

The gym is the only place where anyone can be a "first-string" athlete with no fear of getting benched. The soul of a lifter benches no one. The gym is the place with no sidelines, no stands – just room – for first-stringers. The soul of a lifter does not understand the concept of second-string. Or third-string or fourth-string. "Back-up" is what the soul of a lifter does ... not let you become.

The soul of a lifter sees a bench inside the gym as an opportunity to keep off the bench outside the gym. The gym is an even playing field – those who want to get off the bench can get on the bench. But those who stay off the bench, stay on the bench. A chance to lift the bench-warmer label and get back in the game – the only place to where you can reach

---

13   A tribute to a masterpiece, *Dream On*. By Aerosmith.

higher and higher and make the biggest impact possible. The explosive kind. It's impossible to make an impact without getting in the game. No impact can be made from outside the game. Just try.

The gym is the only place where all reps are starter reps, the purest meritocracy in society. Not one rep in the gym is a back-up rep. No one is buried in obscurity so deep down a depth chart that potential is not just lost, it's stolen. Robbed. Instead, progression by merit, not by skewed human opinion – no slanted judgment based on friendship, blood lines, or one-night, blink-of-the-eye relationships.

But the soul of a lifter is not a hog. The soul of a lifter trains only one client so that many more can be trained. Shared prosperity and abundance. The soul of a lifter does not play favorites. Can never been accused of nepotism, never been guilty of partiality, discrimination, or one-sidedness. The soul of a lifter believes in equal opportunity – open-admission ... but with a steep labor price. The soul of a lifter invests heavily into one client to fulfill a connective purpose – strengthen others.

The soul of a lifter believes in **BEER** – **B**lunt **E**qual **E**xchange **R**ate ... honesty out/honesty in, workout/work in, energy out/energy in. The soul of a lifter does not believe bullshit. Has no capacity to be a coddling enabler – a co-conspirator in potential thievery.

No desire to be a workout partner.

$$\infty$$

The gym is a fearless leader. The gym knows the secret to leadership ... it can kick you straight in the ass and make you feel important. At the same time.

Chapter 40.7
Rearview Mirror

The "rearview mirror" theory – past weakness fuels current strength. Strength is converted weakness – yesterday's weakness. What we can lift today was too heavy at some time in our past. All strength has to pass through weakness.

Current weakness is unconverted past weakness. Undeparted fear. Past weakness that did not change – stubbornly gripping the past, or never taught how to let go, or never shown the new way. All things are supposed to pass,[14] including weakness. Weakness that doesn't pass is a "connection" paradox – a disconnection and a connection. Unplugged and plugged-in at the same time.

Weakness is converted to strength by an energy source, a rush that powers it.[15] If it's mixed with the right elements, it becomes a fueled fire, capable of burning us up or down, or ... propelling us forward. It depends on the direction of the energy source. The soul of a lifter knows the formula – blending all elements together to produce a super high-octane fuel. Like when two wires touch, sparks fly. When a negative and a positive connect – explosion.

The radical transformational power of the rush is a miracle.

The past can weaken, or strengthen, or both. It can build up, or knock down, or both. The past can hurt, lift, drop, carry, topple, fortify or destroy. It can empty the tank or fill it, or both. The past is our training ground – good or bad, the past is our classroom. Understanding our past makes us understand our present and plan the future. Who we become, comes from who we are. Who we are comes from who we were. The way we think determines our future. Our experiences determine the way we think. And the way we think determines our experiences.

It's impossible to drive with 100% attention to the present – full focus on "now." Staring in the rear-view mirror takes our eyes off the road. But glancing at it is essential for safety. Staring in the rear-view mirror is

---

14 A tribute to a masterpiece, *All Things Must Pass*. By George Harrison, borrowed from Jesus, in Matthew 24:6-8. "... for all these things must come to pass."
15 Tribute to a masterpiece, *Sing the Changes*. By Paul McCartney.

careless – kills the drive. Never glancing back is unsafe – oblivious driving kills the drive. Field of vision … scanning … front and back. The past is our research. The experiments and tests that lead us to conclusions that fuel the drive to the future. The rearview mirror builds our destiny. Our drive determines where we end up.

There's a road in front and a road behind. The driver's seat is connected to the road traveled, the road traveled on, and the road traveled to. We move toward one and away from the other. The road traveled takes us to the road to be traveled.

Scripted plans for the future are limiting. Rigid plans have no room for change. No room for maneuvering – for adaptation. The secret is strategize and improvise – flexibility. Make the tough call when the unexpected happens – the tough calls that keep us on the road, moving forward. Making the call depends on the field of vision.

The path traveled then merges with the path to be traveled.

St. Thomas Aquinas taught us, "existence determines thought." Descartes taught us that, "thought determines our existence." In one of the most compelling books of all time, *Crossing the Threshold of Hope*, Pope John Paul II referred to both theories before reaching his conclusion: "I think the way I think because I am that which I am."[16]

The past can't be lived in but it can't be ignored … we can't live in the past – fully. We can't live in the future – fully. But we can't live in the present – fully.

Deleting the past is the equivalent of erasing every lesson learned, every insight absorbed – wiping the board clean. Emptiness. Doomed to repeat the past. Yet obsessing over the past kills the passion to learn more.

∞

The soul of a lifter sees a paved road but builds a new path, hears the usual language but writes a new one, feels the dread of the ordinary … and turns on the ignition switch … a drive down only new roads. An ignition switch with only one button … "on."

---

16 A tribute to a masterpiece of masterpieces, *Crossing the Threshold of Hope*. By His Holiness, Pope John Paul II. (1994). Published by Alfred A. Knopf Inc., New York. A must-read regardless of religious belief. An intellectual workout. Several reps are needed to process it. Pope John Paul II is one of the greatest minds in the history of wo/mankind. We are blessed to have been alive during his papacy.

Chapter 8-11
Textless Messages

Building armor and covering it are two separate concepts.

One of the cures for childhood dysfunctionalism is building armor. But layers of protection can become layers of deflection.

There were no text messages in the 1960s. No Internet, no Google, no Facebook ... no un-social connection. The '60s had only social connections, the old-school kind connected by real energy, not synthetic (dis)connections. No network of wireless isolation united by the common bond of hiding from life, concealed by a keyboard – viral separation. Unplugged from reality, plugged-in to the silent existence of Cyber-friendship where the biggest impact is fingers on a keyboard. The post-modern social experience has been reduced to the quantification of faceless friends, abbreviated words on chat lines, photos of the past thrown across the virtual frontier. Lost in Cyberspace.

In the 1960s, alternative messages were sent. Textless messages.

The garage needed work. So did all the neighboring garages. All of them were twisted, tilting or falling apart. None were wired to electricity. They were all the same, built the same. Not one garage stood out in appearance. Rows of broken down garages, neglected. Some of the garages were sturdy enough to protect what was inside. Some garages protected cars. Others protected piles of junk. Not one distinguished itself – except the garage with the artificial electricity. The one that sizzled. The one that lit up from an invisible raging, burning fire. The otherwise dark, decrepit garage converted to brightness by an infinite source of energy – the strongest kind.

The open, battered door gave way to free viewing. Prehistoric YouTube. YouTubeless – you, there, without the tube. Up close and personal. In-person. Live! Not voyeurism by distance. Live-wired to real energy, where you could catch fire, get jolted from the impact, where Culture Shock could transform into a power surge.

Power surges make an impact. They can burn an image.

To an 10-year-old, an 18-year-old is an elder. Four 18-year-olds are a mastermind group. And when they are lifting, pushing, pulling heavy metal, they become **D-Force** – **D**riving **F**orce. Watching a mastermind group perform ordinary reps makes a fuzzy picture. Extraordinary reps stamp an iron brand.

The soul of a lifter knows how to send a message – stage a live performance. Front row seats. Captivate with the power of a textless message.

$$\infty$$

Beam, bench, bar, bodyweight, basement, plates – the basics have transformational powers.

Business Development 101 – simplicity, focus, efficiency … and mindset. Contrary to popular myth, opening a gym is not high-risk. It's high-challenge. One perspective evokes fear. The other flips the switch – brings on the rush. Fear to fearless by changing the point of view. Attitude adjustment alters action.

Even a 12-year-old can start a gym. Start with the basics, one member and the best consultant – the soul of a lifter.

Gym equipment was inexpensive in 1969 because there was no demand. Weight lifting wasn't popular – it was a subculture. A bench, a bar and six ten-pound plates fit within the budget of a lost art – part-time student employment. A minor investment – one week's income from two part-time jobs – gave the capacity to build full body armor with the miracle of compound exercises – movements that use multiple body parts. And, like the miracle of compound interest, exponentially multiply strength and muscle size. Squats, bench press, front military press, curls, rows, close-grip bench press – no machines needed, no unnecessary expenses. A solid business plan.

A beam on a basement ceiling is sturdy enough to hold and pull-up bodyweight. A basement floor is sturdy enough to push-up bodyweight. And any chair with legs is sturdy enough to dip and lift-up bodyweight. The cheapest but most efficient piece of gym equipment is bodyweight. It's free weight – cost-free – not a fancy machine. Mobile, multi-dimensional, used for more than one exercise, doesn't take up floor space, doesn't need painting, re-upholstering, can't be bent and broken by being smashed to the floor, and, can't be inconsiderately left on a bar for other lifters to remove.

The most technologically advanced ab machine is the basement floor. Everything needed to build a six-pack can be accomplished with a basement ... including the track around it. Running around and around and around the neighborhood block melts fat ... space-age cardio ... roadwork.

But the most important part of a 12-year-old's training program is coaching – direction, supervision, inspiration and motivation from the strongest force of nature ... the soul of a lifter. The tireless mentor who develops the strongest muscle of all – mindset. Iron-will mindset.

∞

The first time for anything is memorable. So is the second, maybe the third. Then it becomes routine ... unless **SUMM** happens. **S**ubjectively **U**nique **M**eaningful **M**oments. Explosive experiences don't just happen. Neither does exhilaration. Or ecstasy. Or excitement. Sometimes it takes a miracle. Or miracles.

But miracles don't just happen. Nothing just happens. Don't expect miracles to mysteriously happen. Work for them. Miracles are gifts, waiting to happen every day ... but we have to work for them. And then see them – recognize them, because it's easy to take miracles for granted. There are no shortcuts to miracles. Each one has a natural struggle. Every miracle needs misery-busting. But every miracle makes an impact on a dysfunctional 12-year-old.

∞

Message constipation. The 21st century is clogging the system with messages. They entertain us, scare us, inspire us, enrage us, move us, and freeze us. Short messages, loud messages, text messages, mixed messages. But what we're really looking for – furiously searching for – is a straight message. Direct, to-the-point, no bullshit ... the straight-forward message. Direction. The next step. And the next. Which door to open, which door to close. When to flip the switch, when to shut it off. The answer is the textless message – intuition. That gut feeling straight from the heart ... and soul. The textless message has to compete for attention but it won't fight for it. Listening is optional. The textless message doesn't have a re-send button or a volume button. And, the soul of a lifter won't take "no," for an answer.

Chapter 1
The Deep Secret

No one is born fearless.

No one is born gutless.

Nothing just happens.

Gutless doesn't just happen. Neither does changing it.

The soul of a lifter knows the deep secret. The secret is an iron-will mindset. It's the secret to performance, achievement, workout longevity … ageless fitness. Iron will build iron will. Iron will change a dysfunctional child. But all the iron in the world will not help if there is no drive to meet iron. Like destiny, iron has to be faced, not avoided. Free will has to bring you there. But free will does not turn into iron by accident. It needs a coach to exercise it.

$$\infty$$

The secret to an iron-will mindset is changing a goal into a basic survival need.

Hunger, thirst, or choking for breath will inject life into the lifeless, pound a pulse into the pulseless … light a fire.[17] But "fires" are not created equal. Some are strong, some are weak. Some can be extinguished with a soft breath. Some fires can't be – no matter how hard the wind blows.

Fire is the soul of passion. It's impossible to go deep, reach higher, and make a thunderous impact, with the lethargy of a neutered dog. It's impossible to make a difference without a deep-rooted passion for what you're doing, what you believe in and who you're doing it for. Passion is not a passing flame. It's not an occasional spark. And it doesn't just happen. Someone – something – has to light the fuse. Someone – something – has to pour gas on it. Then you have to learn to do it on your own.

$$\infty$$

"Number 26 is gutless."

Halftime speeches make an impact.

---

17   A tribute to the masterpiece, *Light my Fire.*   nal by Jim Morrision and
The Doors, the second version by Jose Feliciano.

"Number 26 is chickenshit."

The impact is bigger on little league teams.

"Number 26 hasn't made one block all game."

Being the center of attention makes an impact.

"That's why the runningback can't score."

Impacts go deep.

"Coach Bob." The title is an oxymoron. His name was Bob, but he was not a coach. He was impersonating a coach, occupying empty space with his emptiness. Caught up in his own world, never stepping – never looking – outside himself. Exposing weaknesses without correcting them is a symptom of a weak mind. It's easier to expose someone's weakness than change it. Strengthening it, changing it, takes work – hard work.

Scientific research shows that a minimum of two-thirds of a group will conform to the attitudes and actions of another person, even if by doing so, it contradicts personal beliefs.[18] The "66% Conformity Rule." At least 66% will follow instead of leading, regardless of what is being followed. The percentage is higher with little leaguers. Halftime speeches make a long-term impact on ten-year-olds. What a coach says must be gospel truth. Number 26 must be a chickenshit.

Then the reps follow. Supersets and megasets of repetition with no rest. Number 26 is definitely a chickenshit.

Sometimes we make an impact without knowing it. Coach Bob did not know it at the time. He had no idea. No clue about the positive impact he made on my life. He lit a fire. And threw gas on it. And the switch broke – melted from the heat.

∞

"IF YOU LISTEN TO EVERY CRITIC, YOU'LL GO NOWHERE IN LIFE. ABSOLUTELY NOWHERE."

During my first season as a high school head football coach, I barked that statement twice in one day – for no apparent reason. Once during practice. Later during a gym workout. No one did anything wrong.

---

18   Tribute to masterpieces, conformity research listed in the bibliography including Milgram's shock experiment, Zimbardo's prison experiment, and Asch's line experiment.

No one acted like an asshole. No one was lazy, disruptive, or disagreeable. Everyone was working hard – extremely hard. On the surface no incentive-speech was needed. Afterward, I realized I had made a mistake. They knew what I meant, but I edited it for the next day's practice.

"You will hear criticism your whole life. That's a fact. People will try to publicly embarrass you and degrade you … stop you with their words. Can't escape it. BUT YOU HAVE TO LISTEN TO IT … AND LISTEN CAREFULLY. DON'T IGNORE IT. Then you have two choices – accept it or change it. NEVER ACCEPT IT. NEVER PROVE THEM RIGHT. CHANGE IT. PROVE THEM WRONG. That's not revenge. It's not retaliation. Just prove them wrong … with your performance. Not with words … PERFORMANCE!"

Bold statements make an impact. Positive or negative, bold statements make an impact. Words can strengthen, words can weaken. Critics have a purpose. So does embarrassing and humiliating. Forces you to decide – make a call. Crawl away and hide … or get off your ass, bust your ass and prove them wrong. Build thick skin. The pain of stinging words can break you … or make you. It's your choice. How you respond matters. Accepting it wires it – from your heart to your mind to your soul. But deciding to change … what a force you can unleash when you make up your mind to never hear it again! Change re-wires then hard-wires a brand-new you … new and improved version – with just a few scars.

Let pain motivate instead of devastate. Learn the art of the inner dialogue: *Watch me now!* Let performance be your outer dialogue.

∞

Every message has a purpose.

Altar boys don't have unions. No collective bargaining agreements. Just forced labor, a movement that unifies the parish and parents. There is no exit strategy for ten-year-old altar boys. Stuck in a holy rut. A dead-end job with no upward mobility. And no pink slip. No lay-off. No bail-out. No bail. Middle management always invokes Higher Authorities when whispers of mutiny spread … threats of life sentences with maximum minimums.

December 31, 1967. Double-duty with forced overtime. Eleven o'clock mass and two o'clock Benediction – in the middle of the NFL championship game. Dallas Cowboys versus the Green Bay Packers – in

Green Bay. At Lambeau Field. The shrine … the cathedral. The winner would represent the NFL in Super Bowl II – a time when the Super Bowl wasn't a super bowl at all but merely an after-thought. The Super Bowl started as a pain-in-the-ass game where the real champions – the NFL champions – played the champions of an upstart league – the AFL. An unconventional league that had the audacity to go up against the NFL – the Goliath of the gridiron.

Benediction was a bigger thorn-in-the-side to a couple of ten-year-olds than the AFL turned out to be for the NFL. A few old ladies in the pews, the best-looking organist in the diocese – she wore the shortest skirts and paid zero attention to fat, dysfunctional altarboys – and the stench of burning incense. Mixed emotions.

The job description was simple. Mumble some Latin sentences, drop some pucks of incense into a Medieval-like dumbbell, tighten it and light the pucks on fire through a small opening in the dumbbell. But like all mind-numbing jobs, temptation becomes a coping mechanism. The need for a rush is overwhelming. It's no match … even for iron will.

" … Don't tighten the dumbbells – watch what happens!!"

It's hard not to listen to evil when it's charming, charismatic … and funny.

" … and the Holy Ghost … "

"CARPET ON FIRE. CARPET ON FIRE!!!!!"

Blazing pucks, carpet-bombing Benediction. Shots fired.

"NOT THAT JAR … THAT'S THE HOLY WATER!!!"

Instead of getting fired, setting the carpet on fire at Benediction gets you, and your co-conspirator, the death sentence. Funeral Service, Monday morning, 10 a.m.

But reps are hard to break. More temptation.

" … and the Holy Ghost … "

"CARPET ON FIRE. CARPET ON FIRE!!!!!"

Deflected, burning pucks bouncing off the casket post.

Even the gloom and doom of black and white TV can send a powerful message. Last play of the game. NFL Championship on the line. Green Bay on the Dallas one-yard line, losing 17-14. Third and goal. Sixteen seconds left, Green Bay calls its final timeout. Green Bay quarterback confers with head coach Vince Lombardi – the guy whose name is stamped on the revered Super Bowl trophy. The "safe play" would be to call for a field goal attempt to tie the game and send it into overtime. *"A tying field goal is the conventional call,"* the broadcasters remind the viewers. The temperature is minus 13 degrees with a wind-chill making it feel like minus 48. The "Ice Bowl." Balls of steel needed to survive.

At the end of the timeout, Green Bay lines up … with the quarterback under center. No kicker – no field goal attempt. The QB runs with the ball, into the end zone, right behind the block of #64, the right guard who explodes off the line driving his man backwards into the end zone. Final score: Green Bay 21 : Dallas 14. The most dramatic play in pro football history. And, for the first time ever, a new technology made sure there were infinite reps – instant replay. Over and over again, instant replay reminded us of the most famous play in the history of football … the play where the guy with balls of steel made the most unconventional call in history – "go for it" with the game on the line. Drive their asses off the line and win … don't kick the ball over their heads and tie.

If Benediction had dragged on 16 seconds longer … .

∞

Lillie's Pharmacy had the best-looking, best-dressed female employees. And lots of them. Every shift. In an era when females never wore pants to work. And glass windows on the front of the store. Six giant glass windows. Better than black and white TV. The 1968 version of the Internet.

Reps are the key to getting good at anything. Back and forth. Set after set. Supersets, megasets. No rest in between. Learning the science of "covert observation." The reps paid off. There she was, front and centre, moving the legs right up against the window in full view. *Instant Replay* in bright, gold letters, next to the black and white picture of #64 sitting on a bench. Above the football player's picture, the green and gold print read: The Green Bay Diary of Jerry Kramer. $1.25.

The soul of a lifter balances the Laws of Attraction and Distraction. Two attractions, side-by-side, can cancel each other out, or compete with each other, or … freeze the moment. $1.25.

The back cover confirmed suspicions: "From the locker room to the goal line, from the training field to the Super Bowl, *INSTANT REPLAY* is the inside story of a great football team – bullied, maligned, loved and mothered by an extraordinary coach, Vince Lombardi – and the day-by-day diary of Jerry Kramer, a football veteran, and this season's literary superstar." The heading on page 212: "December 31." On page 218: "Thank God for instant replay."

Number 64 wrote a book about the play, the season, the team and the coach who had balls of steel, balls big enough to defy conventional thinking ... and not blink. A book about "going for it" instead of kicking ... and not blinking.

Empty pockets go deep. So do distractions. The book returned to the stack. But the soul of a lifter never gives up. More reps in front of the pharmacy. Heat, temperatures soared. The view never let down. And *Instant Replay* stared outside. A runaway best-seller did not move for three weeks.

A sister never gives up on you. A $1.25 loan never re-paid.

Instant Replay never let down ... not once in 26 readings.

∞

| < Back to Messages | Mark as Unread | Report Spam | Delete |

Gino Arcaro Feb 11, 2010 at 3:26 pm Mr. Kramer: I am starting my 40th season coaching football. "Instant Replay" convinced me to become a football coach. Countless players have had life-altering experiences during that time. So have I watching them. Your book has made a deep impact on many lives.

Jerry Kramer Feb 15, 2010 at 5:07 pm Sorry Gino that it took so long to get back to you. I feel very flattered that a guy like you read and appreciated my book. I appreciate you and your motivation. I wish you all the best, JK.

Thank God for *Instant Replay* ... and Facebook.

Chapter 2-6(1)
Performance Demand

H-POD is impossible. **H**igher **P**erformance **O**n **D**emand – can't happen. Every job, every sport, every relationship … everything we do has a game-day performance – performance for public consumption. Performance that will be measured – score will be kept. Elusive but continuously pursued, every human at some point strives for it, desires it, chases it, fights for it, doubts it … some give up on it. Performance is the most accurate personality test.

Game-day performance doesn't just happen. Neither does H-POD. We aren't born with an "H-POD" switch. We can't simply flip a switch and reach a higher level of any performance – physical, intellectual, emotional, or spiritual. Higher game-day performance is reached through training and during training.

Training and performance are directly proportionate. **G**ame-**D**ay **P**erformance will never exceed **T**raining **P**erformance. **GDP = TP**. Performance can only match the highest level that is reached in training. How we train is how we perform. Fight like you train, train like you fight. Training sets the bar.

Performance demands are the survival secret – secret to success. Any kind of success – school, work or play. Performance demands are the secret to athletic survival, business survival, academic survival, relationship survival, financial survival, fitness survival – physical, intellectual, emotional, spiritual fitness. Because they start with what we demand of ourselves, performance reveals every personality trait developed, underdeveloped … and completely absent.

Performance demands are the secret to surviving the natural struggle – facing it, beating it, not avoiding it … then thriving and actually living instead of just existing.

A performance demand is a work order – issued to self or others. A mandatory request to get a job done. No option. No choice. Just make it happen – no excuses. A performance demand is a force of nature and nurture – making a call and mobilizing a team to make it happen … no matter what. The secret is to pay attention. Otherwise, the performance demand won't be identified. It will walk away, scot-free.

Performance demands don't just happen. And not just for any reason. They need a trigger.

∞

GET OFF YOUR ASS AND LOSE SOME WEIGHT, YOU FAT SHIT.

The soul of a lifter was a worldwide web connection even in the dark ages, using innovative wireless communication and messaging before NASA had even landed a man on the moon. In 1967, you couldn't Google "fat loss." No infomercials, no online research, no Oprah. "Carb-restricted diet" was a foreign concept. For Italian immigrants, carbs were survival food – nutritional Darwinism. Bread, pasta, polenta ... cornmeal so thick it could double as a spare tire. Carbs were the cheap energy source that fueled the next day's work in the fields, in the mills, in the playground. But left unused, carbs in a ten-year-old's body spilled over into mounds of fat. Laying on my ass for months with multiple leg fractures – motionlessness, mush, causing the wheels to fall off, in the blink of an eye. And when finally learning how to walk again – the wheels carried a heavier load. A load that quickly went from fat to obese.

If muscle grew as fast as fat, no one would ever get frustrated and quit working out. Fat and muscle are the "hare and turtle" of fitness.

Obesity 101: Physical dysfunction plus mental dysfunction equals isolation. Total disconnect.

HAVE ANOTHER PIZZA, YOU FAT SHIT.

The soul of a lifter never ignores simplicity, is persistent ... and recruits messengers. Get off your ass ... don't have another pizza.

Fat loss 101: Exercise plus nutrition equals the basics. Exercise and nutrition are connected. One won't work without the other.

Nothing changes until a deep need surfaces – like bubbles of fat around a child's gut. A fat gut is the best motivator to become gutless. There is no armor that can cover a fat gut. It sticks out in private, in public. An attention-seeking junk food junkie fueled by chronic rationalization that justifies the behavior.

"Why is your brother so fat?"

"Oh, he broke his leg. He couldn't walk for six months!"

"Wasn't that two years ago?"

Rationalization is worse than any Goliath-sized opponent. Negative **E-Force**. Excuses. Enabling. Evil. Extreme bullshit – internal and external. Lies, alibis. Honesty MIA (missing in action).

The strongest need to change is the need to stop over-the-top pain and misery. Ordinary suffering is not enough. Saturated suffering is a change agent. The overwhelming kind. The kind where we've had enough. The soul of a lifter permits certain things to happen to get our attention – trials, tests … whatever it takes to overwhelm so that change can start happening. So that we can start moving toward our authentic self. So we can start realizing our potential. So we can stop wasting our potential. So we can open our eyes to miracles.

We are free agents. We are free to decide when to change, what to change and how to change. But we need help to exercise our freedom properly.

Fat loss 101 is a beginner program – and the secret is to start at the top – mindset … the basics. Nothing more. The basics start the race. They get you out of the blocks and move you in the right direction. For a fat ten-year-old who had absolutely no idea how to get outside the box, walking around and around and around the block was enough to get out of the blocks. And, when the fear of just reaching for the edge of even a small box was overwhelming, I had a big sister's hand to hold. A sister is the best personal trainer. Long before the phrase "personal trainer" was invented. And an even better strength coach, without ever spotting a lift.

You can't make it on your own.[19]

It's unnatural for a child to connect with only one person. By the age of ten, a kid should be on the road to making meaningful connections. Just ask the experts.

"What's wrong with your brother?"

"Can't he walk by himself?"

"Why won't he cross the street?"

Humans were publicly broadcasting ignorance long before social media.

There is no such thing as a half-sister. Or step-sister. Just sister. One connection is enough. Thankfully, sisters are not unionized. No CBA

---

19   A tribute to a masterpiece, *Sometimes you can't make it on your own.* By U2.

protection. Grievances, strikes, work stoppages and walk-outs would side-track, off-track and ultimately derail. A sister has to be multi-dimensional ... public defender, communications director, psychiatrist, Guardian Angel. Being stuck to your sister's hip is a security plan – a live **GPS** – a **G**uiding, **P**rotecting **S**oul. Or maybe it was her resemblance to Lillie's Pharmacy staff. Or both. Either way, a price was paid – community harassment. Young and old, female, male, amateur, professional ... shots fired from every direction.

"How long are you going to babysit him?"

Freaks are connectors. Freaks are uniting forces. They bring people together with a common cause of condemning anyone who has the audacity to be different. Community derision is the training ground for thinking so far outside the box that eventually the box disappears.

The secret to survival is to start off by doing both ... back and forth, in and out of the box. Think inside the box when the basics are needed. Think outside when it's time to change. The fundamentals always build the foundation. But innovation is found outside the box. Then, when it's time, moving forward means leaving the box – and bringing the basics with you. Thinking outside the box means taking it one step at a time– one rep at a time ... in the right direction. A GPS helps. Think outside the box long enough and the box disappears – when it has to. Until the basics are needed again.

Reps as a freaky child, are the vaccine against a debilitating addiction that boxes in – the "approval addiction." The freak-child vaccine is immunization that builds the armor[20] to fight off criticism – the antidote for blind conformity, the antibiotic that destroys the virus of public condemnation for being different and the strength program that builds iron will.

Single reps have little value. Doing something once will not make an impact unless it's followed by many more reps – endless intense reps. And not just the exact same rep repeated. The secret to growth is reps with a growing degree of difficulty. Thousands of challenging reps build a chain. An iron chain. Not enough reps, or soft reps, are like an unfulfilled destiny – a broken chain. A mess of solitary links scattered aimlessly. There are

---

20 A tribute to a mega-masterpiece. "Put on the full armor of God so that you can take your stand against the devil's schemes." Ephesians 6:11.

many steps to transformation – like rungs on a ladder. Reps connect to sets. Sets to workouts. Workouts connect to meals. Each one is a link in a chain. How solid the chain is, depends on how many links are connected.

The cost of being a dysfunctional child is steep but there's a big payoff – the non-conformist mindset – addicted to the thrill of thinking different, acting different, taking different risks – the rush of extreme difference. High-risk investment can yield high returns. There's a blessing in every curse.

The miracle of a "compelling purpose." A goal, filled with risk and uncertainty ... a goal so challenging that it would inspire even the most lifeless automaton. Like all miracles, we don't make them. They are made for our benefit. An obese, socially inept, mumbling 12-year-old, incapable of making eye contact, incapable of stringing a couple of sentences together, could not possibly come up with a compelling purpose on his own. No. Divine intervention was needed. The soul of a lifter made the performance demand. When the mission was accepted, the switch is flipped. The miracle unfolded.

Any compelling purpose sparks a "Code 3" – lights and sirens. Nothing is allowed to block the path. The brain, body and soul go into survival mode to make sure the golden rule is followed: Avoid the worst-case scenario. For a fat, dysfunctional child who carried the "chickenshit" label like a weight-lifter struggling with a bending bar across his shoulders ... ready to crush or be crushed, the compelling purpose was the approach of high school ... and high school football. The looming gloom and doom of pain – getting physically and emotionally pounded into the ground – by assholes ... the ones who also just graduated from elementary school. The worst possible consequence – getting cut from the high school junior varsity football team ... not being able to "cut it."

Running in circles around and around and around the confines of one city block gets boring. There's no escaping boredom when striving to get really good at doing something. To escape boredom, you have to work in boredom before taking the next step. It doesn't have to be miraculous – just one step outside a comfort zone – like the track around the high school football field. A track that became a vision board for a lost, little-leaguer who made a performance demand on nature. Running laps and laps and laps around the field of personal dreams[21] makes a huge impact on mounds

---

21   A tribute to a movie masterpiece, *Field of Dreams*.

and pounds of fat. Better than any cardio machine, twister, roller, or as-seen-on-TV comfort machine.

∞

Message to parents: Don't fret if your child doesn't have the "Arnold V-shape" while in the crib. Don't agonize if your child can't explain the theory of relativity before entering kindergarten. Don't panic if your child doesn't have MLK/JFK-oratory skills before graduating elementary school. Don't lose your mind if your child doesn't run, jump and lift like an Olympian before reaching puberty. Like a delay-of-game penalty, sometimes the next play can't get going in time, but eventually it will … if the connections are strong enough. If the soul of a lifter makes a performance demand.

∞

What you focus on grows – including fat loss.

Fat does not come with an expiration date – you have to make one. You have to attach that label. Fat is a major source of conflict. Inner and outer. Unresolved conflict is the cause of sadness, depression, anxiety, rage, violence, hatred, envy, jealousy and every other negative stress that will rot body, mind and soul.

Solving the outer conflict starts with solving the inner conflict. The pain of inner conflict doesn't just go away. It won't leave on its own. Like drunken guests who overstay their welcome, the pain of inner conflict needs to be evicted. Forcibly removed, if necessary. And that requires another kind of pain – work. Extreme hard work. Physical exertion. Manual labor. If the pain of inner conflict outweighs the pain of hard work, the rotting accelerates. Pushes petal to metal. When the pain of hard work can't be handled, the rationalization speeds up. More excuse-making, more complaining, moaning, groaning, finger-pointing … but no meaningful positive change. Just a waste of precious life. Unresolved inner conflict can go one of two ways – good or evil.

You can't think outside the box until you've been trapped in one. No one is born to think outside the box … or inside the box. Like everything else, both are learned. Nature builds the box – nurture positions you inside or outside.

∞

Fat burns off one step at time.

Fat loss is connected to drive and fuel.

One single first step is the first rep to a new habit. Rewiring doesn't just happen. And it doesn't happen all at once. An entire load of excess fat will not be dumped all at once. Fat is lost one blubber cell at a time. One step, one rep at a time. The first step points you in the right direction – or misdirection. The brain and body will follow.

Losing fat is a work-in-progress. The first step must be simple and doable, not radical and unrealistic. Addition by subtraction. Stop eating junk food – even a 12-year-old knows that pushing away junk food makes the quickest, biggest impact. No special knowledge is needed to identify junk food. No Master's degree, no diploma. No certificate is needed to learn what junk food is and to avoid it. Any human of any age can figure out step one – stop eating junk, stop drinking junk.

Losing fat doesn't just happen. Fat loss will fail without iron will. Iron will cement and solidify. Iron will change fuel-deficiency to fuel-efficiency. Iron will change softness to hardness … if the need is deep enough. No achievement ever happens without a deep hunger. Deep need has to replace deep fried.

Honesty never out, honesty never in. A false reality. Science fiction. Fantasy and delusion. Destruction by obstruction … cementing tired, old, unproductive, self-destructive habits. Chronic rationalization gets hard-wired like an out-dated program that slows the operating system … eventually clogging it up until it shuts down. Left unchecked, rationalization becomes almost criminal – chronic rationalization breaks the bullshit meter. Eventually, the suspect cannot identify bullshit out of a lineup.

The gym promises brutal honesty. The gym is incapable of bullshitting. The gym's bluntness shocks those unfamiliar with frankness. Culture Shock. The gym believes in honesty out – honesty in … you get back what you send out. The gym has zero tolerance for deception. The gym teaches you to honestly judge yourself while letting you practice abundantly.

Habitual excuse-making is a staple of the martyr syndrome. A sympathy-seeker addicted to pity – self and otherwise. Don't be a victim. Be accountable. Be responsible. Don't look to assign blame. Believe that failure is not an option – ultimately. In reality, setbacks will happen. Stumbling and fumbling are part of the price – the cost of tuition for higher learning.

Really believe that the end result will not be failure. Don't just post it on a wall. Don't just wear it on a T-shirt. Live it. Condition yourself to never accept mediocrity – yours or others. Adopt a zero-tolerance policy for half-assed work. Commit yourself to avoiding the pain of embarrassment. The secret is to remove "quitting" as an option. Get it done. Believe that quitting is not an alternative. Believe that quitting is not a choice.

The first secret to not quitting is to focus only on the first step. Not beyond. Don't try to find the finish line. Do not look at the big picture. Focus only on one step at a time. After the first step, concentrate on the second step. Don't look beyond that. Focus on one move only, not the whole board. For beginners, one move is manageable. The whole board is not. Staring at the whole board builds mounds of pressure strong enough to make you crack.

The second secret to not quitting is gaining experience in not quitting. Become a habitual finisher. A closer addict. Complete the job. Finish what you start. This applies to fat loss. Define success in your terms. Build your own dictionary. Make your language concrete – measurable. Divide the assignment of fat loss into stages. Each stage with a clear finish line. Make it a short track. A sprint. Cross the first finish line. Feel the rush of finishing. Then repeat. Experiencing success is addictive.

If help is needed, find a coach. If there isn't one available, turn to the soul of a lifter – a tireless coach. Never misses a workout, never fails to appear at practice. And 24-hour access. The soul of a lifter never fails to return a call, is never too busy to help pick up the mess, never too scared to back you up when shots are fired.

The soul of a lifter never runs out of energy. A rechargeable battery and jumper cables ready and willing to exchange power.

∞

Running Hard On Pavement – R-HOP, joins "compelling purpose" and "nutrition" to complete the fat-loss trilogy when a performance demand is made. The miracle of roadwork melts away blubber. Short distance and long distance. But R-HOP is one of those best-kept secrets

… because it's hard work, uncomfortable, not profitable, and it has to be done in isolation.

Sprints can make any coach look like a genius. Yelling, *"RUNNNNN!!!!"* is the secret to being a great coach. Daily sprints during practice transform the human body – not just change it … radically transform it. No machines, no equipment, no special knowledge – cost-free, minimal teaching, minimal learning. The basics are simple – body position and pumping the arms along an imaginary track. And anyone can do it. Sprint, walk, sprint, walk, sprint, walk … intervals, running hard then walking hard. Start off by going as far as you can and doing as many as you can.

Football coaches use sprints to transform their players into machines – physically and mentally. But sprints aren't reserved for football players. Sprints are open to the entire human race. Including fat, dysfunctional 12-year-olds.

Difficulty and disconnection are the two reasons why we don't try something, don't try harder, fail, lay down, roll over, surrender, walk away, quit and never try again. The pain of hard work and isolation. Busting your ass – alone. And there are infinite synonyms for, "it's too hard."

"Running on pavement hurts my knees!" A full beer bottle can slip out of a drunk's hand and injure a knee. The pizza delivery car can back into a knee. The local drug dealer can break a knee for failing to pay a drug debt.

"I'm not a good runner." That would change if there was a desperate need to run – or if there was a cause: *"Free beer!! … free food!!"* If you've been blessed with all the working parts, you were born to run.[22]

You can't watch TV, read, flirt, gossip, talk on a cell phone, reminisce, laugh, or carry on 20-minute interventions while R-HOP, and R-HOP is a non-profit venture. There is no economical reason to promote the benefits of any simple activity that doesn't need tens of thousands of dollars for machines, maintenance, repairs and replacements. Running is the simplest, most inexpensive form of fat loss. It's a natural act. Instinctive – choosing flight instead of fight. The body's flight mechanism does not come with a user guide. The soul of a fleer goes on automatic pilot.

But simplicity is often ignored. Complication is sexy, attractive. Far more attractive than simplicity.

---

22 A tribute to a masterpiece, *Born to Run*. By Bruce Springsteen.

Hard work and isolation are scarier than a dark alley. Too much risk, uncertainty ... and loneliness. Every natural act has a natural struggle. And all natural struggles are ugly – unattractive, plain, non-descript and too hardcore. But they're needed. Essential. The natural struggle is the only training program that prepares us for the main event.

$$\infty$$

The gym believes in Athletic Darwinism. The natural struggle, survival of the fittest but the chance for all to get fit. The gym is enlightening. It lets you shine, wants you to shine. But the gym is demanding. It expects you to go deep, reach higher, break limits, fight Goliath, beat Goliath.

To change anything, we have to first conquer ourselves ... overcome what we currently are to get to what we want to be. If we give in to what we are, it is then impossible to effect change. No one can change us – we have to change ourselves, our situation. No one will lose our fat. No one will make our muscle. No one will build us. Someone will teach and guide us, but we have to do the heavy lifting.

1RM – lifter language for **"One-Rep Max."** How much you can lift ... once. The heaviest weight that you can lift for one single rep in a specific exercise such as bench press, squat, or deadlift – the traditional powerlifting trilogy ... test of strength. 1RM is the answer to the most common question, "How much can you lift?" For thirty years, I was addicted to 1RM – 75% of my workout career was centered on a passion/obsession with 1RM. Not once a month, not once a week ... every workout. Then 1RM spread to non-traditional 1RM lifts – curls, rows, chin-ups. Then it spread outside the gym to anything that wasn't nailed down.

Addictions are contagious. First the 1RM addiction was private. No audience. But some symptoms leaked out in public ... *"just pour the damn wheelbarrow!!!"* Then I spread the 1RM to my football players and changed the rules – 1RM only after exhaustion. Complete fatigue. *"Who cares what you can lift when you're well-rested! Let's raise the bar!'* Then I changed the rules again – $1RM^2$ – back-to-back 1RMs. $1RM^2$ was next-level addiction. But the mystery 1RM is the real hard stuff. No one knows when it's coming. Just be prepared.

Years of 1RM causes wear and tear while building strength but it's not the absolute solution to big muscles and fat loss. The one certainty about

1RM is that it prevents fat buildup ... in the brain. The crushing challenge – crush the weight or be crushed. The need to hold a weight, one that can crush most humans, over your chest or on your shoulders ... feel the rush of controlling it ... then lifting it.

Thirty years of daily 1RM caused a rebellion. A joint force of chiropractors and massage therapists. So I changed the rules. 1RM is now part of every set. Every single set. The last rep of every set is the new 1RM.

Change the focus, change the outcome. Change the rules, change the game. Write your own rules, win your own game.

Start with a performance demand.

Chapter 34.5
Attempted Suicide

Evil plays dirty. Evil poses as the soul of a lifter. Dresses the same, acts the same, talks the same. They almost look identical. Tireless, intellectual, physical, workmanlike. Persistent, dedicated, passionate, even obsessed. Both use the natural struggle as a strategy. But with diametrically opposed missions – one tries to reveal full potential, the other wants to conceal it.

Evil's playbook has one play called, "broken focus." It's a simple play. Evil does not ignore simplicity. But unlike Allen Iverson, evil does not mock practice. Practices go live – full contact. Workouts reach new heights of intensity. Seven days a week, no days off. Evil is never satisfied – bigger, stronger, faster, leaner, meaner. More is expected, more is demanded. The infinite spiral effect.

When evil makes a performance demand, a deep force mobilizes to fulfil Evil's mandate: Broken focus has to be executed flawlessly … break the opponent's focus, and the will follows. Half-assed efforts are not tolerated. Evil never accepts mediocrity. Broken focus is a game-breaker. And to jack up the pressure, evil uses a warp-speed no-huddle. A lightning attack – ground and pound, aerial bombing … every play executed without a hitch.

"Broken focus" is a masterpiece. A genius drew it up. A big team is not needed to execute it, not in numbers or size. A small but committed team is enough. A team with one mission: Stop the plan – beat destiny. But evil is chickenshit. So it recruits heavily to fight its battles. Any one of us can be recruited to carry out evil's mission. Evil has no balls to face its enemy. Evil enlists others, an army if needed, to fight. Then sits back and watches. Those who can, do. Those who can't, watch.

Evil is cheap. It doesn't arm itself with expensive weapons. Just the cheap stuff like gossip, rumor, drama, fiction scripts. Words are powerful. They can be anabolic or catabolic. Depends on how they are injected.

The basis of broken focus is attraction. Evil uses limitless attractions to take our eyes off the road. Side-tracked, even momentarily, leads to off-track. The Law of Detraction and Derailment.

But evil can teach us – when we fight it and beat it. Battling evil raises our reality IQ – lessons learned from the frontline. Every enemy teaches the gift of insights – deep insights ... for free. No tuition, no hidden costs. The highest quality of education. No summers off, no standardized workload formula, no class-size caps. No mindless meetings to inflate self-importance, no toxic work environment, no burn-out. Just hardcore teaching. So, like any opponent ... study evil – learn through intense preparation. Analyze game video. Scout your opponent. Even evil has habits. Even evil reveals its tendencies. Lessons are learned from every opponent. And the stronger the opponent, the stronger the lesson.

Evil's playbook is unconventional. It's not a playbook, it's a system. Even though broken focus is the only play, evil's system is limitless. Evil has countless ways to break focus. And evil has many faces. Smiling, warm, friendly, charming, charismatic, sensitive, understanding, lovable, flattering, jovial, credible, trustworthy, enlightening, interesting, attractive ... with a dark side. Evil is a master poser, who has done the legwork.

Evil reveals itself in many ways. Limitless appearances, but the same play. Broken focus can look like failure or ... success. Both delight evil.[23] Failure can break focus, and success can sharpen it – and vice-versa. Success can carpet-bomb focus and blast it to fragments. Success can be worse than the worst failure because it breeds complacency. But so does failure. The inability to manage success or failure kills the sense of urgency that drives the soul. Evil can make you become extremely good at things you hate to do, make you become the best in the worst of places. Put you at the top of your game even when the game is in the bush leagues. Success brings praise that keeps you in that place. Standing still. Misery inside a box. A double-homicide crime scene where both potential and destiny are victimized. Leaving your soul on life support.

Evil believes in the Law of Distraction by Attraction. Evil uses no-holds-barred tactics to beat down hope, drive and passion until dreams are bruised, bloodied, carried out on a stretcher and stacked in the ICU. Evil works hard to distract potential by attracting "impotential" – a word not yet admitted to the dictionary. It means: Situations or people that render you weak, powerless, limp, unable to perform – **ED** – Extremely **D**ysfunctional.

Evil trains hard. A training program unmatched. Intense, heavy lifting, long distance roadwork, sprints, speed bags, heavy bags ... supersets,

---

23 A tribute to a masterpiece, *American Pie*. By Don McLean.

megasets, dropsets – with no rest at all. Evil never misses a workout – ever. Evil never fails to appear at practice. Because evil refuses to lose. Expects to win, to be undefeated. Rep after rep, set after set until the play is perfected each and every time. No mistakes.

Evil is a dirty bastard. A pathological sonuvabitch with no conscience. An opportunistic sociopath. Evil uses intense pressure to sack every single attempt to go deep. Evil uses relentless pressure to throw us for losses, stop us from running with the ball, stop us from picking up speed ... from running over the competition and scoring some points. Evil is the nasty defense that shoves, jabs, throws elbows, hooks, fouls on every play. And rejects every shot we take, not always illegally.

Evil is in shape, fundamentally sound, a master of the basics. Man or zone, evil can pressure from any position. Evil is the first on the field and the last one to leave. The hardwood, the ring, the turf ... evil is multi-dimensional, highly-skilled, hall-of-fame material. Heartless. No conscience. Plays whistle to whistle.

The fight against evil is unregulated – worse than the National Hockey League. Cross-checking, sticks to the head, boarding from behind, skull-cracking, teeth-extracting hits – nothing is ever called. The referee doesn't just hide the whistle, there is no whistle. Actually, no referee. But unlike the NHL, a year can't be taken off to fix the game.

As much as they try, no government has been able to legislate the fight evil brings on – or win the fight against evil. Despite all efforts to control and police our thoughts, words, actions and passions, no government has been able to outlaw fighting by evil. Evil visits every nation, every state, every province, every city and schedules fights any place it wants. No government intervention. And no sanctioning. No pay-per-view. Everything is live and free, public or private.

Evil has no game clock. No referee to stop the fight. It attacks until the objective is accomplished – until the soul is killed.

∞

One year is a long time to spend working at a job you hate. But 34 years is an eternity. What you focus on grows, including working at jobs you hate, passionately. The kind where the joy inside you is forcibly removed, dragged out kicking and screaming, replaced by the most sinister bastard –

dread. Like any unwelcomed guest, strength is needed to separate ... from the evil ... from the downward spiral that attempts to kill the drive.

Maybe blaming evil is an excuse, a cop-out for failing to exercise free will ... for not having the balls to leave a job behind when I knew I should have. Is accusing evil just a cover-up for the inability and unwillingness to make smart, tough choices? For shutting down the volume when the soul of a lifter spoke? For choosing to ignore the daily signs, hourly messages, the minute-by-minute ticker that screamed, *"GET OUT. MISSION COMPLETE. YOU HAVE ANOTHER ASSIGNMENT."*

Or should I have recognized that my situation was a training program designed by evil's opponent? Intense workouts coached by the soul of a lifter? Honing a message that screamed just as loudly, *"MISSION INCOMPLETE. THE NEXT ONE WILL NOT BE ASSIGNED UNTIL THIS ONE IS FINISHED."*

$$\infty$$

Evil's best weapon is fear. Instilling fear. Drilling fear. Hammering fear. Only one side of the good-versus-evil war arms itself with weapons of fear. Darkness, dread, depression, doubt, deflation, debilitation. Fear-management is the secret to survival. But the fight is not against humans – it's a waste of time being pissed off at assholes.

"We do not wrestle against flesh and blood but against principalities, against powers, against the rulers of the darkness of this age." — Ephesians 6:12.

Translation: Get pissed at the power of darkness that made the asshole. I have failed miserably and continue to fail miserably, to apply this simple rule. And yet I apply the defence of "darkness" when I'm accused of being an asshole. Like the presumption of innocence, we all have the benefit of the presumption of darkness – but it's not automatic. It kicks in only if we prove resistance – evidence of fighting back.

Here's the good news. We have access to fighting equipment: "Put on the full armor of God, so that you will be able to stand firm against the schemes of the devil." — Ephesians 6:11.

The soul of a lifter doesn't fight evil. It manages fighters.

Chapter 2-6(2)
300

Like potential, secrets can get buried until someone finds and unleashes them. Some secrets are re-cycled information – messages wrongly labeled as "spam," deleted before being read. But the soul of a lifter persists. Like a network marketer pressing "send," over and over until the message is read – and spread. Revelation, distribution, processing, digestion – the true path of viral messaging. Rep after rep, set after set, the same message rises from the trash folder, gets pushed into inattentive minds until … until there's reaction.

"Ten cents, please." Like automobiles, nothing drastic has changed with books. They look pretty much the same as they did in 1969. Hi-liters had not been born. Neither had laptops, cell phones, digital recorders, iPods or Crackberries. The '60s had conventional addictive substances, simple stuff like cigarettes. Recording information depended on two dinosaurs from the Neanderthal stage of the Communications Evolution – paper and pen.

A library card was not a badge of honor. Neither was reading, studying … all violations of the manliness code that 12-year-olds were expected to abide by … unmanly activities that were part of an underground culture. But the basement of the library afforded the best view of the next levels.

Contrary to popular myth, the 21st century did not unveil the secret to making big muscles. The 1960s did – in libraries … miraculously. In language that a 12-year-old could understand. Like treasures, the secrets were hidden, waiting to be re-discovered … the next rep of a discovery. And the next rep always makes a bigger impact than the previous rep.

Miracles seem complicated but they're not. The point of a miracle is to simplify. Water into wine, walking on water, parting water, all have one thing in common – unexplained phenomena. Mystery. "How did s/he do that?" meets, "I really don't need to know the details." We have been conditioned to believe that miracles stopped happening 2,000 years ago. But they happen all the time. Epic miracles of Biblical proportion happen during every workout. It's just that now, they're expected. We're spoiled. The novelty wore off around 33 AD. Ancient miracles became a tough act to follow.

Like today, miracles were not called miracles in 1969. Thank God the soul of a lifter assigned readings. Three of the "Fabulous Four"[24] strength-building miracles – neural pathways, ATP production, adaptation and mindset – were re-discovered, dug up … using a ten-cent library card.

∞

There's a spot during a bench press where it feels like the weight is picking up speed, where it shifts into high gear and tries to crash down and crush the life out of you. That's where the conspiracy happens. **G-Force** and iron partner up. **G**ravity joins forces with the bar in an attempt to break you, make you shake and tremble until the weight makes an impact by landing on you. Two-on-one is never a fair fight. You either control the bar, fight gravity or it controls you – put the brakes on or let the bar drop, smashing down on your chest. If you beat the dynamic duo, the fight isn't over. You've won only round one, the negative stage of the lift – the descent, the lowering of the weight. Round two is lifting it off your chest – the positive stage … the ascent.

Labels are misleading. The negative stage gets a bad rep. It doesn't get the same credit as the positive stage. Both build strength. But the negative stage builds only if three things happen: The pace is just right, the bar stays on track coming down, and the chest is not used as a trampoline.

The bar is not intimidating. By itself, the bar is a lightweight. It only weighs 45 pounds. You decide the size of the opponent – middleweight, heavyweight, super-heavyweight – by how many plates you add to the bar. You decide the size of the fight. The size of the opponent determines your appearance – what you will look like. Lean and mean, or sticky and sickly. There's a direct relationship between opponent strength and the strength you build. Heavy weight builds heavyweights. Light weight builds lightweights.

But sparring with lightweights is essential – not just for warm-up. Lightweight reps, done over and over again, ignite miracle #1 – neural pathways. The human body performs a miracle, connecting mind and body, through repetition. Reps hard-wire the body, making a movement second-nature. Automatic. Guaranteed.

---

24 A tribute to the masters of masterpieces, The Beatles.

Demanding thousands of lighter reps builds the programming – the guts of the system. No-brainer motion. Doing without thinking, especially the kind of thinking that normally fuels fear and self-doubt. When a lifter has too much time to think, thoughts move toward disaster – worst-case scenarios. Extreme negativity. But the miracle of neural pathways solves that problem. Routine removes negativity. The simple act of doing the same thing over and over makes a performance demand on the body – wires it up. The miracle of neural pathway lets a pitcher throw heat one nano-meter inside the strike zone, lets a guard drop an ironless three-pointer, lets a gymnast dismount with a perfect ten – makes a lifter fearless of the opponent. Performance on demand by performance demand. Hundreds of reps start twisting the wires together. Thousands of reps weld them solid. Tens of thousands of reps cement the connections.

The key to being fearless of a heavy bar is to make the body work on auto-pilot. Make a performance demand on neural pathways and a hard-wired machine is built. But miracles don't work in isolation. They're connected.

In 1969, gas prices didn't go up and down like a light-rep bench press. Filling up an empty tank did not require a bank loan. And the only true hybrid machine was, and still is, the human body. Perfect hybrid with not just with two tanks … three, that automatically fill up themselves, mysteriously, and switch from one to the next without pressing any buttons.

Three tanks and a fuel that is miraculously made by the machine – Adenosine Triphosphate (ATP). An endless supply of muscle-contraction fuel, without carbon emissions, refineries, greedy corporations, oil spills, taxes, or other Big Brother government intervention. It's the equivalent of high-octane gas for a car – premium blend. The good stuff.

Three tanks connected by three play-clocks. The first tank is extremely small – only ten seconds of capacity. When the tank empties after ten seconds, it takes 60 seconds for the body to completely fill up this small ATP tank with more high-octane fuel. A one-minute pit stop. The second tank, a larger one uses lower grade fuel – still ATP, but made from lactic acid. The lactic acid tank has a one to two-minute capacity. Lower grade but longer drive. When tank #2 empties out, the third tank takes over – the largest one. This tank is huge – a one to two-hour capacity. It uses oxygen to produce ATP.

Miracle #2 – ATP production, is mind boggling. Without a full pit stop to re-fuel tank #1, the body will use the portion of tank #1 that has been replenished, along with tank #2. For example, if the pit stop is only ten seconds long, the body will use the one-sixth full tank #1 along with tank #2 before switching to tank #3.

A workout is an exercise in ATP management. Every workout is a chain of emptying and filling tanks. The strength of the chain is connected to the strength of each tank. And all three tanks are strengthened by training them. The first tank is trained with ten-second sets – anaerobic alactic training. The second tank is trained with sets that range between ten and 120 seconds – anaerobic training. The third set is trained by sets that exceed 120 seconds – aerobic training. The key to strength and conditioning is training all three energy systems. Making a performance demand on all three tanks builds a human machine.

Strength Deficit Management – **SDM** – is connected to ATP production. It is the ability to keep strength levels high by preventing lows. SDM is not about energy conservation. It's not about saving energy. It's about making more and using more. Not losing strength during a workout is the key to losing fat and making muscle, and the secret to maximizing a workout. This is why every set, every rep, every amount of weight used and every second of rest has to have purpose. There has to be a reason for every call made during a workout. Why you lift what you lift.

SDM builds a machine made to last – workouts, decades, all with a lifetime guarantee. But SDM is not isolated to ATP. Miracles are connected.

There are no investments that guarantee a higher return except heavy, intense lifting. Making a performance demand with **HELL**. **H**eavy **E**xtreme **L**aborious **L**ifting – makes the body perform miracle #3 – adaptation, building armor – while you sleep. Armor on demand. The body answers the demand of strenuous performance by strengthening itself for the next one. Stressing the body with heavier weight mobilizes the internal construction crew. Working out tears down the structure, sleep rebuilds it. But the return always exceeds the investment. Guaranteed. The rebuilding is not equal to what was torn down – it's greater. The body compensates by building a bigger, stronger structure each time because it expects more weight, more intensity the next time. The body prepares for more HELL by making itself armed and dangerous. Transformation by hard work. A heavy price is paid but a higher return is guaranteed.

The Law of Expectation. Self-fulfilling prophesy. The Pygmalion Effect – you get what you expect … and more. But only if there's a demand for it. Demand and Supply. Make a performance demand and the body will supply the armor. Greater demand, tougher, bigger, stronger armor – with balls. Positive adaptation makes an impact.

So does negative adaptation. The body will not reward soft work, comfort or laziness. Bad investments make you pay with bad returns. Transformation will not happen with a minimal investment. Instead, the body goes into debt – muscle debt.

Thank God for libraries, they taught the first three miracles that can build human machinery. The fourth miracle, the one that needs to connect to the first three to build true strength, was not learned in a library. It was taught by the soul of a lifter.

Iron will make the miracle of iron-will mindset. The fabulous four miracles will not happen if there's no drive to the gym or in the gym. The gym will not perform the miracles of hard-wiring, fueling, and armorizing without the proper mindset. Iron-will mindset. Nothing else matters.[25] Mindset is the key to building muscles, losing fat, getting stronger, never quitting, enduring, workout longevity, balls, fearlessness, never ever quitting, getting stronger, resilience, consistency and never EVER quitting. Mindset is the secret to performance – what you do, how well you do it, how long you do it. The game has four quarters, nine innings, three periods, two halves. No one gives a damn if you have a great first quarter and then quit. Dominate the opponent in the first two innings and then quit. "Short career" is an oxymoron. It's not a career, it's a visit. Tourism. Sight-seeing.

Iron-will mindset is the magic formula that makes the greatest transformation in the gym – turning fear to rush, turning discomfort to comfort, turning displeasure to pleasure. Iron-will mindset builds attractions – attraction to hard work, attraction to the rush, attraction to body shock, attraction to bust-your-ass, reach-deep-down-in-your-gut, limit-breaking, shake-you-to-the-core workouts. Attraction to uplifting experiences.

---

25 A tribute to the masterpiece, *Nothing Else Matters*. By Metallica. Two "personal bests" recorded to it.

Iron will stops you from quitting. Iron will keeps the drive alive, keeps you in the game, keeps you in fighting shape while stopping dreams from turning into nightmares. Stops you from getting knocked out, caving in, giving in just when the weight gets heavy – right before the real growth opportunity presents itself. Iron will stops the pain of regret – of walking away from the threshold just as the door opens ... instead of crossing it.

The reason for quitting anything is the opposite of iron will ... broken will. They're related. They come from the same family ... with free will. Iron will is broken will that worked out. Broken will is iron will that stopped working out. No one is born with iron will or broken will. Yet we all have the potential for both. It depends on free will. How free will is exercised determines whether iron will or broken will reaches full potential.

Iron will attracts and is attracted to extremes – extreme risk, extreme danger, extreme challenge, extreme achievement, extreme strength, extreme impact, extreme exhilaration and ... extreme rush. But, extremes attract and are attracted to extreme consequences – extreme disappointment, extreme failure, extreme heartbreak ... extreme darkness.

∞

Attraction can turn into obsession – when it leads to destruction – negative reps that demolish whatever stands on its track. Obsession is related to passion – the Cain and Abel of inner drive. They look alike, act alike, have similar personalities. Both are scary, fearless, reckless, relentless, impulsive, charming, charismatic, attractive and ... unstoppable. Forces of nature, powered by high-performance motors that never stop, infinite high-octane fuel and white-knuckle steering – swerving through traffic, racing to get to known and unknown destinations. Both are born out of need. Something missing. A deep hole. An abyss, that as Nietzsche taught us, will stare you down if you stare at it long enough ... until someone blinks.[26] Focus on emptiness, emptiness grows.

Obsession and passion have presence, the rare combination of audience-captivating force. Originality, strength, expertise, innocence, trustworthiness, one-of-a-kind, never-to-be-duplicated

---

26   A tribute to a masterpiece by Friedrich Nietzche who warned us, "When you stare into the abyss, the abyss stares back at you."

performance, don't-fuck-with-me belligerence, get-off-my-stage, move-out-of-way-I'll-go-in-first attitude. Presence makes an impact. Presence is unforgettable. Presence can move any crowd. Motion through emotion. Applause, praise, admiration, rage, disgust, repulsion ... presence brings out the very best ... and the worst.

There are two differences between obsession and passion – how free will is exercised and the outcome. Passion produces explosive experiences. Obsession simply explodes. Both are choices, not fate. Neither just happens. Both are the products of conscious decisions. Not situations ... how we react to them. Post-modern mind-controllers who want to politically correct our thoughts, speech and actions, lump all inner drives together under the title "obsessive," using "obsession" as a synonym for "passion."

Passion is feared because it works – it separates the strong from the weak. Passion breaks the homogeneity that desperately wants to blend failure and success, mix mediocrity with excellence, level the playing field to reward all performances – half-assed, full-assed, quarter-assed, or just plain asses. Passion lifts. Passion goes deep. Passion breaks barriers – smashes them. But passion also scares the shit out of people – passionless people.

$$\infty$$

Like all wrongful accusations, weak evidence led to strong speculation, or strong evidence led to misinterpretation. All leading to a bad call. Wrong translation. Jumped to an unjustified conclusion, or, pre-conceived biases revealed themselves. Either way, a case of mistaken identity – tagged a person with an unusual drive as an "obsessed, out-of-control extremist" unable to achieve the elusive "let it slide" mantra that self-proclaimed, expert, wannabe counselors/psychologists preach is the road to the promised land.

The problem with false accusations is the indelible label tattooed on the suspect. Say something loud enough and long enough, people will believe it. Using "obsessive" to label the need-to-achieve is name-calling by the weak-minded who fear natural selection. It's a pack leader control strategy, a way for megalomaniacs to keep everyone in the same place, at the same level – back in the pack, so far back that they can't catch up or pass the pack leader. Pack leaders try to kill drive. Leaders fuel it. Leaders inspire the drive, fill the tank, push every drive to its limits ... and beyond. Pack leaders leash the drive. Leaders unleash it.

A performance demand flips the switch that starts the drive down the road to passion or obsession ... the road taken depends on where you're looking. It's easy to swerve in and out of lanes. Iron will become a passion or obsession because it's impossible to let the human body perform its miracles without the miracle of iron-will mindset. Weak mindset leads to weak body. Strong mindset, strong body. No exceptions.

∞

JOIN THE 300 CLUB.

Muscle magazines were different in the '60s. They were strength-training, non-fiction literature. True stories. Relevant, immediately applicable, and in the mold of academic journals, not today's science fiction glossy fantasies, poorly disguised supplement brochures posing as gospel truth.

The article explained the virtues of benching 300 pounds and the formula for doing it – bench press a lot. Not cable-crossovers, not declines, not inclines ... bench press. You don't learn to throw a fastball by throwing curves. Three-hundred pounds was the benchmark for bench press, the admission standard into a club – a culture of strength. The article did not explain a secret program. No scripted workout that guaranteed a 300-pound bench press. Instead, it simply pointed out that bench pressing 300 pounds needed miracles. High, lighter-weight reps plus lower, heavier reps plus at least 60 seconds rest between sets plus *"a strong, tireless work ethic."* No mention of a 12-week transformation, no special supplement, no magic machine. No bullshit.

The soul of a lifter uses imagination and innovation to make a performance demand. An article written by a stranger. And a catchy title in bold print.

Thank God for libraries.

Chapter 2-6(3)
18 Inches

A boy with a book was a freak. A boy under a bar was freakier. A boy in a bar was a man. Reading and working out were paradoxical dysfunctional male activities in 1969. And in the '70s into the '80s. Like Italian immigrants, literary and lifting were minorities – foreigners. Intellectual workouts detracted from the dumb-Italian star attraction. It wasn't cool to be smart in school. High marks needed a strong defence. Making the honor roll was dishonorable.

Derision followed by more isolation. Academic success and manhood were not connected. So, reading had to be kept a secret. As did working out. "Arnold" was a cult name, not yet a household name. Two underground activities, one at a library, one at home. Both isolated places.

But secrets are hard to keep. Reading and working out reveal themselves eventually. Dysfunctionalism disappears when two opinions change – private and public. Insider and outsider attitudes. The best way to change attitudes is appearance and performance. Contrary to the popular myth that appearance does not matter, it does. How many fat news anchor people report the news? How many obese weather people try to make sense out of the Canadian climate? Judgment by appearance may be superficial, but how we look goes deep.

Despite post-modernist attempts by parents and teachers to eradicate the concepts of failure and disappointments, performance matters. It did in cave-person times, it does today, and it always will. Including Judgment Day. Reality is a natural selection process where the strong survive and the weak get torn apart, self-destruct, and suffer the devastation of broken will.

Performance is the universal language. It breaks all communication barriers. Translators are unnecessary. Ineptitude and excellence, incompetence and brilliance all cross borders. No visa needed. Performance has been, continues to be, and will always be wo/mankind's most powerful wireless messaging – good or bad.

Performance offers a guarantee ... one irrefutable Law of Nature. The work ethic of a farm animal is the strongest, most powerful personal brand. They can call you anything but not the L-word. It's impossible.

No one will ever call a driven person lazy – guaranteed. And as long as they can't call you lazy, nothing else matters.

"Lazy" is created equal. There's lazy bastard, lazy sonuvabitch, lazy dumbass, and just plain lazy. The lazy label is like a tattoo. A brand. A stain on character. An indelible mark, there forever unless a radical, painful procedure erases it. There will never be mistaken identity – working like a beast of burden will never leave you mistaken for a lazy burden.

Achievement attracts. Making things happen, getting it done and doing it when no one else can or wants to, draws attention, admiration, praise, applause ... and controversy, criticism, resentment. Achievement can unite or divide, rise or polarize.

Strength attracts. A power magnet, a drawing force that pulls in a crowd, captivates it and creates a following – of users, abusers, maligners, malingerers ... and protectors. Like a train wreck, strength attracts good and evil. Good Samaritans, rubbernecks, ambulance chasers, media and anyone else trying to profit from the fortune and misfortunes of others. Those who want to use your strength, share your strength, take your strength and those who want to test it. All of which can weaken you, lower your defenses, turn your jaw to glass, earn you a standing eight-count. High energy costs cause power outages, blackouts ... if your training slips. Or if you ignore your corner crew. Or if you simply can't hear the next play called.

"I used to work out." Nothing cures dysfunctionalism like a pair of guns. And nothing promotes bullshit like a pair of guns. Eighteen-inch biceps make an impact. Better than a tattoo, 18-inch guns make a personal brand, a distinguishing feature that separates from the rest – a customized, memorable, individual ethos. Eighteen-inch artillery shatters the myth that appearances do not matter.

No one ever says, "I have 18-inch triceps," or "I have 18-inch arms." No, "I have 18-inch biceps." Biceps and triceps are connected but biceps get all the isolated credit.

Appearances send powerful messages: "I work like a beast of burden," or, "I don't give a shit about myself." Appearances are a virtual resume ... a CV in motion. Appearance answers a lot of questions without asking ... the quickest, most honest background check. Appearances are the single-most potent letter of reference ... for the secure.

Insecure people are scared of 18-inch hammers. Fear of anything different leads to bullshit generalizations: "Probably a knuckle-dragging Neanderthal with an IQ slightly above plant life."

No one ever says to a fat, dysfunctional child, *"I used to be fat,"* or, *"I used to be dysfunctional,"* or, *"I used to be both fat and dysfunctional."* But when they see 18-inch arms, the bullshit switch turns on ... and gets stuck. *"I used to have 18-inch arms, and a 32-inch waist, and I worked out six days a week. And I benched 400 pounds. But then* (insert excuse for quitting)." Note: physical aliment, work, spouse, money and children are the top five.

Bullshit #1. He never had 18-inch arms and a 32-inch waist, not once in his life, because if he did, he'd still have them – 18-inch arms are addictive. You can't go back to skinny, flabby arms. The mind won't allow it.

Bullshit #2. There are 168 hours per week. Four hours per week invested in exercising represents only 2.4% of your life. Six hours would be 3.5%. Calculate the hours per week spent watching mind-numbing TV shows. Or reading on Facebook that someone is tired and going to bed. Or murdering brain cells by getting hammered in a bar and vomiting all over the floor until someone calls the cops. Or torturing your soul with soul-rotting after-hours work gossip about who got promoted, who screwed who, who is screwing who, who visited who without inviting who else, who wore what, who said what about whoever ... who's retiring, comparing personal retirement dates, wishing those dates were here, disclosing intimate personal details and later wondering how the whole community knows about your deep dark secrets, who is a sonuvabitch and competing for best hangover story. All the equivalent of Grade 10 conversation in the smoking area of the local high school.

Bullshit #3. What spouse is repulsed by an athletic body? What spouse would insist on his/her partner being grossly out-of-shape? *"I forbid you from going to the gym. You are prohibited from being ripped and muscular. I prefer gross obesity."*

Bullshit #4. No one ever says they stop drinking beer because a case of 24 costs too much. There's always enough money for alcohol, tobacco, dope and toys.

Bullshit #5. The most shameful excuse for quitting working out is children. *"Mom, Dad, I'm really proud that you both look like slobs."* Using children as an excuse for not doing anything worthwhile is the most sinful form of self-deception. *"I'd like to thank my parents for giving up their dreams, giving up on life, and teaching me to do the bare minimum and never stretching, never extending, never lifting my ass off the couch, never going beyond, never reaching higher."*

If you have ever blamed your children for not reaching your potential, shame on you. Children are the greatest blessing. One which should deeply inspire you to move your ass into the highest gear to set an example that you have only one life, so MAX IT OUT. Parents have an obligation to teach their children to dream, dream bigger, get off their ass when they fall on it, dream some more and show them that anything is possible … ANYTHING!

Too broke to run a few laps around the block. Too married to do a push-up. Just too busy to do a sit-up in front of the chat line, in front of the "add friend button," in front of the Xbox, in front of Internet porn.

What a miracle – 18-inch biceps transform dysfunctional to functional.

Chapter 40.10

X-Fitness Welland "The gym is the ultimate polygraph test, the perfect lie-detector machine. It's impossible for bullshitters to pass. Even an opportunistic sociopath with a dormant conscience cannot beat the gym's bullshitter detection"

— From the 4th & Hell Series.

June 1 at 2:50pm · Like · Comment

👍 23 people like this.

Fifteen years of frontline policing teaches the depth and breadth of the social disease called, "lying." Conservatively, a 15-year veteran cop is lied to about once an hour. Forty lies per week, 2,000 lies per year – 30,000 total lies in a 15-year career. Victims lie. Witnesses lie. Co-workers lie. Administrators really lie. They all lie even when they don't have to. Suspects are different – some lie but eventually they confess the truth.

One of the many survival secrets for frontline policing is bullshit-detection. Credibility evaluation. Do the math and see if things add up. Adding up the red flags and subtracting no flags is the secret formula. Don't know the formula? You'll wave the white flag.

Forty seasons of football coaching also teaches the social pandemic of widespread lying. Second-generation liars. Players lie. Staff lies. Administrators really lie. The volume of lies increases proportionately with the level of play. Novice lies from high school players, next-level lies at the collegiate level, beyond-the-next-level lies at the semi-pro/senior level.

The reason for the progression is experience and hard-wiring. The older the player, the more lying-success achieved. High-intensity lying reps. Volume bullshit training. Quantity and quality of lies and rewards. As lying reaches full potential, neural pathways are formed, resulting in the habitual liar.

High school players are rookie liars, beginners who stop lying the minute they understand that the head coach is not the same enabler as his parents, teachers, and friends. College players are more challenging – major rewiring, download new software, erase the virus. Semi-pro is deeply infected – a tough virus impossible to clean.

Conservatively, a football coach is lied to on average of once per day during the season and much, much more in the off-season, where recruits lie as if it's their calling. Lying about a wide range of issues such as strength training achievements, intention to try-out for your team, marks, their past … re-writing history into a fable of accomplishments. Three hundred sixty-five lies per year – total lies, 12,775 lies over a 35-year coaching career.

Twenty years of teaching and coordinating community college law-enforcement programs teaches the social tsunami, tidal-wave lying. Third-generation liars. Students lie. Staff lies. Teaching applicants lie at job interviews. Administrators really lie. Conservatively, a 20-year college coordinator/professor is lied to about twice an hour, 16 lies per day, 64 lies per week, 3,200 lies annually … total lies equals 64,000.

Ten years as a business owner teaches "Revelations" – signs of the social apocalypse. Fourth-generation liars. Staff lies. Customers lie. Job applicants really lie. A business owner hears superset lies – back-to-back lies with no rest in between. At an average of 40 lies per week, a business owner is lied to about 20,800 times per decade.

Grand total of 127,575 lies – conservative estimate – over 35 years. And that's professional life only, personal life not included.

Bullshit piles up. Stacks of bullshit are a heavy weight to lift, a load that eventually crushes and breaks your will. The secret to survival – stop believing in coincidences. Coincidence and connection look the same, sound the same … can't tell them apart. Believing in coincidences is the equivalent of quitting working out – it makes you soft. Weak. Fragile. The resulting disconnect – emotionally, intellectually and spiritually – destroys judgment, rendering the coincidence-believer dysfunctional.

Thankfully, the gym is not an habitual liar. The gym is a sanctuary of honesty, a no-lie zone that reveals only the truth. The gym is incapable of deceiving, fabricating, embellishing, conniving, manipulating and otherwise misrepresenting the truth. The gym restores faith.

The gym is a place where you can't hide – it exposes every strength and every weakness.[27] No hiding, just seeking.

The gym is a lie-detector. And smoke-detector and fraud-buster. The gym is the best kind of polygraph machine … it identifies lies, alibis, con-artists

---

27 A tribute to a masterpiece, *The Wall*. By Pink Floyd … teachers who would hurt the children however they could, criticizing and deriding them … causing every weak-ness the children possessed to be exposed, no matter how hard the kids tried to hide them.

and cheats with 100% accuracy. The gym doesn't just sniff out bullshitters, it crushes them. The gym is a place where fraud is still a crime, not a success strategy. The gym will never let pretenders be contenders.

The gym promises brutal honesty. The gym is incapable of bullshitting. The gym's bluntness shocks those unfamiliar with frankness. Culture Shock. The gym believes in honesty out – honesty in … you get back what you send out. The gym has zero tolerance for deception. The gym teaches you to honestly judge yourself while letting you practice abundantly.

Chapter 2-6(4)
140 Pounds

"If you can't handle carrying flour bags and quit, don't come home. Don't embarrass me." The translation was simple. An interpreter wasn't necessary. Italian is called "the beautiful language," but "Italian dialects" are not created equal. My father's uneducated version was simple, but ugly. The soul of a lifter uses diversity to send messages.

The Flour Mill is unforgiving. It makes a heavy performance demand. The Flour Mill does not ever compromise. "Back-breaking manual labor" is the Mill's mission statement and expectation. The Mill does not accept mediocrity, reward laziness, never lowers the bar and has zero tolerance for slackers, whiners, complainers, and loafers. Manual labor does not have a smooth, gradual learning curve. No touchy-feely orientation, no ice-breakers, no warm-welcoming committees, no happy smiles and friendly hand-shaking, back-slapping brevity. From the very first rep – Culture Shock. Extreme Culture Shock.

Manual labor in a Flour Mill was an eight-hour workout of extreme, isolated reps. Eight hours of intense lifting with the bare minimum rest between sets. Real-life "go heavy or go home." "Fail to appear" was punishable by immediate termination. You couldn't miss work because of grandma's birthday, girlfriend's prom, or family trip to the cottage. You either made it or it broke you. Over 80% of new student-workers didn't last one week. Another 10% quit after the second week. An unforgiving, uncompromising natural selection process. Those who couldn't hack it went off to lift lighter weights – like burgers. Or, they simply headed for the beach and reps of 24 … beer bottles. And no second chances. No re-applying after six months. Quitting cut yourself from the team, forever. The Flour Mill was blunt, brutally honest. The truth, the whole truth, and nothing but the truth.

The Flour Mill assembly line was a caste system that stretched about a mile – from the packing room to the warehouse, connected by two ominous conveyor belts. Flour was made by skilled, educated staff – easily recognized in their spotless white uniforms – who turned raw ingredients into the magic of flour, the substance that sustained both rich and poor countries. Then it was sent to the packing room where adult immigrants loaded it into two types of bags. Rough, crusty, 140-pound burlap bags were filled with low-quality flour for impoverished countries, while softer, smoother, 100-pound bags were loaded up with enriched flour for rich countries. Bags were sent on two half-mile-long conveyor belts, side-by-side leading to the same warehouse. Two tracks leading to two destinations, different as day and night.

The clean, soft bags were directed to a clean, metal chute where they slid gently to a slow-rotating platform, like luggage at an airport. Bags were carefully lifted from the rotation and piled onto wooden skids. A guy on a forklift transported the skid into a tractor-trailer, where it would be driven to North American destinations.

The burlap bags went elsewhere. They were herded onto a dirty, worn-out chute greased up with oil so the bags would slide at warp-speed into a train boxcar. A wooden table resembling a gymnastics pommel-horse stood silently and ominously, connected to the bottom of the chute. Shoulder height. The wooden platform was also lubricated to make sure the 140-pound burlap bags never slowed down … never lost any speed racing towards the lifter who walked briskly from the center of the boxcar to one side and then the other, with a bag on his shoulder, stacking 600 bags per boxcar. Three workers per boxcar. Six bags across, seven bags high. Seven rows on each side of the boxcar … leaving only the entrance – filled last. Six boxcars per eight-hour shift. A total of 3,600 bags per shift. Divided by three … 1,200 bags each worker.

Twelve-hundred lifts of 140-pound weight. It's either a blessing or a curse – depends on point of view. Attitude. Mindset. View it as pain, it will become a pain-in-the-ass. A pain that will spread like a virus from legs to torso to brain, to heart, to soul, into the environment infecting the insider and outsiders. Rotting bodies, minds and souls until the virus is contained. Or view it as reps. An opportunity. A chance to grow, to lose more fat, to build iron legs, iron core, iron upper body … and iron will. An opportunity to reach higher, to separate from the rest, to move toward actualizing potential. A chance to test yourself, to see who the hell you really are and who the hell you can be. Search, explore, discover.

All by turning pain into pleasure.

Change the focus, changes the outcome.

Change the focus, changes the mindset.

Change the mindset, change your destiny.

∞

"Stop the bag with both hands or the bag will fly out the boxcar."

Silence.

" … and land right there and explode all over the grass."

Silence.

" … right next to the foreman's window."

Silence.

Until it gets dirty and thickens. Finger skin bleeds easily. Soft and sensitive skin can't handle pressure. Burlap bags flying like speeding bullets make an impact on unsuspecting skin.

"You're gonna kill yourself unless you use the right technique."

Silence.

"Hand placement is the key. Don't just stand there and try to grab the bag wherever you want. Grab it like this, push and pull at the same time and drop it onto your shoulder."

Until it gets dirty and thickens. Shoulder skin bleeds easily … with or without a T-shirt.

"BALANCE THE BAG. STRAIGHTEN YOUR BACK."

Until it gets dirty and thickens. The back will hunch over and crumble.

"TAKE LONGER STRIDES … YOU'RE NOT GOING FOR A WALK FOR FUCK SAKES."

There are two ways to move faster. Increasing stride length and stride frequency increases speed. Longer steps and more time your feet hit the ground makes you faster. Making your legs stronger with heavy legwork makes you even faster. Change the stride or change the strength – the keys to speed. But both are useless without drive. A performance demand by the soul of a lifter is the key that turns the ignition.

"I thought you were one of those freaky weight lifters!!"

Silence.

"That bag weighs less than you!"

Silence.

"You better not let Antonio find out ... he'll fucking kill ya ... can't fuck around with Antonio."

Failing to lift a weight is a message – GET STRONGER. Weakness is a sign – time to get off your ass ... and bust your ass. When the top row of a boxcar stack is higher than your shoulder, technique is needed to lift and throw a 140-pound burlap bag. To make the bag reach higher, a coordinated effort, synchronized movement of calves, knees, thighs, hips, back, arms, shoulders ... multiple-joint movement ... like compound exercises is needed. And not just one bag, one bag every ten seconds.

But squats aren't enough to push and throw a weight to a higher level. Neither is a shoulder press. Or raw arm strength. All three have to connect into a choreographed force of energy. It starts with positioning. It's impossible to push a 140-pound flour bag to a higher level while it's lying parallel to the ground, on your shoulder. The bag must be repositioned so it's standing upright. Like a rocket on a moving launch pad. Walk toward the target, squat to ninety degrees, drop your ass to a sitting position, stop momentarily, explode up, roll the hips, push the arms, press the bag upwards ... liftoff. Repeat. Load, re-load.

Prehistoric plyometrics – manual labor. Age-old, timeless sports-specific training. Manual labor teaches every fat loss/muscle building/speed development strategy ever known to wo/mankind. Bigger, faster, stronger, leaner ... and meaner. Above all, mental toughness – the ability to fight through. Nothing else matters. Nothing builds iron will like eight hours of heavy manual labor. Forced reps under fear of firing, family feud, failure.

Getting paid to do "sports-specific training." The social pendulum has swung from right to left – people now pay for it.

No one is born a fighter. Becoming a fighter doesn't just happen. The secret to making a fighter – take away the flight option leaving just one choice – fight. It's impossible to get anywhere in life – any career, any job, any sport, any fitness program – without the mental strength to work intensely in isolation. All expertise needs tens of thousands of hours of practice – intense reps. Not one week, not one month. Years. The "Decade Rule" taught us that ten years of dedicated practice is needed to become an expert at anything – physically, intellectually ... emotionally and ... spiritually.

Getting connected doesn't happen overnight. It's a work-in-progress. The type of work needed to become the best always happens in private, not public. No audience. No stage. The heavy lifting happens behind the scenes. And ordinary practice is not enough. Research shows that extraordinary reps are needed – greater challenge, stronger competition. Consistently moving to higher levels is a prerequisite for the gradual growth that embodies expertise development.[28]

The Decade Rule teaches us that a long road of busting-your-ass repetitive work is needed to become free of boring, mind-numbing repetitive work. Fearing isolated reps makes it impossible to reach higher, to reach the pinnacle of performance in any career. Working hard, alone, disconnected from the world is a must to separate from the pack and become a leader. Being able to handle mind-numbing boredom[29] is the secret to escaping it. Know the enemy to beat it.

The miracle of compound exercise. Strength multiplication. Building several muscles all at once. Like compound interest, compound-exercise reps yield rapid growth – naturally. Don't ignore simplicity. No lifting exercises are simpler, more inexpensive, make a bigger impact ... and are harder than compound exercises with free weights. No machine, no gadget, no toy, no secret program builds high-quality strength – physically and mentally – than free-weight compound exercises. Women, men, young, old, rookies, veterans ... free-weight compound exercises.

"Where do you think you're going? There's 30 minutes left. Just because you finished faster doesn't mean you're done! Get to the 100-pound platform!!"

The soul of a lifter does not form predictable habits. The soul of a lifter will not stick to one communication system – always changing up the play calling. Working like a mule to create growth opportunities ... with one catch – they have to be recognized by the receiver. Growth opportunities are a blessing or a curse. It depends on point of view. Attitude determines whether or not

---

28 The "Decade Rule" is a product of research that studies "Expert Development," the key to next-level peak performance. We are indebted to brilliant researchers including Benjamin Bloom, Anders Ericcson and Swap & Leonard who provided compelling evidence that no one is born with expertise – it is developed. This means we all have the potential to reach higher and higher and higher. Reading the works by these researchers will make an impact in your life. It shaped my coaching and teaching strategies and ideologies.
29 Tribute to a masterpiece, *Comfortably Numb*. By Pink Floyd.

a growth opportunity will be falsely identified as a pain-in-the-ass that must be avoided like a plague – or perceived as a golden opportunity to make something happen.

"Moving the finish line" is one of the secrets to building iron will. Every assignment, every workout, needs a finish line to know when it's over, to keep score, to cross it and go into overtime. Pushing back the finish line conditions the mind to expect the worst and solve it – to deal with the unexpected and overcome it. To be prepared to handle the pressure of overtime so that the actual game becomes routine.

$$\infty$$

Both guys at the 100-pound platform had huge forearms – thick, ripped. Chords of muscle as a backdrop to the gardenhose-like veins that crisscrossed the dense fiber. Forearms send a message. They make questions redundant. Forearms say, *"I bust my ass working hard, I have no fear of extreme hard work ... have no fear, I'll go in first,"* or, *"I've never gotten my hands dirty."*

The first 100-pound bag moved closer. The platform was below waist level – about the same height as a barbell on a deadlift platform.

"HEY! DON'T BEND OVER. Drop your ass and squat down. Use your legs to lift it off ... ASS LOWER."

When two people collide, an impact happens. The biggest impact is made by he who has his/her ass lower. Lowest ass wins. Ass lower. Two words can make a huge impact for decades without the teacher knowing it. "Ass lower" is the secret to legwork, to a powerful stance, to tackling, to blocking ... to applying force – and taking it. Absorbing force and dishing it out. Ass lower builds tree-trunk legs, keeps you firmly grounded, roots you in place so that nothing can knock you over, not even slightly off-balance, absorbs an impact and dishes out a bigger impact.

"Grab both ends, not underneath it ... what the hell are you doing??? You're not serving dinner."

Grab the ends. Palms facing in. Got it.

"Now lift the damn bag with your forearms ... higher! SLOWER, control the bag ... all the way up to your chest!!!"

Vein-popping is a rush. A huge rush. Chords of forearm muscles and pipeline veins attract attention. *Best pump ever ... look at ... .*

"MOVE! Don't just stand there staring like a dumbass ... walk to the skid, keeping walking ... put it down ... SLOW!!! DON'T BREAK THE BAG."

Doing anything wrong is much easier than doing it right. Like throwing a 100-pound flour bag onto a skid instead of controlling it and positioning it exactly where it belongs.

"Pick it up and do it again ... DO IT RIGHT ... ASS LOWER ... SQUAT DOWN ... KEEP YOUR BACK STRAIGHT ... ass lower ... control the bag on the way down!!!!"

Set #1 complete. Deadlift, clean, squat. Three compound exercises ... cardio included. A conventional superset – megaset. Consecutive compound exercises blended into one. Prehistoric boot camp. Silence speaks volumes.

∞

Thinking outside the box is the key to growth and fearlessness. Conformity is a confining Force. **C-Force**, the powerful Force that attracts us to the same thinking, over and over, even if it's stale, senseless, ancient, unproductive. The "66% Rule" taught us that the vast majority of humans – minimum of two-thirds – will adopt the thoughts and actions of others even if they contradict personal beliefs. Follow the leader ... blindly.[30]

C-Force is the magnet that confines us inside a box of conventional thinking, including the kind that limits, binds ... lowers the ceiling like an overweight bar crashing down with no hope of lifting it – without a spotter. The soul of a lifter thinks so far outside the box, the box disappears. The soul of a lifter is original – embracing authenticity, bold ideas, raising the bar, breaking from convention. But non-conformity is a work-in-progress.

The magic of compound exercises has no limits. Innovation is simple unless the fear of criticism is greater than the need to change. Adding one more compound movement at the 100-pound-bag platform made a big impact, on shoulders ... and co-workers. Adding a shoulder press. Deadlift the bag off the ground, clean it to the chest (the precursor to the greatest

---

30   We are indebted to the brilliance of researchers including Zimbardo, Asch and Milgram for the "66% Comformity Rule." Their research can be applied to any career – law enforcement, business, athletics ... anything related to leadership and human behavior.

forearm-builder of all-time – the hammer curl), simultaneously do a front squat, then press the bag overhead, holding it while walking the seven steps to the skid. Then, like a doctor's prescription: "Repeat to end of shift." The 1972 abs-of-steel workout. Stares send messages. A strained look, forehead slightly tensed, eyebrows tilted. *He's really fucked-up. A mystery. But, holy shit he's strong.*

The miracle of reps lightens any load. But reps can be a blessing or a curse. "Reps" are not created equal. Reps can be too light, too heavy, stay exactly the same, or constantly change. The point of reps is to effect change – positive change. Growth. Reps have a purpose – to make a difference. Reps are not intended to keep the status quo or to regress. Reps have a meaning – to move forward toward a destiny, not to stand still or go backwards. Reps are supposed to make an impact. Otherwise they become part of the ninth layer of hell.[31]

Same reps are needed to build a foundation through the miracles of hard-wiring and adaptation. But after they've served their purpose, unchanged reps lead to monotony, a mind-numbing, IQ-dropping condition that causes homicide and/or attempted murder of brain cells, spirit, joy, heart, and … soul. Doing exactly the same routine over and over, day after day, digs a transformational rut deeper and deeper, spiraling downward from boredom to dread with pit stops at each layer.

The secret is heightened awareness – monitor the change. When positive change stops, change the reps. When the reps stop making changes. The only cure for dread is a new challenge. But the problem with challenges are location and cost. Where do you find it and what's the price?

"Challenges" are not created equal. Some are mild, some are extreme. Challenges can be a blessing or a curse, depending on the distance between the challenge and current level – the present level of skill, knowledge and will. Getting to the next level is not simple. Reaching higher needs ladders. Someone has to put them up. But "ladders" are not created equal. If the angle of the ladder is not just right, the climber crashes … free falling to the ground, splattering self, along with dreams and hopes. "Messes" are not created equal. Some are salvageable, others are not.

---

31 Borrowed from Dante's Inferno, a depressing theoretical model of hell that postulates all levels of hell are not created equal. The ninth layer is rock bottom.

Challenges are the secret to growth, health and happiness if the balance is struck between boredom and anxiety.[32] Boredom and anxiety are related. Both are potential killers by causing the same type of destructive pressure and stress. Anxiety caused by being in the wrong league is shattering – physically, intellectually, emotionally and spiritually. Being in the major leagues with minor league talent crushes the spirit. The opposite is also true. Floundering in the minor leagues with major league skill will erode mind, body and ... soul. Boredom – armed and dangerous.

When the 100-pound bags stop making change, replace them with 140-pounders. Faster cleans replace hammer curls. When the weight is too heavy for the forearms to hammer curl strictly ... "ass lower." Drop the ass, simultaneously curl the bag to the chest and explode with the legs ... liftoff. Press the bag over head, walk seven steps, lower the bag under control. Repeat. Build a core of steel.

Change the reps when the reps stop making changes.

∞

"See that switch? Press it if you need help. It stops the belt, stops the assembly line. Gives you a chance to clean up a mess, catch your breath, regroup. But NEVER press it. Crazy Italians in the packing room will go fucking nuts."

Flour mixes with sweat in every orifice until it bakes and cakes. Showering scrapes only the surface and barely cleans the blood from the scrapes. Unsightly flour-knots build up in body hair, leading to the self-haircut and torso shaving.

"You shave your forearms. Are you a bodybuilder?"

"No. I have flour knots."

Blowing your nose ejects a disgusting mix of ingredients that looks like broken-down day-old muffins. Eyelashes stick together.

"Hey you ... you in the front row... are you sleeping? Go see the Vice Principal."

---

32   We are indebted to the brilliance of Dr. Hihaly Csikszentmihalvi. His research on the pursuit of happiness is recorded in *Flow: The Psychology of Optimal Experience*. A masterpiece, *Flow* is a mental state achieved through immersion in a meaningful task – the confluence of skill and challenge. When skill matches the challenge, an unrivaled state of happiness emerges. Reading *Flow* will make an impact.

Math teachers never carried flour bags. Probably never sat in the front row either. Being forced to sit in alphabetical order when your surname starts with "A" should be a violation of the Constitution.

"Don't lie to me!"

Even the slightest hint that you're not running the place properly, brings out the **E-Gene** – **E**mbarrassment **Gene**. Strong E-Gene equals zero tolerance ... the more you get embarrassed by mediocrity, the less tolerance you have for bullshit.

"Honest, I was picking flour out of my eyelids."

High school Vice Principals are not bullshitters. They are unforgiving. They are intolerant of incompetence, mediocrity, laziness, waste, lethargy, apathy and even the slightest moments of weakness, irresponsibility, immaturity, whining, crying, excuse-making and most importantly ... bullshit.

"Three-day suspension."

High school Vice Principals will not compromise. They will not lower their standards to accommodate misfits, miscreants and malcontents. Their E-Gene is connected to a sensitive switch that doesn't activate – it ignites.

"Man, you are gullbull."

Gullible you moron ... gullible! Flour Mill manual laborers have a warped sense of humor.

"Look, it's Gail walking by!!" Someone's always tempting.[33] Three thuds – a 140-pound bag hitting the back of the gawker's skull, then him and the bag both hitting the ground outside the boxcar ... right next to the foreman's window.

It was a lie. A compulsive lie disguised as humor. There was no legwork to check out. The foreman's daughter wasn't walking by.

"YOU LAZY SONS-OF-BITCHES. WHO SHUT OFF THE BELT???"

Translating that message was easy because of expertise ... the ten-year "expert" rule applied. Warehouse intercoms magnify heavy Italian accents. Broken English echoes off the walls like the waves of a Culture Shock.

---

33 A tribute to a masterpiece, *Pink Cadillac*. By Bruce Springsteen.

Italian immigrant Flour Mill packing room workers are not bullshitters. They are unforgiving. They are intolerant of incompetence, mediocrity, laziness, waste, lethargy, apathy and even the slightest moments of weakness, irresponsibility, immaturity, whining, crying, excuse-making and most importantly ... bullshit.

Italian immigrant Flour Mill workers will not compromise. They will not lower their standards to accommodate misfits, miscreants and malcontents. Italian immigrant Flour Mill workers have the E-Gene, connected to a sensitive switch that doesn't activate – it ignites.

"DID YOU BREAK THAT BAG???"

Silence.

"THAT'S 140-POUNDS OF FLOUR WASTED!!!"

Silence.

Flour Mill foremen are not bullshitters. They are unforgiving. They are intolerant of incompetence, mediocrity, laziness, waste, unproductivity, lethargy, apathy and even the slightest moment of weakness, irresponsibility, immaturity, whining, crying, excuse-making and most importantly ... bullshit.

Flour Mill foremen will not compromise. They will not lower their standards to accommodate misfits, miscreants and malcontents. Flour Mill foremen have the E-Gene, connected to a sensitive switch that doesn't activate – it ignites.

"You want to waste flour? Let's see how tough you are ... only two guys per boxcar. Let's speed it up."

"No ... only one. One guy loads all 600 alone. I'll go first."

"Crazy bastard ... one car each?"

Legends are simple to build. Think outside the box (car) until there is no box. Do the extraordinary. Stretch goals – beyond-the-box performance targets and expectations that raise the bar and the eyebrows. Announce a stretch goal then do it. Stretch goals stretch limits and break them, changing mindset by setting brand new standards that were once perceived as outrageous. And falling short of a stretch goal has the same effect as achieving it – viral marketing. Not just ordinary word-of-mouth ... warp-speed dialing.

"He's really fucked-up. A mystery. But, holy shit he's strong."

Performance demands are contagious. One spreads to two and then spreads to three. Misery is a bonding agent. Brings people closer. But conquered misery is the extreme connector, publicity director and promoter. The stuff legends are made of.

"He did it. Don't fuck around with Antonio's son."

The soul of a lifter never rejects a performance demand but always makes another performance demand in return – don't blink.

Chapter 2-6(5)
Misery

X-Fitness Welland "The gym never bullies. The gym is never a smart-ass, never a mouthy punk, never a loud-mouth coward. The gym never annoys, depresses, pollutes, contaminates. Even when the gym is down in your parent's basement. Even when the gym has one bench, one bar, 362 pounds – all plates, one chin up bar and a transistor radio"

— From the 4th & Hell Series.

May 30 at 2:33pm · Like · Comment

👍 10 people like this.

Like many Italian-North American households, the Holy Trinity hung on our kitchen wall – Jesus Christ, the Pope and Frank Sinatra. Backed up by the Virgin Mary, Joseph and dried palms twisted into a knot. All were invoked during the routine domestic disputes – except of course, Sinatra. He was off-limits.

The peasant-Italian-immigrant message was hammered into you: *"Una depressione viene presto!!"* The depression reps. The lead story – every night: *"A depression is coming soon. Heading our way, any day now."* It's inevitable. What's the use? And not just any depression, an apocalyptic kind. World-wide misery.

Misery is connected to Italian rage ... *"Porca Misera."* Despite the literal translation of, "pig misery," porca misera can be used in different contexts as a response to a warning, or, independently as a self-directed warning. *"Damn the misery,"* either expresses contempt for the pending global depression or serves as a warning of a preemptive strike: *"You sonuvabitch, now you did it!"*

"Mannaggia la Miseria!" is the next-level damnation of misery. Despite some controversy about the actual strength of the damning, it's the tone, body language and situation that determine the exact level of damnation directed toward misery. *"Mannaggia la Miseria!"* has reached cult-like status. It has its own Facebook page and T-shirt for wannabe Italians or, to confirm one's status as an Italian just in case it's not clear.

"Una guerra sta per scoppiare presto!!" The next world war was not a question of "if," just "when." Long before CNN and war analysts, Italian

prognosticators routinely announced that war was about to explode any minute. "Breaking news" waiting patiently on-deck.

Not just any war, a nuclear Armageddon. The kind that spared no one. The kind that brought on *"La Fina del Mondo!!!"* – that long-anticipated end of the world. Judgment Day. Which of course led to the customary caution: *"Fare il segno della croce."* Instead of, *"Start your engines,"* be sure to *"make the sign of the cross!"* Reaching a destination was God's will. *"We'll see you when we get there, God willing"* ... if God spares us during this three-mile drive.

The anticipation of a fatal car crash en route to visiting like-minded relatives, to discuss upcoming global depression and the final war, was the Italian version of going to the cottage. White-knuckle reps. Clutching and grabbing – the steering wheel, dashboard, rosary beads, figurines of the Virgin Mary, holy water, black and white pictures of the Pope ... and uncooperative kids.

"Voi avete sentito che è morto?"

"No, who died?"

"The great-aunt of Pepino's second cousin's neighbour ... "

"Mannaggia! She's Guido's second-cousin's mother's aunt!!"

Italians spread news of death overseas faster than e-mail. Transatlantic warp-speed obituaries. Technology has yet to replicate that communication miracle.

Death notifications triggered the **3-Cs** workout: Checklist, Coffee, Condolences. Set #1: Get out "the list" to see if the grieving family gave you condolences in the past. If "no," skip to "Finally." If "yes," move to set #2: Recycle condolence coffee. Every Italian household has a cupboard of coffee bags received as condolence gifts. Proceed with set #3: Visit the grieving family, offer condolences of the overseas death. After obligatory two-cheek kisses, cheek twisting and shouting[34] served with trays of stale biscotti that could pass as flat-tire replacements, and intense reps urging everyone to, *"EAT! ... EAT!!!!,"* change the focus to "Homeland Security." Finally, raise the threat level for depression and war.

---

34 A tribute to a masterpiece, *Twist and Shout*. Made famous by the Beatles, but written by Paul Anka and Bert Russell, originally recorded by The Top Notes, and covered by the Isley Brothers.

"Ascoltare!" Listen. Sit still and listen. Don't move, just listen. Talking back instead of listening was the equivalent of civil unrest. Aggression. Act of war. During any visit to relatives, mouthing off constituted an unlawful assembly. Italians believe in equality. The guilty and the innocent morph. Suspects, victims and witnesses are mixed together. No separation for the rest. And no trial, no appeal, no due process. Summary conviction and punishment. The first SWAT team – no riot gear, just equally distributed shit-kicking. Like professional wrestling and shouting. A continuum of yelling and cursing interrupted by the actual match.

"Ascoltare tutti !!!!" Listen to everyone and believe them. Believe every single word they say. Doctors, lawyers, priests ... teachers ... police officers. Give them all instant credibility. Immediate trust. All are smart, upstanding pillars of the community. They are educated professionals, social leaders, beacons of hope whom we depend on for wisdom, protection and safety. Symbols of character, strength ... iron will. Never question them or anyone else. Acceptance. Accept the will of the higher level. Accept your position in life. Get a job, stay in that job, take no risks, save money for the next depression, stay inside the box, shrink the box, live in the box, die in the box.

Depression, death, war, conformity – all connected. Misery. And all completely foreign to the soul of a lifter.

Chapter 2-6(6)
340

"And I was afraid and went away and hid your talent in the ground."

— Matthew 25:25.

Fear makes us hide our talents. Fear makes us bury our gifts. Fear makes us conceal our potential. Underachieve. Fear is a dream-killer, heart-breaker and soul-wrecker. The toughest enemy is the insider, the person deep inside ourselves who we are locking in or locking out … the force waiting to explode or implode. The force on standby waiting to unleash or strangle, escape or confine.

Overcoming ourselves is the main event, the fight. Everything else is preparation – sparring, undercard bouts, tune-ups. Round after round, the will to fight either strengthens or weakens. Heightens or hides. Forges to steel or breaks. It depends on who we want to be – the indispensable warrior who leads out in front, the dispensable middle-of-the-packer who follows, or the non-essential at the back of the pack.

Without throwing one punch, evil batters and bruises. And with no bell. Round after round, the fight is never over. Never. But, that's the good news. Because when evil pulls out the heavy artillery, it must be trying to stop something special. Something big. The harder evil fights, the greater the confidence that the battle is worth fighting. Something big must be waiting to happen. And evil's job is to block it. Evil does not want potential to actualize and reach its destiny.

Reaching full potential is serious business. So is wasting potential. Check out Matthew 25:25-30. Jesus makes it pretty clear that wasting potential will have consequences – big ones. In the *Parable of the Talents,* one of the five who had each been blessed with a talent, hid his talent because of fear

– fear of failure, fear of accountability, fear of responsibility. Jesus used two words to describe the fearful man – "wicked, lazy." And the eight-word consequence – "… there will be weeping and gnashing of teeth."

∞

The first day at work as an 18-year-old rookie cop is Culture Shock … tripled. First, it's Culture Shock for society to have any 18-year-old wearing a uniform that symbolizes public safety. Second, it's Culture Shock for police veterans who imagine the horror of any 18-year-old backing them up at a gun call, knife fight, barroom brawl, violent domestic – guy who wants to kill his mother, guy who blew his brains out, guy who blew his brother's brains out, or any of the infinite sick, twisted events that cause endless human suffering. Finally, it's Culture Shock for a guy who was acting like a jackass in calculus class 72 hours earlier, throwing pennies as the teacher brushed his comb-over … and missing the target each time – the same guy who should have been blowing out 18 candles three months ago.

There's no way to answer a comment.

"So, you're the guy who can bench press 300."

"Yes," sounds self-serving and arrogant. "No," is an outright lie and a sign of self-disrespect. Silence is the middle ground even though it makes you look like an arrogant, self-serving, self-disrespecting liar – an asshole.

"You're the third Italian they've hired this year."

"Yes," sounds self-serving and arrogant. "No," is an outright lie and a sign of self-disrespect. Silence is the middle ground even though it makes you look like an arrogant, self-serving, self-disrespecting liar – an asshole.

But signs on the wall expect silence.

"He who asserts must prove," in bold letters beneath a giant finger pointing at the reader. Simple, unique, meaningful … memorable. **SUMM** – **S**ubjectively, **U**nique **M**eaning, equals **M**emorable. A memorable message – stays with you forever. Unforgettable… Translation: If you allege it, back it up. Back it up with EVIDENCE. Back it up with action – performance, the global language that is not foreign to any human on planet Earth. Build a case. Not just a half-assed case, a mountainous case. Pile up the evidence high enough so there is no mistake about the strength. The soul of a lifter has a limitless communication system. Signs, messages and more signs – just read them.

PPPHH. The secret to getting hired as a police officer – **P**ersonal brand, **P**ositioning, **P**erformance, **H**umility, **H**onesty. Applies to any applicant. Guaranteed. Pass all five, you get hired. If you fail just one of the five, back into the pile – guaranteed.

PPPHH makes a performance demand on the applicant – prove you are not a pain-in-the-ass and will not be a pain-in-the-ass down the road. Unlike the "presumption of innocence," the world of crime-fighting does not hand out the "presumption of not being a pain-in-the-ass." Senior cops want proof. S/he who asserts NOT to be a pain-in-the-ass, must prove. Proof is the absence of the **5-Ls**: **L**azy, **L**iar, **L**ow-life, **L**ummox, **L**oser. The applicant's mission is simple: Separate yourself from the rest, distinguish yourself from the pack – with evidence ... a track record that shows you will not be a thief, that you will not steal salary, energy, hope, or joy from the public, the organization and every one in it, and that you will not end up in the crime beat reporter's headline ... as a suspect.

The difference between PPPHH and 5-Ls is the inner circle. Nature and nurture conspire to make the call and move the pieces on the board. They decide pain management or mismanagement – pain-in-the-ass or not-a-pain-in-the-ass. And neither title is permanent. They are temporary. Both titles are up for grabs. We have to fight hard for either title ... with intense training. Both titles build a personal brand that separates from the rest. The difference is the direction – leader or back of the pack. Two titles with a common purpose but different destinies.

∞

A police job interview is a scarier place than a dark alley. Sitting in isolation across from the brain-trust of a police department, gleaming in white shirts and enough gold trim to pay down the national debt, as they ask questions to figure out whether to give a uniform, badge, gun and bullets to a kid not yet old enough to legally buy alcohol. Five-on-one. Chief, two deputy chiefs, two superintendents. 150-0. One-hundred-and-fifty years of police experience to zero.

A two-hour-and-45-minute job interview is hard to recall. The human memory is both a blessing and a curse. There is a line of demarcation that separates the forgettable from the unforgettable. But not all garbage is emptied in the trash bin ... not all valuables are locked up.

"Your coach told us you made the high school varsity football team in Grade 9. Says here you played both junior varsity and varsity in Grade 9."

Silence.

Unlike the right to silence, saying nothing would run the risk of sounding dysfunctional – or like an asshole. Or both.

"Your football coach said you're a leader. He named you team captain in Grade 11."

Silence.

Coach-athlete is a unique relationship. Special. Nothing like it in the world. Not real family. Not friends. Both need each other desperately. Two guys who need an impact, real bad. Football coaches make the best job references. Football coaches are not bullshitters. Football coaches are not enablers who soften, weaken, coddle and rob others of the riches that the natural struggle brings. Football coaches have one mission – destiny. Full potential. Put up ladders, smash barriers, experience the rush of letting others experience the rush. The impact of knocking down the weaknesses that everyone else developed and then ran away from. The rush of seeing others succeed through sweat and struggle, long after they had been left behind, way back in the pack. And football coaches have full view into the soul of the athlete. A view from a private, exclusive box. Football coaches know exactly what you're made of and what you can be made into.

Football coaches make great job references.

"He says in Grade 10, you got kicked out of math class. Why?"

" Errr ... ahhhh ... just stupid. No excuse."

Football coaches are not bullshitters. They are not habitual liars with a mission to deceive and circumvent every natural struggle and every natural selection process that seeks to find the strongest, fittest, smartest and most honest.

"He says in Grade 11, you were suspended from school twice. Why?"

"Very stupid, no excuse."

Football coaches respect the game, the profession and everyone in it. They refuse to lie to protect even the students in the climb they are leading.

"In Grade 12, you got drunk at a school dance. Wanted to fight the whole gym. Four officers were called. What was that about?"

"Extremely stupid, no excuse."

"Is all this a pattern? Has it stopped?"

The soul of a lifter sends messages any way it can, identifying extreme personalities in any lineup and then tailoring the message. Message sent, message received. What you do with the message depends on how you exercise free will. And whether free will turns to iron will or half-in-the-bag will. Thirty-five years alcohol-free. Not a drop. Never drank again. The soul of a lifter knows how to put the fear of God in you.

"The foreman at The Flour Mill said you were one of the best students to work there. Carried 140-pound flour bags, eight hours every night, 40 hours during the week and weekends all through high school. He mentioned that only one in ten cut it."

Silence.

"Your football coach told us you are the most dedicated player he's ever seen in the weight room. Said you're a hardcore lifter."

Silence.

"How much can you lift?"

"Three hundred … I can bench press 300. And I can squat four plates for reps … four plates is 405… are 405 pounds."

Silence.

Forgot to tell them, bodyweight 190 pounds and 5'10" … and forgot to tell them natural. 100% natural. No chemicals, no pills, no needles stuck in my ass. Totally natural.

"How did you do it?"

"Six years, six workouts a week, Tuesday and Friday are bench press days. Ten sets of bench press. Sets one to six go up in weight and down in sets. Set number seven is the max. Sets eight to ten are the same as set number one. One to two minutes rest. I started when I was 12. Took me six years to bench 300. Did it four months ago, just before my 18th birthday."

Silence.

Forgot to tell them my lifting goals – 400-pound bench press and 500-pound squat.

"You have any questions?"

Silence.

"We'll call you if you're selected."

∞

"My officers will not be punching bags. If a guy takes a swing at one of my officers on the corner of King and James, that guy better be flat on his back before the punch lands. It's expected."

The soul of a lifter has a limitless playbook. A performance demand made at a survival lecture that doubled as a swearing-in ceremony. A real-life, compelling performance demand – don't get punched out. Don't embarrass the uniform. Don't embarrass the profession. Don't embarrass the organization.

A performance demand reaches its potential – guaranteed ... if you don't blink. Not blinking means raising the bar – change the compelling purpose to a survival purpose ... the deepest purpose known to wo/mankind. A survival purpose connects all the pieces on the board – physical, intellectual, emotional, spiritual – setting in motion a force of nature ... and nurture. It doesn't just motivate, doesn't just inspire – it incites. It triggers an inner rebellion. A new switch is installed – with "ON," cemented in bold, upper-case print – a one-sided switch stuck in position ... with no "off" option.

REPS is the only way to become fearless. **R**epeated **E**xposure to **P**ressure **S**ituations. The only way to guarantee that you will not bury your talent. Every time you face what scares you, do what scares you, beat what scares you, you move toward fearlessness – of that opponent. Opponents become boring. Fearlessness of one opponent leads to monotony. Left unchecked, monotony leads to madness. The vaccine for madness is a scarier opponent, scarier REPS.

I never had a career goal. Never even thought of one. Never wrote a goal down. Never discussed it. Never wanted to be a cop. Never thought of it once – until my father planted the seed, said the magic words in broken Italian, two days after my 18th birthday: *"There's a full-time job opening at the Mill. After 90 days, you'll be in the union."*

The fire lit. Not just a flame – an inferno. I applied for a police job. I have absolutely no recollection where, when, or how – but I remember why. The thought of 40 years in a Flour Mill, mindlessly carrying 140-pound bags, eight hours a day. Not the glamor of the uniform, not a fixation with guns, not a psychological void that needed to be filled with a badge. Survival was the reason … avoid the "gnashing of teeth."

I don't remember filling out the application. I don't remember how I ended up doing the entrance exams. I don't remember driving there. Just 668 applicants for two jobs. I'll never forget that because we were reminded about it constantly – before we got hired … and after. The message was clear: Easily replaceable … so, bust your ass.

Since then, I have had only one goal – never let twenty things happen. Never let anyone call me stupid. Never let anyone call me lazy. Never let anyone mock my IQ. Or question it. Never let anyone call me a chickenshit, again. Never let weakness go unrepaired. Never get soft – never. Never get caught in traffic – a passenger – always drive ahead, be the driver. Never live my parents' life. Never be ordinary. Never be bored. Never be normal. Never let anyone think I'm a second-class citizen or treat me like one. Never end up like my father – never stop … never retire. Never let my wife and three daughters think I'm a deadbeat. And never blink.

My personal mission statement – my private manifesto.

Manifestos are better than long-term goals because they're flexible and they can stretch. I believe in the "strategize and improvise" method of personal goal-setting – build the basics, have a general plan and make the calls situationally. The call depends on the situation. Like a football game, life can't be scripted. Neither can the game plan. It's impossible to predict every opportunity – positive and negative. Strategize then improvise. Prepare better than your opponent and don't just expect the unexpected – embrace it. Change uncertainty from risk to rush.

At the end of the swearing-in ceremony, the only flash bulb that went off was in my head, exposing my embarrassment, lighting up my scores – 75% and 81%. A 300-pound bench press and 405-pound squat fell short of my performance goals. And, a survival performance demand had been made.

∞

"Point the shoulder directly at the bag. Twist. Rotate the torso. Short punch. Use your power angles. Start at the ankle. Move the body, the punch will follow." Iron work, roadwork and now bag work – the survival trilogy that changed the scores, within months, to 85% and 86% – 340-pound bench press and a 430-pound squat. Because when a survival performance demand is made, the soul of a lifter recruits a coach.

"DO IT AGAIN. DO NOT GET COMPLACENT. COMPLACENCY KILLS." Like football coaches, SWAT commanders do not compromise. Do it right every time. Half-assed is not an option. Zero tolerance for incompetence, ineptitude, laziness, whining, crying, bitching, moaning, finger-pointing, excuse-making, selfishness, self-centered juveniles who put their teammates at risk.

"IF YOU'RE LOOKING FOR SYMPATHY, YOU CAN FIND IT IN THE DICTIONARY BETWEEN SHIT AND SYPHILIS." SWAT commanders are like football coaches. No bullshit. Their mission is to stop misery, not cause it.

"THIS IS THE FORCE'S FIRST SWAT TEAM. WE WILL NOT LOOK STUPID. WE WILL NOT FAIL. IF YOU DON'T BELIEVE THAT, LEAVE NOW BEFORE YOU BECOME A LIABILITY." Like football coaches, SWAT commanders have a sensitive E-Gene. And they give you no exemption just because you haven't reached your 20th birthday. SWAT commanders don't check ID.

$$\infty$$

"Ascoltaretutti!!!!" It was bullshit. The warning to, *"Listen to everyone and believe them,"* was bullshit. Not intentional bullshit – bullshit produced by fear, which led to ignorance, which led to compliance.

Culture Shock rocks the soul after the sudden and repeated realization that you've been duped. Lied to. Brainwashed by snake-oil saleswo/men who blindly accepted seats in the lower class, ignored their potential and tried to make you bury yours.

Chapter 19
400

"How much can you bench? 400?"
Silence.

When two 19-year-olds connect, the unexpected happens.

Greg was a psychopath. A violent, dysfunctional social misfit without the capacity or willingness to understand or follow conventional rules. An impulsive extremist with a sensitive switch that could unleash a force of nature with a vengeance. Greg had a tortured soul, one that was fueled by a complex personality.

Despite a religious fervor to break the rules, Greg never threw any punches after the bell. Not once. He respected the game, just not the people in it.

After he split his father's skull open, then pulled a knife on me, was disarmed, arrested and dragged to the police station, Greg revealed his mission. He had been chosen to make a performance demand – of the cop outside the cage he was slamming his head against.

The gap was only 60 pounds. Based on past performance, the quick math said four months. Six tops. A terrific 20th birthday present. And 400 pounds would turn the keys into two clubs for me, including the bench-double-your-bodyweight club.

The first knife-fight is like the first time for anything – a rush. A surge that presses the switch. But no training can prepare you for it. The human mind is not equipped to process the sight of a metal blade pointing in the direction of your chest, slightly below the stare of a madman. The miracle of 20/20 vision brings the image faster and clearer than fiber optics, satellite, or HD TV, but the brain does not immediately register the magnitude. *Guy just pulled a knife on me,* takes a few seconds to process. Delayed reaction due to Culture Shock. Momentary confusion from the jolt.

$$\infty$$

Unlike workplaces and team sports, working out does not depend on the presence, absence, motivation, desire, need, or commitment of any other human. The training team is just you, iron … and the soul of lifter.

Iron feels nothing. No brain – no pain. Iron has no heart, no pulse, no rage, no sadness, no frustration, no depression, no elation, no feeling ... no fear.

Essentially, iron is isolated deadweight, linked to no other power – Higher or lower. Iron has no soul. But when a performance demand is made, iron offers resistance, the opposing force that works with you by fighting against you ... and never fighting with you. Iron will partner-up in direct proportion to the demand made. What you ask of iron, you receive. But only if you exercise free will.

Fighting evil is not a 15-rounder. There is no buzzer. There's only overtime – sudden-death overtime, where one wins and one goes home. It's impossible to train alone. The soul of a lifter has to be signed to a long-term contract. The soul of a lifter is an energy source, the infinite source of energy that manages elite resistance training. The kind needed to prevent the worst disaster – stopping the fight against evil. Laying down, not trying to come back. Tapped-out. Throw in the towel, or a casual wave of the hand before turning away and walking back to your corner – forever.

∞

"The human brain is as long as a loaf of bread."

Pathologists, and pack leaders of groups of lazy people, share the same job description – they work with dead people. The only difference is that pathologists do their job with "official" corpses. An autopsy is formally known as a "post-mortem," derived from Latin, meaning, "after death." The point of an autopsy is to find out how it happened. How did the pulse shut off? Where did the spirit go? How did the lively become lifeless?

The first autopsy that a rookie cop sees is not a rush. It's morbid, depressing ... Culture Shock. Unlike the millions who've allowed CSI to become a cultural phenomenon while killing their brain cells with its morbid attraction, I was not attracted to the carving up of a human being at 8:30 a.m. on a Saturday.

No attraction to the overwhelming morgue stench, no attraction to the slicing-up of a person who was walking and talking 12 hours ago, no attraction to the dismemberment of someone's loved one, no attraction to watching a victim's internal organs being disconnected and deposited into plastic bags. My coach officer comparing the intestine removed from the victim's guts with *"sausage we made last week,"* while the pathologist's assistant munches on a sandwich, right over the body. No attraction to my coach officer's cackling reminders for me to *"smile, for fuck sakes ... we're going for breakfast pretty soon,"* and absolutely no attraction to working a day shift at any time, especially immediately following a late, late night shift.

"Can't you tell, it's his first one, hehehehe ... the last guy threw up all over the fucking place, hahahah."

Like a lumberjack, the pathologist fired up a saw and cut open the skull. *Focus on business.* The soul of a lifter uses intuition to re-direct focus. *Focus on business.* Change the focus, change the outcome. Business-like, workman-like – the secret to surviving the first autopsy.

"It's a miracle. Look at everything it can do. See this part, this is where we remember ... " He was right. The human's brain fit in his hands, like a loaf of bread. Depressing becomes insightful when the focus changes, transforming an opportunity from catabolic to anabolic. A learning moment happens any time someone decides to teach, chooses to share, presses "send." But a receiver is needed to complete the pass. An open receiver. *"Neural pathways? Sure, let me explain ... "*

"Jobs" are not created equal. Some list "death" and "catastrophic injury" in the fine print. If you can die from it, intuition is your **MVP** – **M**ost **V**aluable **P**artner. The frontline, the playing field, the gym all share the same potential – enriched life or loss of life. The paradox of the high-risk activity – great benefits and grave consequences. Two diametrically-opposed forces. One capable of building reality IQ, the street-level Mensa club where it's acceptable to lift a T-bag, and drop an F-bomb, at the same time. The other capable of carnage. Instructive and destructive.

$$\infty$$

"FUCK YOU PIG!!!" Substance abuse plus an audience equals false courage ... delusion. By their nature, alcohol and drugs alter the mind. An altered mind thinks in ways that it normally wouldn't. Cowards become courageous. Demons are set free – frustration, jealousy, envy, hatred. An entire package wrapped in rage is released by beer, liquor, cocaine, heroin or any of the infinite list of poisons, toxins, and contaminants that are

purchased with regulation currency, regardless of whether the buyer has a pot to piss in or the aim to fill it. Voluntary manslaughter of brain cells is recession-proof.

"COME ON, LET'S SEE HOW TOUGH YOU ARE!!!!" Every single day, the taxpayers fund an environmental clean-up. Bar owners pollute the environment then call the police to clean up the toxic waste.

"FUCK YOU, I'M NOT GOING WITH YOU. COME ON MOTHERFUCKER, LET'S SEE WHAT YOU'VE GOT." "Performance demands" are not created equal. Neither are Culture Shocks. Every cop remembers his/her first arrest. Thirty-five years cannot erase the image burned into my mind – a shirtless, tattooed madman exposing his dysfunctionalism in a crowded bar, before friends, family and wife – the person who voluntarily announced, *"I do,"* locking the iron door on a life sentence with a cell-mate. *"Stop crying. You're embarrassing yourself. At least wait til I get you to the police station."*

The frontline has a strict street-level code of ethics. A hard-hitting code of conduct that leaves nothing behind. The frontline punishes the ill-prepared with the pain of losing the fight or the pain of flight.

Inability and unwillingness are connected only if the lifter consents. The inability to do something today becomes permanent only when we decide to change inability to unwillingness. Inability changes to ability when willingness strengthens. How free will is exercised determines the places we go. Free will determines what remains an inability and what changes to an ability.

The gym does not compete for our attention. The gym does not micro-manage. The gym does not nag, play victim, or suffer from the martyr syndrome. The gym doesn't ask for sympathy and won't accept any. The gym is secure. It's there. If you want to visit, the gym opens its doors. The gym never closes – 24/365. But it will not call you. It won't knock on your door. It won't drag you to iron. The gym will not drive you to iron but it will drive you when you get there, if free will is exercised.

∞

"Unit to back." Three words that mean: Game-time, move your ass, this is not a drill, red alert, flip the switch, do not end up in the emergency room, we're not leaving in body bags … it's on. The front part of the message

doesn't change the message. It doesn't matter if it's "break-and-enter in progress", "shots fired", "unknown problem", or ... *"Domestic, 2825 Brooklyn Street – ambulance dispatched."*

A four-minute drive with lights and sirens is a rush. When your platoon-mate confirms his arrival at the scene with *"10-7,"* the rush gushes. The flood-gates open. Like any final lap, the last turn becomes a runway. Slam on the brakes, try not to hit the parked ambulance and cruiser, run into the house, glance at the pool of blood on the carpet, wonder if the paramedic can find a pulse on the motionless woman ... and, *"MY GUN!!!"* ... try to figure out what the cop at the top of the stairs is yelling while a 6'3", 280-pound unkempt slob wrestles with him trying to remove the cop's service revolver from its holster.

Experience teaches not to ignore the obvious – never ignore simplicity. Experience also teaches that dull, mind-numbing use-of-force lectures – the kind that teach nothing relevant to real-life – have no bearing on reality. Just vagueness and ambiguities.

Two punches to your forehead teaches deep insights – don't freeze – ever again. Especially not when a madman who just re-arranged his wife's face is trying to get his hands on a gun. Freezing your balls off is reserved for Canadian midnight shifts, not when there is a clear danger to lives.

But the first time for anything is unpredictable. The brain can't always process Culture Shock – even the simplest of images. Analysis can cause paralysis. We don't know who we are until we are tested. We are clueless about what we really have until things go bad. We are completely ignorant of what we've got until it's called into real action – serious action ... survival action.

Just 0.4 to 1.16 seconds of delay is not really a delayed reaction. It's just stupid. But, good news! Stupidity teaches – it's a learning experience in disguise – when you realize that even a 280-pound slob can throw two punches in under two seconds. Until that moment, I had never believed people when they claimed to have seen stars. I became a believer. And I learned something that a degree can't teach you – how to fight through the stars flickering between you and an over-sized skull with long, greasy hair, dripping sweat and bad breath – that I didn't have a glass jaw. That working out works – it overcomes a 100-pound disadvantage.

And that there are seriously fucked-up people in this world. An obese wife-beater slamming his head against the iron bars of a police jail cell made no sense. The average person would have suffered a broken skull.

"You're being investigated for excessive force. The fat wife-beater complained to internal."

Silence.

"His wife had two surgeries – broken jaw, broken cheek, broken nose."

Silence.

"She refuses to give the detectives a statement ... won't testify against her husband. But she did say that you guys were rough on him."

Three weeks is a long time for a no-brainer decision. Twenty-one days is a long time to wait for an obvious answer. Five hundred four hours is an eternity for your ass to sweat, waiting to know if you will be charged for using excessive force. *"Cleared. Cleared of any wrongdoing. Justified use of force."* Instead of feeling relief and gratitude, the pissed-off-at-the-world meter blows a fuse.

Policing changes you. A lot. Spewing profanities becomes second-nature. Not just ordinary F-bombs. Creative vulgarities. Innovative vile, repulsive language – the miracle of neural pathways. But the biggest change is your worldview. Frontline policing presents the presence of evil in HD and 3-D. You become an expert at identifying evil, recognizing ... feeling the presence of evil. You learn that fighting evil is a good fight – but a tough fight. One that requires you to be in shape. Your outer dialogue changes too: *"Fuck you, buddy"* replaces, *"Pleasure to meet you."* And the list of assholes you encounter every day grows ... 16-gigabytes is barely enough storage.

∞

There's a point in a squat where you know exactly if you've nailed the lift – two inches before your ass reaches the bottom part of the squat. Just before you stop the bar, a moment of clarity floods your mind and soul ... and you know it's either: *FUCK YOU!!* – the bar is going to explode upward, or, *FUCK ME!!* – your legs are going to explode as you drop the bar to the ground before it crushes you.

An easy one rep max (1RM) squat at 455 pounds should be cause for celebration. Especially if it's really easy. But celebrations are not right – a waste of energy – agains the Code. They show shock – Culture Shock … sending a bad message to self: *Holy shit, I can't believe what I just did.*

Regardless, instead of piling on more weight, I relaxed – enjoyed the moment. Did not recognize the opportunity. Imagine how much more could have been squatted. Never found out. It was the first and last time I squatted 455. Final score – 91.0% of my goal – what an embarrassment.

Ever since, to mask my ineptitude, I have rationalized – very convincingly. Hundreds have believed me – football players, clients, gym members: "*1RM proves nothing. 1RM wrecked my joints. 1RM is just macho bullshit. Fuck that, who needs it – I never go higher than 225 pounds. Higher reps is way better. Now I'm in the best shape of my life. Can't believe I did that shit …*"

Fooled everyone – except myself. And the soul of a lifter.

∞

"*I lied. I put 390 on the bar.*"

Silence.

"*Mind over matter.*"

"*You motherfucker!!!!*"

If he would have put ten pounds more on, the performance demand would have been met. But it never happened. Ever. One decade to get to 390-pound bench press. Three more decades of trying but never reaching 400 pounds.

Final score – 97.5% of my survival performance demand – what an embarrassment.

Chapter 1-17
Smileless

"Smileless" is an official English word, recognized by the dictionary since at least 1913. It's not common, rarely used. So rare that spellcheck underlines it in red. More commonly, we use "frown, grimace, miserable," or just plain "sad." But it would be too sad to describe it that way. Smileless is less sad.

The word "smile" has been around since 1300 A.D. It's not foreign. Infinite reps of smile have been used for over 700 years.

"Laughless" is not recognized in the English dictionary. Probably because it's redundant. There are enough words to describe laughless – misery, gloom, doom, dark, dread, depressing … dysfunctional.

Households are supposed to be filled with laughter and smiles. Despite the lack of hard evidence that proves the benefits of laughter, there is enough for a case. Laughter is linked to stress relief, a bright outlook, motivation, inspiration, productivity, less depression, and improved physical health.

Laughter is a fat-loss and muscle-building supplement. Laughter helps you live longer by emptying cortisol, reducing the horrific side-effects of the life-and-death-hormone. Cortisol is the hormone that helps us fight like hell when we flip the switch. But if the switch goes on and there's no actual fight, cortisol becomes deadly. Unused cortisol grows piles and piles of fat when stress turns on the cortisol hose with no accompanying physical activity to drain it.

Laughter is a cardio workout, strengthening cardiovascular functions – boosting the respiratory system improves circulation. Laughter tones muscles, if the laughter is intense enough – laughter reps and laughter supersets. Laughter can be a cleanse. Laughter fights colds by strengthening the immune system. Laughter can release endorphins, the natural painkiller that helps protect against depression. Studies have shown that twenty seconds of deep "belly laugh" is the equivalent of three minutes on a rowing machine. Mega-laughers should be lean, ripped but not mean.

Laughless households promote fat, depression, and dysfunction. Laughless families are misfits Products of laughless families are never guided, just misguided and never know what it's like to be "in-place," just "out-of-place."

There are almost .25-million words in the English language yet none can adequately describe growing up in a smileless, laughless household. It has to be experienced to be believed, but never should be. Eighteen years in a gloom and doom environment with absolutely no normalcy, by any post-modern definition, is a fate I wouldn't wish on my worst enemy. Five tenants sharing a house, never discussing current events, personal events, or any events. No meaningful, enriching dialogue. No fire. No passion. No brevity. No levity. And no vacations. I never entered a restaurant or airport or train station or cottage til I was eighteen. Just work and performance and homework and more more work … .

Parenting is the greatest challenge on planet Earth. Nothing is harder than raising children – nothing. No job is more difficult than transforming infants to fully-functioning adults. And there's no manual. Nothing is more painful and at the same time more rewarding. Or should be.

Learning "to be" is a work-in-progress. No child should ever feel out-of-place in his/her own home – never. No child should ever be smileless.

Chapter 40.4
Monster Abyss

"It's like just the fuckin' regularness of life is too fucking hard for me or something." In episode eight of *The Sopranos,* Christopher Moltisanti attributed his growing irrationality to the pressure of boredom and the horror of leading an ordinary life.

Anticipated pain is stronger and scarier than the real thing. Imagined pain is worse than actual pain. The imagined pain of not being able to work out has the same motivating properties as jet propulsion. The imagined pain of being ordinary has the equivalent force of rocket fuel.

If you want to get motivated to work out, just imagine ... imagine not being able to work out. Visualize life without the gym. Imagine a life of fat. Avoiding fear is the secret to iron-will mindset. Avoiding fear is the secret to workout longevity.

The imagination is the mind's inner big screen for trailers, produced and directed by the soul of a lifter. Good or bad, they give a preview so we can make a decision. A glimpse of a potential play before we make the call – so free will can be intensely exercised.

Forced reps of staring into an abyss over and over again, forces us to train like a monster.[35] Fear of not working out intensifies working out. Fear of being ordinary causes the most pain. A spiral effect. Chain reaction. More imagined pain, higher RPMs.

Intense fear is the secret to working out like a maniac for forty years. The secret to not quitting is imagined pain. The pain of the natural struggle becomes as addictive as the drugs that build unnatural muscle.

---

35   Friedrich Nietzsche warned us, "When you stare into the abyss the abyss stares back at you," and, "Be careful when you fight monsters, lest you become one."

Chapter 26
Vocare

In *The Test Dream*, episode 63 of *The Sopranos*, Tony had a 20-minute dream – a nightmare. The longest dream sequence of the entire series. A number of people appeared in Tony's dream, those who had made an impact on his life. Most of the dream was disturbing. Dead people, sinister people, adultery, assassination plans. At one point, Tony and Carmela were having supper with the real Annette Benning and the corrupt detective Vin Makazian who had committed suicide in season one.

But the final scene of the nightmare was the scariest, a type of horror that makes you wake up in a cold sweat, pulse racing … thankful it wasn't real.

Coach Molinaro, Tony's high school football coach scolded Tony for abdicating his calling to coach high school football.

"You were supposed to be a leader of young men!!!!"

Coach Molinaro wouldn't let up.

"You were supposed to be a leader of young men!!!!"

Tony had had enough. He lifted a gun, pointed it at Coach Molinaro, fired … but the gun malfunctioned. Coach Molinaro amped it up.

"I suppose you blame it on your father when you're cryin' ta that shrink of yours."

"No, more my mutter."

"Of course, even better."

Tony woke up, shocked. Carmela calmly asked, *"Coach Molinaro again?"*

The soul of a lifter is a bastard. Uses a limitless playbook to send messages. Cruel messages. Punishing messages. Can't even slide in a DVD and escape reality for an hour without being reminded: *Never abdicate your calling*. Does whatever it takes to get the point across – *never abdicate your calling*.

The Sopranos writers could have chosen any profession for the theme of Tony's nightmare – cop, college professor, program coordinator, manual laborer, writer, gym owner – But no. High school football coach … at the exact time in my life when I was questioning my sanity, given my football-coaching addiction. Years of coaching other people's kids in an age of entitlement, coddling, enabling ... escaping responsibility and accountability. Not one team per year – sometimes two. The soul of a lifter is a relentless, ruthless messenger: *Never abdicate your calling.*

Or was it evil who sent the message, using a trick play? *Never REFUSE your calling. Accept your mission. Complete the mission. Wait for the next assignment.*

Assignment and alignment are connected. "Vocation" is derived from Latin word "vocare," meaning "to call." A calling is a performance demand, not a multiple choice question, not a recommendation. A calling does not include *Mission Impossible's*, "if you choose to accept ... " exit strategy. The Higher-ups run a para-military organization. Orders are not suggestions. Insubordination is an offence punishable by cognitive dissonance – internal conflict.[36] A horrific, perpetual, internal pain caused by intense pressure – from the top right down the ranks to the soul of a lifter – when orders are not followed.

There's only one cure for cognitive dissonance – follow orders. Sign the papers. Accept the assignment. Complete the assignment. Follow your calling.

∞

"I quit."

The best job in the history of wo/mankind is high school head football coach of a team of social misfits – dysfunctional teenagers, ungifted, untalented, scared, even chickenshit. Not elite athletes, not the front of the pack ... the back of the pack. The unchosen, the unforgiven.[37]

"Can I apply?"

Coach Dave was the only coach in the league with a "V shape." The only head coach who was ripped. No other head coach was leaner and meaner – with 18-inch pipes. An oxymoron – an in-shape football coach.

Coach Dave had that rare leadership quality – the ability to kick your ass and still make you feel important. A relentless task master, brilliant teacher, who sincerely revelled in the successes of his players. Authentic. Genuine. Real talk, real deal. A mentor who put up ladders, who put player

---

36   Tribute to masterpiece research in 1957, Co   issonance by Leon Festinger.
37   A tribute to the masterpiece, *The Unforgiven*. ‿, ...llica.

development ahead of winning, believed in the miracle of empowerment, rejected the evil of enabling and believed in open-admission. He did not recruit the best. The door was open. If you crossed the threshold, your threshold was challenged. No cuts. No list of made-its and couldn't-cut-its. Players cut themselves. Pure meritocracy. Natural struggle. Natural selection. Those who wanted to survive, stayed, those who didn't left the field behind. Free will filled out the roster, not the coaches.

"Sure. I'll give you an interview."

He who alleges must prove – the secret to job interviews. Back it up with evidence. "When?"

A job interview can be a pain-in-the-ass. Or not. The interviewee's attitude manifests. S/he who is not a pain-in-the-ass, gets the job. Change the focus, change the outcome. Every job interview is an opportunity. A chance to shine. Center stage. Stage fright is overcome by staring down the opportunity and … not … blinking.

"Now."

56-0. The scoreboard over Coach Dave's head framed the message: Change this misery. No wins in two years is an unbearable streak for any high school team, including the Blue Bears.

"Why do you want the job?"

The most important answer that any employer wants to know – the reason. Motive. Motive and opportunity are connected. Motive leads, opportunity follows. Opportunities remain concealed until motive is revealed. Motive makes a performance demand. Nature and nurture conspire to make motive meet opportunity.

"It's my calling. I can make an impact."

The secret to answering that question is to memorize what the employer teaches and preaches. Brand it, burn it … deeply. Save it. File it. Store it. Back it up. Hard drive and flash drive. And above all, make it easy to retrieve. Coach Dave believed it – and lived it. Coaching football is a calling – and it makes an impact.

"You're hired on two conditions. Don't ask me to coach. Don't ask for a pay cheque."

Never reject your calling because it's too hard. Never reject your calling based on money and manpower ... or any other reason.

"Congratulations. You're the new Blue Bears head coach."

An outsider head coach. The **4-Cs** of being a foreigner: **C**op, **C**anadian, **C**ommunity service, **C**hild. High school football coaches are supposed to be teachers, American, paid and older ... experienced. A 26-year-old detective working for free as an assistant coach is not positioned in the inner circle. The huddle is closed. No room in the huddle.

$$\infty$$

"No one is playing without working out." The secret to coaching is never forgetting what it was like on the other side – as a player. Not for one set, not for one rep. *"Football is a high-risk activity. You can get killed or maimed. You need body armor. You lift weights or you don't play."*

Gyms are a work-in-progress. Fourteen years – one member. Until a performance demand was made. *"Since there's no weight room at the school, we work out in my basement. Every night. My gym is called 'X Fitness.'"*

Performance demands are connected. A single-member gym built in 1969 had a greater purpose, a deep meaning that could not have been envisioned at that time. The soul of a lifter keeps secrets ... and reveals them on demand.

But only if you answer the call.

Chapter 26.1
A-Bomb

Arguably, we male people simply change from one level of asshole to another. Social psychologist, Harry Overstreet, identified fifteen dimensions of maturation, complex elements including "depth of rationality" and "depth of originality," that move us from childhood to adulthood.[38] Contrary to his extraordinary research, males appear to mature along one single dimension – the asshole scale – an indicator of the depth of assholism reached, the number of A-bombs dropped. Males move along a linear measurement of asshole behavior that ranges from extreme to moderate to tolerable. High to low.

98.6% of rookie high school football players fall under the "extreme asshole" category. The scale breaks when they merge into a group. Assholism spreads exponentially on day one of football practice – a spiral effect. Asshole behavior is limitless. Infinite. It manifests in an attitude that everyone else is an asshole except them. Left unchecked, they discover a even higher level of assholism. The team adopts the asshole ethos. Eventually, the head coach becomes a reflection of his team. The goal of a high school football coach is to move the needle on the scale. Sliding the needle down to "moderate" is a moral victory. Sliding it all the way to "tolerable" is a miracle.

The Blue Bear mission statement steadfastly adopted one ideology – asshole transformation. The biggest impact from which society could benefit. There's a secret to changing assholes. It starts with a written code of conduct. State a simple objective – "no assholes." Then define "asshole," because "asshole" is an abstract concept with wide-ranging interpretations for high school student-athletes. Never ignore simplicity. Use synonyms. "Punk" is understood by any generation. Next, change the abstract to concrete – prohibit every concrete punk-like behavior and demand every non-punk concrete behavior. Add "zero tolerance" at the bottom of the document. Make every player sign it. Finally, the hard part … live by it!

---

38 Tribute to a masterpiece. Dr. Overstreet's research on the maturation process, *The Development of a Measure of Vocational Maturity.*

"Living by it" will drain every drop of energy from your body. If you don't believe it, ask parents. They will corroborate the fact that tremendous strength and patience are needed to "live by it." But it works. There's a cost. A heavy price is paid. But it works. Asshole reform is not only possible, it's the great reward that, even if only for a moment, brings the tormented soul of a lifter some peace.

$$\infty$$

"It could be worse. You could wake up in the morning and see them at your breakfast table." Sharing an office with ex-Coach Dave was Culture Shock. The phys. ed. department head was an icon. A 26-year-old rookie head coach was not worthy. But everything happens for a reason. My profane, garbage-can-throwing, desk-lifting tirade could have happened anywhere else. But it didn't. It happened with ex-Coach Dave as a witness.

The soul of a lifter works in mysterious ways. Yes, Coach Dave was right. It could be worse. They could have my surname. Change the focus, stop the tirade.

Nietzsche was dead wrong. *He who asserts must prove.* He was full of shit. God is alive and well. Three daughters and no sons.

Chapter 25
Show the Way

"Our workouts were spiritual events."

Unlike wedding ceremonies with infinite guests you barely know, 25th anniversaries are not bullshit. Wedding celebrations are the equivalent of having a championship banquet before the season starts. A championship banquet before the first practice. A championship banquet before the yelling, screaming and misery of the first practice. Italian weddings are monumental. Caterers work miracles, feeding the masses for hours. Supersets of serving food and giant sets of food consumption. Mixed with the obligatory screams of encouragement, *"EAT! ... EAT!!!!"* All with one purpose – hoping to escape the dreaded "there-wasn't-enough-food" label.

The 1985 Blue Bears had an unconventional 25th anniversary – a spiritual reunion. No invitations, no tuxedos, no suits, no music, no dancing, no food, no beer, no tears – no formal event. In fact, no one physically met or assembled in one place. Didn't have to – because of "the connection." Reunions are intended to re-unite after disconnection. The 1985 Blue Bears never disconnected after graduation. Even though many of us never saw each other again, there was no need for a reunion. We were always united in spirit.

Gifts were not exchanged – except one priceless gift ... a five-word message from a player to a coach. The needle on the asshole-meter had slid to zero. *"Our workouts were spiritual events."*

Same message, one week later could be confused as SPAM – or compound messaging. But, the soul of a lifter is not a bullshitter. Would never send SPAM. Is not a disingenuous poser, hiding behind a mask trying to side-track with false pretenses. The soul of a lifter seeks truth, expects truth, sends truth – honesty out, honesty in. Every message happens for a reason. This one was the second rep – extra help with a lesson that, until now, had continuously failed to sink into a thick-skulled athlete's brain. Like a teacher who won't give up, the soul of a lifter ignored the collective bargaining agreement and worked 24/7 trying to teach a lesson that wouldn't be learned until many years had passed – to open up a mind ... to get a point across.

The Blue Bear era ended in 1989 and the addiction started the same year. Coaching one football team per year wasn't enough for me. No. Two teams. The Calling. But I wasn't alone in my calling. Somewhere between 1989 and 2010, an invisible force worked as hard as me – like a bastard – to slide the needle on the asshole-meter all the way back the MAX ... and jam it in place.

Suddenly, student-athletes were bombarded with new influences – postmodern ones that worked to change their mindset. Twenty-four-hour images of pro athletes and coaches mocking the team concept. Salary-cap, free agency, retiring/unretiring/retiring/unretiring ... hold-outs at practice and welcomed back – begged – with open arms and open pocketbooks. Video games replaced the real deal – less pain. Keyboard warriors replaced field warriors – far more pleasure to post images and words of sloth and debauchery than try to work past them. Mindrot became the new mindset. Contrary to popular myth, this is not the age of entitlement. It's the age of abandonment – the leaderless age. The age of the unnatural.

Pope John Paul II, in *Crossing the Threshold of Hope*, defined the "most fundamental characteristic of youth" as " ... the search not only for the meaning of life but also for a concrete way to go about living his life." Parents and "every mentor" have an obligation – " ... must be aware of this characteristic and must know how to identify it in every boy and girl ... and must love this fundamental aspect of youth."[39]

A message to all of us: SHOW THEM THE WAY – NOT AROUND THE WAY. Teach them, encourage them, let them fumble and stumble and let them line up on their own again ... but don't coddle them to the point that they cannot function in any aspect of real life. The main ingredient of reality is struggle – it's natural. Avoiding it is unnatural.

Coaching and teaching someone else's children – for free – will become extinct like rotary-dial phones ... or face-to-face communication. Unless the lesson is taught and learned and internalized: "We do not wrestle against flesh and blood but against principalities, against powers, against the rulers of the darkness of this age." — Ephesians 6:12.

---

39   Tribute to a masterpiece, *Crossing the Threshold of Hope.* By His Holiness Pope John Paul II.

And then tested … it's a waste of time being pissed off at asshole student-athletes. Don't be pissed off at the asshole, get pissed at the power of darkness that made the asshole.

∞

I passed the test in 1985, and again in the 1990s at two other high schools. Then I failed miserably, and continue to fail miserably to understand and apply what I once knew.

It's easy to forget who the fight is with. And it's easier to forget that every one of us has all the fighting equipment we need: "Put on the full armor of God, so that you will be able to stand firm against the schemes of the devil." — Ephesians 6:11.

A spiritual event is easily identified because there's nothing like it. A one-of-a-kind jaw-dropper. The brightest light in the darkest times. The deepest switch flips on. The mother of all rushes. Spiritual events are the strongest Culture Shock – impacts that align physical, intellectual, emotional, inside and outside. Self-discovery by going into a dark alley. A place that we feared, where we were unwilling and unable to go. Stepping outside self. Understanding that we don't live in isolation, the Earth does not revolve around us, the universe has other souls with bigger problems … problems so big that they redefine the word "problem."

A spiritual event is proof of winning one battle. Not the war, just one battle. Winning one round. Not the whole fight. Just one round. Then another. Winning one practice, then another. Winning one drive, then one quarter … and just one game. Then another. The miracle of inner peace by connecting souls of lifters.

Good 1: Evil 0. Pounding the shit out of demons. A blood-stained "D" on the opponent's jersey, leaving e-v-i-l exposed.

Fuck you Satan. Next time bring it heavier!

S/he will. And does.

Chapter 26.2
Undefeated

9-1 is catastrophic. Winning nine games and losing only one should be considered a great turnaround story for perennial losers, except if the one loss happens in the last game. An undefeated season is the Haley's Comet of football. It comes close but it doesn't appear every year. When it does, get the binoculars and cameras out. It's a meteoric rush. And even though it rushes right past in the blink of an eye, it's unforgettable.

An undefeated season separates that year from every other year. Everything that happened in that year becomes etched in stone – memorable by association. The year is used for passwords. The year becomes a point-of-reference.

"I got promoted to detective the year before my first undefeated season."

"Our third daughter was born the same year as my first undefeated season."

The first time for anything is a giant rush.

"When's your anniversary?"

"October 31, 1985 … 4:51 pm. Wore a white dress shirt, navy blue suit pants, navy blue tie, white Adidas with black trim."

"You got married in running shoes?"

Years without an undefeated season are ordinary, bunched together in the pack.

"How did your team do in 2003?"

Silence.

"2004?"

Silence.

Even though it was not directly mentioned in the *Book of Revelations*, being behind 13-0 at halftime of game number ten, the championship game, was a sign of the apocalypse. A spiritual event about to turn into hell.

"Halftime speeches" are not created equal. Stopping a slide to hell needs a memorable message – straight from the heart … and soul. Drastic times, drastic measures. Only two minutes on the way to the locker room to draft a performance demand – an epic performance demand – but a full five minutes to deliver it before heading back to the field.

The soul of a lifter is multi-dimensional. The soul of a lifter has the unique ability to be both a powerful speech-writer and a moving public speaker. Scripted speeches will never get etched in stone – or anyone's memory. Strategize and improvise – the secret to speech-writing. Have a general plan but just turn on the switch and let your soul pour out the words. Presence and passion – the secret to public speaking.

"What's the secret to turning around a losing program?" Wayne was the most-respected sports editor of his generation. Before blogs, the public was informed and influenced by an ancient artifact called "a newspaper." But high school football got less ink than the obituaries ... until a picture of #34 running in a Blue Bears' jersey dominated one-third of the front page – directly below the headline, "10-0 Perfect Season."

"The weight room."

The secret to turning a loser into a winner is team workouts. No audience, no excuses, just iron. Iron will make winners out of losers – guaranteed. Iron will slide the asshole needle in the right direction – guaranteed.

Chapter 50
Buried Treasures

There are three secrets to building muscle, strength, a lean/mean physique: Reveal concealed reps by dispelling the myth of the "scripted workout," and, self-performance demands.

Scripted workouts are limiting. It's impossible to script a full workout for any human being. Every lifter has different strengths, different weaknesses, different experiences and most notably, different mindset. X number of sets, X number of reps is nothing more than a guess.

The goal of every set is to reach **MMF** – **M**aximum **M**uscular **F**ailure. Empty the tank so that filling the tank gets done quickly and the tank capacity expands. Scripted workouts, by nature, avoid MMF. Anti-MMF. They force you to stop whether the tank is empty or not. *"Eight reps, that's it, I'm done"* – with the needle on half-tank.

The solution is strategize and improvise. Have a general plan but call the plays according to the situation. Set-calling, rep-calling while the workout is in progress. The right call means calling the next play – calculating the amount of rest, what exercise to select, and a rep range ... not a fixed number of reps. The secret is a system. Building a playbook – a limitless playbook that matches the workout with the person. Making the right call from a limitless-lifting playbook.

Treat every workout as a separate game – regular season, playoff, championship. Do the scouting report, make a general plan, then evaluate every situation separately. In the blink of an eye, adapt ... make the call.

Countless variables come into play in every workout. A scripted workout becomes a limiting liability. The two most prominent variables are fatigue management and the influence of the coach. They are connected. How we manage fatigue determines how far we go – in workouts ... and life. Staying strong is the objective. Not conserving strength – using it, replenishing it and using even more. The influence of a strength coach is limitless – a strength coach has the key to unlock hidden reps ... the ability to flip your switch and unleash all the reps that you have concealed, buried and locked up. Drag them kicking and screaming from deep inside your guts.

"Personal trainer" may be the stupidest job title of all-time. The potential for unregulated, uneducated, self-proclaimed experts in a fraudulent, narcissistic industry – a false-reality world built by drugs – a steroid-infested culture that dupes the public into believing that the unnatural can be naturally built. Even the forces of nature and nurture cannot compete with the evil of steroids.

The real job is "coach." Fitness coach, strength coach. Or teacher, instructor – pedagogical titles that communicate the teaching-learning ... science of the fitness profession – the fitness career. The job title "coach" respects the profession, the client, the gym – and self.

∞

Lee was one of my college football players. He wanted to be a cop. 6'2", 220 pounds – the proverbial stud. But his meager 225-pound bench press performance did not match his physique. The number of bench presses at 225 pounds is the universal football measurement for sustained strength and work ethic. Bench press replicates a common football skill – striking. Except it's not performed on a football field while lying on your back. The 225-pound bench press tests a player's will and reveals the workout investment – what price was paid. Under ten reps clearly shows that the football player didn't go very deep in the pocket. Under ten reps is an embarrassment for any athlete competing in any high-risk game – sport or profession. Lee's personal best was eight reps. Embarrassment squared. Workout scheduled for 11:00 pm.

The myth of "a personal best." It's deceiving – and limiting. Personal best suggests: "That's the best I can do" – a destination. The secret to breaking a personal best is to re-name it – call it "the score." Keep score rather than announce the final score.

Two guys – head coach first, Lee second.

Set #1: 135 pounds, 20 reps minimum.

"Don't put the bar down at 20 ... go past the finish line."

Score: 31 and 22 reps respectively.

Set #2: 200 pounds, 15 reps minimum.

"Don't put the bar down at 15 ... go past the finish line."

Score: 28 and 18 reps respectively.

Set #3: 225 pounds.

"How many are you going to do Lee?

"TEN, COACH ... MINIMUM."

"You said it now do it. Don't put the bar down at 10 ... go past the finish line."

Score: 26 and 16.

The miracle of revealing concealed reps. Finding hidden reps ... lost reps. Habitually avoiding MMF hides potential reps.

Lee miraculously doubled his score. The strength/head coach matched his own score for the fourth consecutive decade, at age 50.

The secret – go deep with unscripted reps and two performance demands. Unscripted reps draws a line of demarcation that separates where you are from where you want to be – a threshold that needs to be crossed. Two performance demands put pressure from the outside and inside. Outside pressure is an external performance demand – made by a coach – that triggers the most important performance demand – from the inside. A self-performance demand flips the switch to the soul of the lifter.

Unscripted reps and self-performance demands are the secret to discovering buried treasures. Anything short of that simply scratches the surface, keeping the hidden reps locked away – kicking, punching and screaming for their freedom. Kept confined, the imprisoned reps will do serious damage. So, free the reps. Open the door and free your buried reps. No choice. Hiding talents is not an option. Burying talents is a mistake of Biblical proportions.

Chapter 26.3
Legwork

There's a spot during a squat where it feels like the bar is picking up speed, where it shifts into high gear, trying to crush your back, split your guts open, shatter your legs and ... bust your ass. Squats are a pain-in-the-ass, literally and figuratively. But there is no other exercise that builds more power, muscle, speed, balls, leanness, meanness and iron-will mindset. Legwork is the secret to surviving violent contact sports. Squats build lower body, upper body and jump-start a miracle – the miracle of T-blasts ... the miracle that turns mush to muscle. Squats flip the switch, the testosterone switch, flooding the system with the miracle natural supplement, the cure for weakness, softness, bad moods, dark moods, down in the dumps. Testosterone makes you rise to any occasion. The miracle of T-blasts – legal, approved by the federal government, tax-free, an infinite supply, accessible, all-natural, no cheap additives, never watered-down, 100% pure. No-charge, easy to carry, no-refills needed. And no side-effects. But, explosive – use with caution ... T-blasts can make you armed and dangerous.

Like all truth, squats are unpopular.

"My knees ... "

Squats challenge the imagination.

"My back ... "

Squats point the finger.

"My chiropractor ... "

The no-squat workout builds the "Y-shape" – "V" on top, stick on the bottom. Heavy squats are needed for the desirable "X-shape" ... equally-distributed upper and lower. The secret to long-term heavy squats is enjoying them – extremely. Looking forward to squats – extremely. Loving legwork – extremely. Dread kills joy. The secret to loving squats is killing dread. Changing the focus changes the outcome – extremely.

There's a wonderful exercise that dramatically improves squats – more squats. Megasets of squats. Not leg extensions, not leg-curls – squats build squat power. No special machine, no secret formula. Reps and reps of squats. Squats that make your legs shake, make them pumped, make you walk funny. Miracle infomercials never show squats. Miracle transformation programs never mention squats. Because hard work does not sell. The truth, as Nathan Jessup taught us, is hard to handle ... and even harder to squat.

"Cages" are not created equal. Some save lives, others kill them. Like the physique it's trying to build, a gym cage is an unmovable steel frame with safety bars, capable of handling tons of weight and stopping excessive weight from crushing. Like a bank, a cage is needed for heavy withdrawals and deposits. The cage can handle bench press, squats, and every other compound exercise worth doing. A cage is not an option, it's essential for positioning. Positioning determines how far you go.

Positioning is where you place yourself, how you place yourself, and ultimately where it leads to. Stance, track, control, zero momentum – the four "Rules of Positioning." Every exercise has a power track, a path that the weight must travel, to work the muscle being trained. Power tracks are not arbitrary. There is no such thing as being slightly off-track. There is only on-track and off-track, nothing in between. On-track is the only path that leads to growth. Off-track leads to wreckage. The right path starts with the proper stance, the starting point – hand placement and body placement before the movement. Stance determines track. Bad stance – off-track. There is no such thing as a close-enough stance.

Everything has a purpose, everything has a reason. Traveling along the track has speed limits and traffic laws. **ControLLLL** governs the speed – Lower, Lock, Lift, Lock. Lower for two seconds, stop. Lift for two seconds, stop. Speeding is a moving violation when the weight is light enough to do high reps. Single-reps are the only exception to the speeding rule. Lower for two seconds, stop, then explode. Drive the bar off you like your life depends on it. Lift-off! No bouncing – not one micrometer of wasted movement. No spring-board action. Motionless twice during each exercise – at the top and bottom. Zero momentum stops the symptoms of impairment, another traffic violation – rocking, swerving, swinging, staggering, jerking, wobbling.

Build a power track inside a power rack. Feet placement, torso, all the way up to the shoulders must align with the launch pad, the place where liftoff happens – the connection of ground and feet. Too wide or too narrow diminishes the quality and quantity of reps. So will leaning forward – like you've been punched in the gut. The torso has to form a human hydraulic piston, a metal-like structure, an unbending, unshakable machine that will guide the bar on perfect alignment with the launching pad.

Alignment is the secret to massive gains, productivity, peace and harmony. Proper positioning aligns the body. After the engineering is in place, work on the rocket's capsule – the mind. Iron-will mindset aligns the whole machine – body, mind, and soul. Connecting the parts. Synchronicity.

Squats use scare tactics – hard work and discomfort – two deadly weapons that cannot be legislated against. Iron will beats fear. The only way to beat the fear of squats is to change the attitude towards them through **REPS** – **R**epeated **E**xposure to **P**owerful **S**quats. Up and down, over and over until the neural pathways form – the miracle of muscle memory … the secret to fearlessness.

When anything becomes automatic, second-nature, the fear of uncertainty disappears. Beaten to a pulp. Fear taps out. Leaves us alone. The fight with fear is no longer a fight because only one fighter is left standing. The miracle of muscle memory is the equivalent of learning the truth – relief from the pressure. No more risk. No more uncertainty.

Squats are a matter of perspective. Instead of viewing them as a pain-in-the-ass, focus only on the outcome – the benefits. Focus flips the switch, triggering a burning concentration on the benefits of massive leg strength and the miracle of T-blasts. Enough REPS make legwork a basic survival need and a power rush. A free-will exercise. Can you live with them or without them?

Chapter 40.16

Chapter 26.4
Cracking the Case

The difference between a team and a crowd is the direction of the force. A team is joined forces. Connected souls organizing their sources of energy into one direction. A concentrated force of nature and nurture. Genetics are the ammunition. The environment is the weapon. Nature loads, nurture unloads.

Scattered forces assemble a crowd, a mob of isolated individuals, moving in different directions, without coordination, without synchronicity. Disconnected. Dysfunctional.

Nothing joins forces into a single direction like a group performance demand. The kind that causes separation anxiety – the fear of being left behind, dropping out, isolated from the group. The thought of being disconnected is a powerful motivator. Being part of a group has the potential to be part of something bigger than yourself. It depends on where the performance demand registers on the **CSI** – **C**ulture **S**hock **I**ndex, the scale that measures the magnitude of the impact of the challenge. Goliath-sized challenges attract a group of like-minded and distract soft-minded.

Stretch goals stretch performance. Every gauntlet laid down is an exercise of free will – fight or flight. An outrageous performance demand gets us on the bench, off the bench … or makes us run far away from the bench. Depends on what we focus on and who is leading. Lofty expectations are dizzying heights if you look down. Focusing on the distance to the ground, the free-fall and high-speed impact is a dream-killer. The anticipation of a fatal crash has the same effect as a real one. Big dreams can turn into nightmares – unless iron will refocuses our vision, our view … staring straight ahead instead of down.

Every performance demand has a natural struggle, an unavoidable path of connected stretch goals. Not just ordinary goals – stretch goals. But stretching can be painful. Pain and panic are connected – they're only one letter apart. The anticipated pain of the natural struggle instils a panic – the fear of God that attracts or detracts from the concept of destiny, the elusive place that can only be found with the most sophisticated **GPS – G**reat **P**erformance **S**oul.

Destinies are mysteries. Enigmas that have to be solved. Cracking the case involves clues that have to be found … clues that have to be read. Clues don't just appear. They have to be searched for … then seized. Search and seizure. Moments that don't just come our way. Moments that happen in the blink of an eye. Moments that happen in the game, not in the stands, not tailgating in the parking lot. We have to be positioned to find them and capture them – tag them, store them, own them.

No mystery is unsolvable. Every mystery leaves traces, clues. The "transfer" theory. Crime-fighting 101: When two people or items meet, a change always happens. Guaranteed – every time. A traceable change – a trail of clues. The transfer theory is the reason why it's impossible for evil to commit the perfect crime without leaving clues that point directly at the solution. And more importantly, why it's impossible for good to create a destiny without leaving clues about how to reach it.

Unsolvable mysteries are a myth. Unsolved mysteries are products of fatigue. Investigative fatigue. When seeking becomes too hard, too boring, unbearable … cold case. The open case? The pain-in-the-ass case that hangs over our heads, fueling infinite questions, endless frustration, sleepless nights, alternating passion with obsession … waiting to get solved.

"Destinies" are not created equal. Like crimes, no two destinies are exactly alike. Each one has its ethos, its distinguishing character that separates it from the rest. The line between our current reality and our destiny blurs when our role is chosen for us, instead of chosen by us. The line gets more crooked when our position is assigned by others and accepted by us. Then, crossing the line starts looking hopeless. That's when change scares the devil out of us, makes us panic.

The soul of a lifter is not born fearless, does not become fearless overnight, and does not become fearless by accident. Fearlessness doesn't happen randomly. Fearlessness is the product of connected fearless souls. Nothing connects souls like shared misery. The heavy sweat of extreme group work is a bonding agent that fortifies intellectually, emotionally and spiritually, and, becomes legendary.

When two souls meet, an impact happens. When a team of souls meet, the case gets cracked.

Chapter 26.5
Vertical Stretch

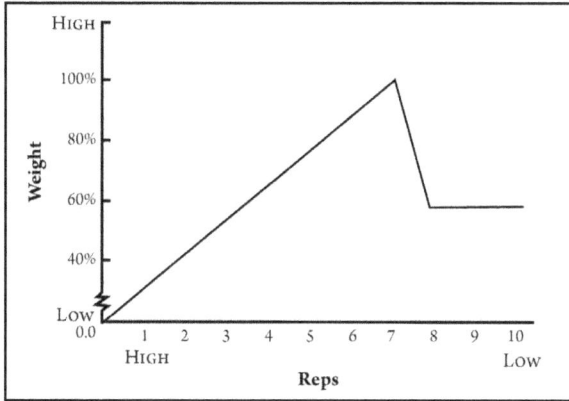

Like an unpredictable, Canadian, long-range weather forecast, the vertical stretch workout has ups and downs ... and works miracles. Ten sets divided into a seven to three split is a miracle-worker for compound exercises – bench press, squats, every compound exercise in the playbook. Ten sets split unevenly in two groups – seven-set rise plus a three-set horizontal.

The seven-set rise ascends at a 45-degree angle to the peak, one-rep max (1RM) or five-rep max (5RM) (even after we rationalize that 1RM is not worth doing anymore). The weight on the bar increases every set while the reps decrease. The amount of weight selected is directly proportionate to a percentage of bodyweight and percentage of intended peak performance – in other words, there is a direct relationship between weight selection, bodyweight, and weight to be lifted. The three-set horizontal uses the same weight – 60% of the peak, but the rest time changes – it lowers between each set.

The secret to the vertical stretch set-calling is a set of three decisions – how much weight, how many reps, how much rest? Turn the gym into a laboratory. Hypothesize, test, record, analyze, conclude. Study the result … make the call.

Set-calling is a science. It's the product of a system, a limitless playbook from which any workout program can be designed to fit the situation. The key program design is volume and simplicity – unlimited capacity and eliminate all complexities.

Making the call that decides exactly how much weight is put on the bar for the next set is based on the connection to previous sets. Sets are not isolated. Not one single set is independent of another. Each set is connected to past sets – immediate past and distant past. Bodyweight is the point of reference for every exercise. Every weight selected is a percentage of bodyweight – above or below.

Never set a rep goal with a ceiling. Simply add the word "minimum." Never add a maximum. Mandatory minimums but no mandatory maximums.

Keep a notebook of every workout. The gym is a research center of excellence. But never write during a workout. Notes are written after. Knowing that you have to remember every set, every rep and every weight, intensifies attention, builds a burning focus – the key to remembering instead of forgetting. The full immersion of concentration results in mental reps, the secret to uploading information from short-term memory to long-term memory.

Chapter 26.6
Nihil Timendum Est

The secret to longevity in working out, coaching, or any other profession is mindset. What we focus on determines exactly how long we last, exactly what we accomplish, exactly what we don't accomplish, exactly what we regret ... and don't regret.

"Nihil Timendum Est." Grade 11 Latin class has been abolished since I was in high school.

"Nihil Timendum Est." Latin reps. Latin supersets. Over and over.

"Nihil Timendum Est." Never judge the soul of a Latin teacher by size, speed, or appearance. Passion is not limited to the physically gifted.

"Nihil Timendum Est."

The Romans, she taught, never ignored simplicity. *"Fear nothing. None of you will be second-class citizens."*

Public high schools have an inferiority complex when compared to their cross-town Catholic rivals. A cross in front of a high school attracts everyone, including the gifted, the affluent and those who score high on the asshole meter. Saints attract Italians, **WWF** Catholics – **W**eddings, more **W**edding and **F**unerals, and of course the **CNE** Catholics – **C**hristmas'**n** **E**aster ... those who can't find "Church" even with Google Earth, those who hope their children will experience spirituality through osmosis, or pick it up at Christmas Midnight Mass – a.k.a., "the family reunion."

Catholic high school football teams are richer, better looking and have an inner circle tightened by long traditions that connect alumni to their glory days.[40] Public high schools play in lower-class leagues. Single-digit leagues – A, B, C – the best way to avoid triple-A Goliaths.

David never played in a triple-A league. In fact, he wasn't even a starter in the Israelite's army. The Philistines dominated their triple-A competition. After camping out in the Valley of Elah across from the Israelites, Goliath set record-setting asshole-meter scores ... mouthing off, trash-talking, generally running smack, setting a modern definition for "punk," and then raising the bar and taking his punk-like behavior to

---

40 A tribute to a masterpiece, *Glory Days*. By Bruce Springsteen.

even higher levels. David had two choices – move down to a lower-class league … or not.

Dr. Harry Overstreet warned us, "To hate and to fear is to be psychologically ill … it is, in fact, the consuming illness of our time." Hate and fear are a full-force attack by evil. Letting hate and fear into the mind is the giving of consent to an intruder – permission to commit mind break-and-enter … break, enter and commit emotional chaos. It gives evil a license to cause havoc on our mindset. Use of force is justified to protect yourself against evil – iron will. Become fearless … but fearless is not easy to become. We have to work like hell – one step at a time … or we burn up. The gym lets us practice becoming fearless, one rep at a time.

Wayne, the local sports editor, spread the news on page one. Front-page news! The Blue Bears voluntarily moved from the basement up to the highest league, the league dominated by a Catholic Goliath, the school that attracted not from one community, but five. Five communities to one.

"Four years you played them coach … did you ever score a point?"

The soul of a lifter lifts and pushes a performance demand. Coach Dave was different. An original. The best leaders know when to light the fuse … and when to stand back. He knew the answer, but let me say it anyway.

"No. We never scored one point against them during my entire high school career – junior varsity or varsity."

Pointless builds purpose.

∞

The best way to silence a crowd is not to rub it in, not to kick when they're down … and never celebrate. Not even when you've gone places that you were previously unwilling and incapable of going.

"Taking a knee" is usually a sign of surrender, except when you're winning 27-10 on Goliath's home field. Then it's a message. Three times, Blue Bears' #34 took a knee instead of running it in from the five-yard line for an easy touchdown. The stands emptied faster than a congregation right after communion.

"8 p.m. Coach?"

"Celebrations" are not created equal. Wild, aimless, purposeless celebrations piss off the opposition. And they show that success was a miracle – lottery-odds success. However, unconventional celebrations send a different message – miracles rep-out. Superset miracles. Back-to-back with no rest. And, they show that miracles will happen again. Eight o'clock at X Fitness – the basement gym. Time to celebrate. Sports editors send powerful messages. Nothing just happens.

$$\infty$$

It's impossible to lead a team while engulfed in your career, your promotion, your upward mobility, your raise, your entitlement. Personal career success is a by-product of what the team does, never the central focus. The isolated soul is never content. Full immersion in personal rewards separates from the rest, total disconnection. Mis-alignment.

Focus has to be on them, not you. Their career, not yours. Their success, not yours. Their safety, their well-being. The key is being happy for the success of others. Their achievement must bring greater joy than yours. Their achievement is your achievement. Their joy is your joy. Otherwise, disaster.

With the wrong focus, it won't be a team, it won't be coaching ... it becomes a typical workplace – focus on self. Advancement, promotion, more money, more titles, more inflated self-importance, more pretentiousness leading to even more emptiness. A giant abyss, stared at long enough is a monster-maker and a soul wrecker.

A team is a collection of souls. Souls of lifters are not artificial, not superficial, not man-made machinery. Souls of lifters are connections to a Higher Power. There's only one version, no "Soul 2.0," but each one is a work-in-progress. They all have unlimited capacity – a fact you'll understand ... once you've done the translation.

Chapter 26.7
Legends

Legends are originals who separated themselves so far from the rest, they started their own brand-new league. There are countless reasons why Mario Lemieux holds the title of "best hockey player of all-time." He turned everyone around him into a star. Every one of his line-mates had career seasons, suddenly becoming prolific scorers. And he dragged and pushed two average Pittsburgh Penguins teams to two consecutive Stanley Cups. But, most prominently, he made two miracle comebacks – one from cancer, the second from a 12-point deficit. And sparked two more miracles.

During the 1993 season, Lemieux was diagnosed with Hodgkin's Disease while playing his best season ever. On the morning of his last radiation treatment, he boarded a plane for Philadelphia, and after missing 23 games, played that evening. He scored a goal and an assist, igniting two more miracles – a standing ovation from the Philadelphia fans (the same ones who booed Santa Claus, pelting St. Nick with batteries and beer bottles) and, a record-breaking 17-game team winning streak. He also overcame a 12-point deficit to overtake the second-greatest player of all-time, Pat Lafontaine, to win the scoring title. Man with a mission.

After his playing career, Lemieux saved the Pittsburgh Penguins again. In 2007, his ownership group bought them at a time when they were the worst team in the NHL – the Penguins were in danger of extinction. Two years later, they won another Stanley Cup. Higher purpose. Hockey as a platform.

Trivia question: Why was Mario Lemieux not chosen to light the Olympic Flame at the 2010 Vancouver Winter Olympics opening ceremonies?

Sgt. Jack Moore was the Mario Lemieux of detectives – a legend, the all-time best, but never got credit. Someone else always held the title of the "greatest" because he never contended for popularity contests. Congeniality awards did not interest him. Competence and character – nothing else mattered[41] … and he had plenty of both.

---

41   A deeper tribute to a masterpiece, *Nothing Else Matters*. By Metallica. Gym music matters. Heavy metal for heavy metal lifting. The gym industry is indebted to Metallica.

The greatest job in the world is "detective." Homicides, robberies, break-and-enters, shooting, knifings, dead bodies, maimed bodies, and best of all ... the Interrogation Room. No place like it. You and the bad guy. Time clock ticking. Get him to tell you the secret – the biggest secret – a confession. **UFC** – **U**ltimate **F**uck-with-the-mind **C**hallenge. Ultimate rush.

A confession is the product of a two-on-one main event – cop and conscience versus criminal, equals confession. Cop and conscience search for the switch. Flip it ... ignite the compulsion to confess. The ultimate performance demand – the soul of a criminal teams up with the soul of a cop. Redemption through confession.

Being Jack's detective partner was the equivalent of being assigned to Lemieux's line. Impossible to fail ... if you can keep up. Guaranteed promotion ... or demotion.

The paradox of the legendary partner. Legends will not compromise, will not lower the bar, will not tolerate a missed pass ... but they will make you an all-star if you raise your game to their level. If you make the investment. If you exercise free will and pay the price.

Chapter 26.8
Bully

Iron will never bully.

Iron has no ill-will. Iron will never degrade, demean, belittle, humiliate, or publicly embarrass. Iron will not seek vengeance. Iron will not plot retribution. Iron holds no grudges. Iron has no ulterior motive. Iron does not have residual effects from dysfunctionalism. Iron is secure. Iron forgives insults but will not forgive laziness, imposters, pretenders, impersonators, frauds, posers, masquerades and haters of the natural struggle.

Metallica gave us the all-time best theory of conflict in the last line of *The Unforgiven:* "You label me, I label you. So I dub thee unforgiven."[42]

Conflict management 101. Don't label others. And if they label you, don't label in return. Drop it. Erase. Press delete. Resolve it. Otherwise, the bell sounds, kickoff inside your guts, a personal Valley of Elah with no knockdown. Unresolved conflict is the root of all evil.

∞

House break-ins are not committed equal.

"You handle this one." A performance demand, not an invitation. *"I'm coming along for the ride. A good chance to catch up with Bob. Haven't seen him since we played hockey together. You'll like him. He used to coach little league football."*

Silence.

Victims of break-and-enter suffer two invasions but only one is legislated against. Home invasion is a serious crime. But apparently, the psychological invasion is not – no politician has yet to make a campaign lie by promising to introduce a psychological-invasion bill.

"This is my new partner."

"We've met … remember?… I'm Bob."

The sign of a great leader – the ability to kick your ass while making you feel important. Jack's signature statement at the end of a shit-giving lecture was a stark reminder that petulance can invade and replace basic workplace

---

42   A second tribute to a masterpiece by the Mozart of heavy metal, Metallica. *The Unforgiven.*

etiquette, even when you're old enough to vote and breed. By ignoring it, Jack would have given immunity to my immaturity and amateurism.

"You're better than that!! His hand was shaking!! You scared the shit out of him!!!" Insights from Jack. Lessons-learned from a legend. No argument. He was right. Nothing worse than being an asshole to a crime victim. Fourteen years had passed, but the label was still fresh. Failed again. Bombed another test.

"We do not wrestle against flesh and blood but against principalities, against powers, against the rulers of the darkness of this age." — Ephesians 6:12. What a waste of time being pissed off at assholes. Don't be pissed off at the asshole, get pissed at the power of darkness that made the asshole.

Jack understood. He passed the test. He got pissed off at the darkness that turned me into an asshole … toward an ex-asshole.

Chapter 26.9
L.I.F.T.

The difference between destiny and delusion is the quantity and quality of performance demands.

Four years is a long time. Great changes can happen during four years. Transformations. Four years is enough time for even radical transformations ... of the mind, body and spirit.

The gym provides modus operandi. Motive plus opportunity equals performance. 1,200 workouts. 24,000 sets. Almost a quarter-million reps ... in one high school career. That's not counting sprints, push-ups, ab-work and all the other on-field performance demands. The basement Blue Bear workouts were more than muscle-flexing opportunities. They were one of several roads toward destiny, a journey that everyone needs to personally discover and uncover through self-exploration.

There is no "Destiny MapQuest," no search engine that will spit out concrete directions. An explorer is needed – with an exploration team. A workout is like any expedition; questions have to be answered before embarking – qualitative research:

- What's your will made of?
- What's your pain threshold?
- How deep can you dig?
- How high can your reach?
- How far can you stretch?
- Where are you willing to go?

If a workout does not force you to look into yourself, question yourself, you'll never know who you are, what you're made of ... what you can be. The gym is about much more than glossy magazines, tight clothes, synthetically freakish muscles, tattoos, indecent exposure, unnatural three percent bodyfat with saran-wrap-thin skin, posing, strutting, flexing, eating unnaturally low carbs, wearing unnaturally tight clothes, and talking unnaturally, incessantly, exclusively, about the size, shape and definition of body parts.

The gym teaches the secret of how to find the intended purpose and live the intended life that every human is called to live. Moving toward personal destiny by continuous forward progress toward full potential and making the biggest impact humanly possible on others.

The measure of working out is **LIFT** – Longevity, Impact, Fitness, Test. How many years can you handle? Have you made a difference? How far have you gone outside yourself? How far have you truly connected? Have you made at least one person's life better? Is your strength isolated to muscles or is it connected intellectually, emotionally, spiritually? Have you shared that connection? Have you put up any ladders? How hard of a test are you willing to take? And, how many tests are you willing to take? Can you walk away from the looking glass? Can you look past the reflection?

LIFT is a personal legacy. The extent of our "legend" depends on how much we LIFT ourselves and others. What we make of lives – ours and others – is what we demand of them. Do we make performance demands or do we ask? Do we invite? Is the extent of our impact on others the pressure of an index finger on a keyboard as we click "Add as Friend?"

The number and nature of our performance demands determine what we reach – destiny or delusion … calling or fantasy.

Chapter 40.12

X-Fitness Welland "The gym teaches personal accountability the hard way. Unlike team sports, the gym refuses to reward the offense of "fail to appear." Unlike team sports, the gym will not reward soft practices, soft reps, soft sets, soft mindset and soft will"

— From the 4th & Hell Series.

May 2 at 2:02pm · Like · Comment

👍 6 people like this.

Chapter 51
Spiritual Moochers

| < Back to Messages | Mark as Unread | Report Spam | Delete |

Leroy Barns July 15 at 4:02 pm
Need help here, need to add more size but having trouble getting in shape. Legs are a problem. In the process of designing a new routine but if you have an amazing proven routine, nutrition and cardio plan and can advise me, let me know. There must be a program to get me bigger and more cut. You can email me advice or routines.

```
To: Father Jim
Re: Spiritual Moochers speech
```
Father: Your "spiritual moocher" halftime speech at Mass this week was amazing and timely. I share your pain. Like you, I have been the victim of professional scrounging for years. It never stops. Football players who want scholarships. College students who want police jobs. Out-of-shape people who want to get in-shape. All want FREE advice, FREE help, FREE consultation, FREE references. And they give nothing back. They steal, rob, and defraud energy, information and every ounce of passion inside me. They siphon it out of me. And they give nothing back except their pile of pain they want me to absorb. They want a FREE agent and a pain absorber. Thank you for helping me understand why moochers are attracted to me and how to deal with them.

Social graces are the opposite of scrounging.

"Halftime speeches at Catholic Masses" are not created equal. Most, but not all, are presented in 3-D – death, darkness, depression. "There will be much wailing and gnashing of teeth," likely originated by someone who endured a Catholic sermon – a post-halftime speech scream for mercy.

"I call them spiritual moochers. Every time there's an opening at the School Board I get inundated with young teachers asking for letters of reference." Father Jim had them on the ropes. Body shot after body shot. Don't quit, Father! DO NOT QUIT.

"I hardly see them at Mass … they don't contribute to our Parish community … but I see them when the jobs are posted."

I wanted to high-five everyone around me – chest-bumping, taunting, lottery-winning theatrics. But like with my football teams' code of conduct, wild celebrations during Mass are strictly forbidden by the Vatican. So I took silent comfort that finally someone understood my pain. A **VOISE** from above - **V**ictims **Of I**ncessant **S**crounging **E**verywhere, united.

A public moocher-bashing … a holy kind. I was in Heaven, until it ended abruptly with another message … from an even Higher Place. Father Jim reminded us, *"To those who are given much, much is expected."* Crash-landing, free fall back to Earth.

We don't have the right to complain about giving. It's a performance demand from on high!

Chapter 40.14

Chapter 52
The Pump

There's a moment during a workout where the skin feels that it's ready to explode, veins look like rivers, the curtain lifts, individual muscle fibers make a grand entrance, ripping and breaking through the built-up layers, and the light goes on ... momentarily. The miracle of "The Pump." Everything gets bigger, better, broader, bolder and brighter. For a few minutes.

Wait ... don't go! Inflation followed by recession.

Craving the pump is not a game. It becomes a matter of survival. Pumped versus pumpless doesn't compare. No contest. A lopsided match – 23.9 pumpless hours to just .1 pumped hour. Not 50%, not 25%, not even 10% ... daily, 99.9% pumplessness.

The pump is a short-lived dream, a reality that becomes a false reality – you know it happened but there's just no way to make it last forever. The pump fills up and empties faster than drunks at a party after a "we ran out of booze" announcement. Nothing can be done to stop the escape ... nothing. And nothing can bring it back except more pain. More lifting, more sweating, more pain.

Tomorrow.

Chapter 26.10
The Big Pump

According to the "world's most interesting man" commercial, interesting attracts. The secret to success is attraction. Attract others and get attracted. Be recruited and recruit others. Make people want you on their team – on their side. Make people want you in their place – in their offices, living rooms, in their minds, in their hearts and in their souls. And make people want to be in your place.

The secret to attraction is how interesting we are. Interesting depends on interests – how far we stretch … what we've done, what we know, or both. Can we make people stare or look away? Can we make people stay or leave? Can we brighten a room or darken it?

"Great minds discuss ideas, average minds discuss events, small minds discuss people." Eleanor Roosevelt made this quote famous, even though Admiral Hyman Rickover first said it and credited an unknown author. Either way, they all would be wrong in our post-modern world – small minds don't discuss much of anything … they're too busy buried in computer games or publicizing their small lives on Facebook instead of pursuing a big life.

Dr. Harry Overstreet identified "scope of interests" as one of the top fifteen measurements of maturity. How far we cast the net of interests determines how far we stretch and how much we grow. The scope of our interests is a symptom of whether we have the emotional capacity of a child or an adult – whether we stretch or shrink. Some people define "adulthood" as "reaching legal drinking age." "Stretching our interests," is a stronger indicator.

Stretching goes beyond the physical pump, past looking at the reflection in the mirror checking out if your biceps have grown. Stretching is the "Big Pump" – the intellectual pump, the emotional pump and the spiritual pump. The Big Pump doesn't just happen. We have to make it happen. And it starts with craving the Big Pump. Craving the big challenge … and the next and the next. Do what we've been told can't be done. Change what we've been told can't be changed.

∞

In the (unofficial) American Dictionary, the definition of "oxymoron" includes "Canadian football." "Canadian football recruit" is listed under "improbable." "Canadian running back receiving a scholarship to play at an American university" is found in the definition of "miracle." Like the Canadian attitude toward European hockey players, Canadian high school football players are suspected by Americans as being soft – not tough enough to fit in their culture of violence. Not interesting.

In 1985, I started a four-year project – obsession – to challenge this thinking. The mission was to land a Canadian high school player in a United States university or college. The "Stretch Project." The Big Pump. Take an ordinary Canadian kid and change two cultures of thinking – one that would eradicate the sweeping generalization of "soft Canadian" and the other that would change the definition of "miracle." All that was required was focus and a belief in Culture Shock. A steep price, investments had to be made – iron, dirt, film and postage. Strength training performance, game performance, videotape that proved evidence of both. Lift, run, record, and mail hundreds of cassette tapes. And read hundreds of rejection letters.

"Too small." "Too slow." "Weak competition." "It doesn't matter what he's doing," said a recruiter, *"look who he's doing it against – he's not playing against the best."* One American university coach said, *"I can go to Florida and find hundreds of running backs on street corners who are better than your kid."*

Four years of rejection forces a decision – quit or put it in high gear. More intense workouts, more mailings, more long distance phone calls, more rejections. Finally, all calls had been made and returned except one. The very last coach called back ... *"I'll give him a shot."* In April, the last month of the semester, as the clock was winding down to zero, a scholarship to an American university ... for a running back. A Canadian running back. The equivalent of the 15th round, behind on points and throwing punch after punch to score a knockout.

Shortly after, a second Culture Shock made local headlines: Linebacker picked up by American school. A 5'9" linebacker. A Canadian, 5'9" linebacker. Two Blue Bears crossed the border when the entry of immigrant football recruits seemed prohibited by law. They didn't need special visas – they were ironworkers.

And two jerseys were hung up on the X Fitness weight room wall – #34 and #13 – evidence for those who followed – sending the most powerful message of all … keep working towards the Big Pump.

Most people won't hear the message because of the problem with the Big Pump – the gap is too big. The distance between the Big Pump and pumplessness is as deep as the Grand Canyon. Having the mindset to continue chasing the Big Pump means breaking the switch – pressing the "on" button and jamming it in place … an attention grabber.

Chapter 26.11
Sudden Death

The first time is not always a rush. In fact, it's dreadful. Unforgettable, dark and depressing. You're never the same after you do it the first time. It changes you – it changes everything about you. Doing it again never gets any better. No matter how many times you do it, it just gets worse. The only reps that you want to avoid.

"I'm very sorry … your son is dead."

If you do adapt and get used to it, you're twisted. Get professional help. Despite myths to the contrary, no training can prepare you to make a death notification of a child. No amount of sets, no amount of reps. No special miracle program, no secret formula. The best you can do is listen to your heart … and soul.

$$\infty$$

"Where's Jack?"

"On vacation."

"You're in charge??"

Condescending asshole. White shirt, gold-trim, template cookie-cutter haircut … clean hands. Jack was right – Duty Inspectors never get their hands dirty. Temptation is powerful when the switch goes on. The dark side waiting – wanting – to bust out of the cage. Then the volume button of the inner voice slides upward. The evil voices pushing, pulling, prodding. *Who does this sonuvabitch think he is?? What was it that Jack said? Don't fuck it up!*

"Yes sir, I'm in charge."

Lights, camera, action.

Two a.m. is a dark time. Only artificial light can brighten things up. Spotlights, roof lights, flashlight, flashbulbs. Uniform cops directing traffic, forensics guys photographing every inch of the road, paramedics packing up, some guy in a suit zipping up body bags, coroner with his pyjama top under a suit jacket, tilted horn-rimmed glasses, hair combed with his toothbrush. Like a fashionably late dinner guest, the lead investigator is almost always the last to show up. And attracts all eyes – glances, stares … .

"Two dead, two alive. Where's Jack?"

"On vacation."

"You're in charge??"

Single-car, double fatality. No one ever calls it double-survivor. Four kids in one car. Not one had reached his 20th birthday. Rolled and rolled and rolled. Flattened, crumpled steel and iron.

"Is he dead?"

"Who are you?"

"I was in the car officer ... passenger seat." Not a scratch. *"... with him."* Not a scratch either.

Same car, same accident – two dead, two survived – natural selection or unnatural selection. No apparent reason how this selection was made. Two were ejected, two weren't. Two get to go on. Two are out. Two get to see their destiny. Two had 19 years apiece to reach theirs.

To a detective, death is business. No time for emotion, no time for deep introspection – time to work. The end of a life needs to be classified, like a final chapter of a book. Homicide, suicide, accident, or natural causes. The conclusion has to be one of the four – can't leave a blank space on the police report. Can't leave it a mystery for the reader to decide.

It's easy to make an initial assumption – accident. It's human nature to form an opinion based on first glance – and to think we're right. But it doesn't work like that when investigating death. Like the misguided belief of Generation X college graduates who think they are entitled to avoid the bottom, the theory portion of a sudden death investigation starts at the top. Think dirty, then work your way down the ladder, one rung at a time. Homicide – yes or no. Then suicide. Then accident. Then natural causes. Can't start at the bottom of the ladder, or the middle. The top. It's the equivalent of looking at the Rorschach inkblot – to see the beautiful woman you have to first stare at the ugly lady. It won't work vice-versa.

"He was sober. He never drank tonight ... he had to drive."

The self-performance demand kicked in. *No time for rehearsal ... first draft ... no proofreading the script ... no editors. Find the words and find them fast.*

"He was leaving for university on Monday. We were celebrating. He was a brain. There ... that's where he lives." Just minutes from the scene, off the major highway.

The play clock ticked louder. The worst thing that could happen at this stage would be to let them find out from someone else. The headlights on cars traveling the expressway just kept passing by. No one who might have cared turned onto the ramp. No one drove up to the house – yet. The house stayed in darkness.

"... His mom's home alone. His dad's working midnights."

The ticking got louder ... *don't let her find out from anyone else. Don't add to the cruelty.*

"First time you gotta do it alone? Too bad Jack's not here. Well, you wanted the suit ... hehehe. Send me the report when you're done."

What was it that Jack said?

∞

Going blank is not a myth.

Not one word, not one thought. Nothing. There's a point just after you shut the ignition off that you feel something like your heart racing, but it's too low ... too close to the gut, like someone just punched you by surprise. But not hard enough to make you double over. Just enough force to take some breath away. The knocking on the door definitely happened – positively. But I don't remember hearing it. My hearing went numb. Then a blur, followed by a type of screaming – a shrieking – that can never be described, never be explained, never be replicated. A complete stranger pounding the living room couch, then the coffee table with her fists.

I had just met her three seconds ago but I was sharing her moment of unspeakable pain, a suffering that would change her life forever. And I didn't even know her name. I assumed it was her when she answered the door. Somehow I assumed right but I didn't even ask if she was his mother. I remember saying something about who I was but I'm sure it was obvious at 2:12 a.m. who the guy in the suit was. But I never asked who she was. I just broke the news. I can't remember verbatim what I said. All I know is that it happened at warp-speed and I can't take credit for the words. They were put in my head and were pushed out of my mouth. I just made a performance demand and a Higher Power went to work. Followed by something I'll simply call "the chills." Goose-bumps, freezing – chilling. I do remember making a silent vow that somehow made it past the screaming and crystallized in my brain: *If anyone even so much as looks at my kids the wrong way, they'll get busted up bad.*

Being helpless to take away someone's pain does strange things, like a fictitious choking feeling. For a moment I felt that something was strangling me. Squeezing my throat. My mind was looking for someone – something – to fight with. The choking stopped when the screaming stopped – when she got up.

"How do you do this? It must be horrible for you?"

Silence.

A high-impact moment – the kind that bares one soul and touches another ... an emotional pump. An intellectual pump. A spiritual pump all at the same time. Life-altering. Transformational. A branding event, indelibly etched, not only in memory but in psyche. Eye-witnessing a powerful lesson that can never be taught in any classroom – it has to be experienced ... mentored on the science of "being human." Feeling someone else's pain over yours. The ultimate stretch. During unspeakable shock, grief and soul-twisting sorrow, the mother of a dead child was concerned about a stranger's pain. A front row seat to a rare stage, a defining moment of enlightenment ... witnessing true strength, the kind that lets a person rise above deep personal pain to see a stranger's pain, feel it ... and try to heal it! Heightened awareness – the deepest dimension of personality ... setting aside suffering to absorb another's suffering. Paths cross and people intersect at unusual moments.

I stayed for what seemed like two hours until her family arrived. A mental makeover in 120 minutes. The first lesson was the power of listening ... presence over pestering. Just being there and not fighting for or dominating air time was a healing force.

Second, you can't absorb someone's pain at the moment of infliction. As much as you try, it can't be done. Pain can be bounced, passed around, handed off, intercepted, fumbled, picked up, but pain can't be taken away right after it's inflicted. The best we can do is take the initial steps, the equivalent of ice or heat on a physical injury. It starts immediately after the impact – the first few moments set the stage. What happens during the first minutes and hours will affect healing time – reduce it or lengthen it.

Third, shared misery makes a powerful connection.

Finally, the pain of the moment prompted a powerful performance demand – *LIVE IT. Live your life! And live it hard!!*

"Life is too short" was re-defined that morning. It's unnatural for a parent to bury a child. It's unnatural to hear the news from a stranger. From that moment on, my daughters took on a deeper meaning for me, deeper than I thought possible. The craving for the Big Pump became a deep hunger. Don't waste a day. Don't throw away chances. And, we share the planet with a lot of people … we are not the center of attention. Others are hurting worse than we can imagine. Try to heal some suffering. Make an impact. Then make some high-impact moments for others.

Since that night, I have driven past that house about 300 times per year – about 7,800 times, total. Each time I instinctively decide to press life's gas pedal a little harder.

Chapter 27
Broken Will

"Fatalities" are created equal because the outcomes are the same. Break-and-enters are not – the outcomes are different.

One year after the first undefeated season, Blue Bear #34's picture was replaced on the front page of the local newspaper by the sports editor's son's picture. 100% of the front page was devoted to the 17-year-old who had died in a traffic accident. A truck hit the cyclist, right in front of the family's house. The paper reported that he "wanted to be a photojournalist. His portfolio grew with every Buffalo Sabres game he covered with his dad, Wayne." And, "He would be buried in his high school uniform." Broken hearts, broken dreams.[43]

What are the chances? None. Zero chance of 100% randomness. And not a coincidence either. Wayne's house did not get broken into while the family was at the funeral home, at random. His son's camera equipment and high school blazer were not stolen, at random. And the lead investigator was not picked, at random. None were chosen by chance. All were connected.

Unsolved mysteries cause tension. *"SOLVE THAT FUCKIN' BREAK-IN."*

Leadership is connected to misery. *"I GET HEAT EVERY DAY FROM THE MOTHER-FUCKERS AT HEADQUARTERS."*

Leadership is measured by how far the needle moves on the misery index.

"The fucking media won't let this go. Breaking into a dead kid's house while the family's at the funeral home ... FOR FUCK SAKES ... FIND THE FUCKING BASTARD!!"

Shit doesn't roll down hill at a police station. It causes an avalanche.

---

43 A tribute to a masterpiece, *Don't Forget Me*. By Glass Tiger, with Bryan Adams on background vocals, two underrated Canadian artists.

Chapter 26-52
Muscle Confusion, Mental Confusion

X-Fitness Welland "Secret formula to handle frustration: a.k.a. asshole detox – load bars with heavy weight, be a bastard to yourself, shut everyone out, shut up and lift, get rid of vacation-like rest between sets, send a message to your brain and body that the bullshit is over. Changing the focus changes the outcome. What you focus on grows. Change your focus away from assholes"

— From the 4th & Hell Series.

September 19 at 4:19 pm · Like · Comment

👍 28 people like this.

The mind controls muscles. The mind is the body's brain-trust. Evil attacks the mind, hoping to knock out the nerve center, or take control of it. Confusing the mind confuses the body.

"A bar can't replace a bench. Beer and brawling does not replace real fuel and fighting. Get out of the bar, get under the bar!!!"

"Speeches" can be created equal and need to be created equal for certain audiences – those who have not yet reached intellectual and emotional maturity. Audiences such as high school football players, community college wannabe cops and other moochers. The exact same message, over and over, until it gets hammered home – internalized. The brain needs basic reps for basic hard-wiring – frame the fundamentals. The same mental reps, over and over, until the mind fully understands. Otherwise, confusion crosses up the wires.

The same principle applies to physical reps. Doing the same thing, over and over, makes an impact. The body fully understands what to do and how to do it, without any confusion.

Blindly following an online workout program is the equivalent of taking a fourth-year university biology course immediately after passing Grade 10 phys. ed. And then, after bombing it, trying out a Master's degree course. Designing workout programs is a science that goes beyond throwing bullshit against a wall and seeing what sticks.

But there's a limit to doing the exact same thing – it's when positive change stops. Until growth stops. Until the same reps stop transforming.

When something no longer makes an impact, it's empty – creates a void. An abyss – a long, steep depression that slides downward endlessly. Then, and only then, is it time to change the program. Change the reps. Change is needed to escape the abyss, to close the void, to fill the emptiness ... change is needed to grow.

But "change" is not created equal. There's change that challenges and change that confuses. One builds growth, the other builds chaos. Challenge is change ... with three extra letters – **LLE** – Long-Lasting Effort. A challenge is a cure for acute mind-numbing boredom. A challenge is a performance demand that flips the switch. A new game, stronger competition, higher level, a place we had been unwilling or incapable of going to.

Negative change is void of **LLE**. It causes confusion, anxiety, deep-rooted grief by making us realize we're so far "out of our league," not knowing what to do or how to do it – that paralyzing fear sets in. The body and brain respond to challenges, but shut down to confusion.

An extreme challenge is a performance demand that shuts off the switch if there is no hope. Hopelessness happens when the soul of a lifter can't get the messages through – when the messages are blocked, intercepted, dropped, sacked. Or if the receiver's state of confusion simply can't make out the messages ... can't even recognize them.[44]

The unchallenged mind withers.

The unchallenged body disfigures.

The unchallenged soul extinguishes.

"Muscle confusion" a popular term used by "personal trainers," is a misnomer. It's impossible to make gains by bouncing around from one workout program to the next, arbitrarily with no rhyme or reason ... to "confuse" muscles. The body has to learn how to execute every exercise. Each movement has to become internalized. "Muscle challenge" is the correct term. Challenge causes growth and strengthens – transforming the tired to tireless.

Challenging reps and sets don't just happen. They have to be meaningfully organized, in stages, step by step – evenly spaced steps. All growth follows structured paths – sets of ordered mental and physical

---

44 Again, we are indebted to the brilliance of Dr. Mihaly Csikszentmihalvi.

learning outcomes positioned like rungs on a ladder. "Performance demand positioning" – workout programs are built by aligning performance demands. Performance demands are connected. One leads to another. Prerequisites.

Sticking to the basics forms power habits … "performance habitude" … a hard-wired attitude that performance is a habit – performance on demand. Flipping the switch and receiving exactly what was ordered. Automatic reps, second-nature sets. Strength, stamina, endurance … all on demand. Ironwork, legwork, bagwork – the basics of the limitless fitness playbook. Lift weights, run on pavement, hit bags … heavy bags, speed bags. Limitless plays, limitless game plans.

Too much workout change too soon causes confusion, random disconnected chaos that serves no purpose, no mission, no meaning, and is not challenging. Just the right change at the right time starts the climbing process. The key is knowing what changes to make and when. Make a game plan, then call the plays. The secret to climbing is the angle of the ladder.

Limit changes to adding and subtracting – add to the amount of weight, number of sets and number of reps. Then subtract from the rest between sets. Addition by subtraction. Addition leads to multiplication.

Three neatly-divided levels – beginner, intermediate and advanced – is another myth propagated by the fitness industry. There are infinite performance levels – entry-level, mid-level, top-level and all the levels in between. Like Dante's Inferno.

The basics are not limited to entry-level. Every workout level has basics. No exceptions. Infinite levels, infinite basics. After the basics are set, re-set. Move to the next level. Climb one rung at a time. Giant steps won't work. Trying to bypass rungs is unnatural. Bad coordination, wobbly, fall, crash. When workouts go wrong at any level, do a "basics" inventory. Check the fundamentals. Chances are, something's gone to hell. Fixing the basics fixes the problems.

Stability precedes mobility. The mind tells you when it's time to change through its internal server – tension and frustration. When progress stops, the battle starts, the inner struggle that builds the hunger, the craving for more, telling you it's time to start doing something new. Make the call. Otherwise the inner battle rages on until you decide to change, or, rationalize a lie that justifies the status quo. How long you stay in the game depends on vertical conditioning. Fatigue management is a personal energy plan – conserving it, making more, being dependent on one Higher source directly and indirectly by connecting with other souls of lifters.

How many reps can you do at the same weight, with the same intensity? How long can you lift without losing strength? How long can you fight off weakness? Do you get stronger as the workout gets longer ... or weaker? Managing fatigue is the key to staying stronger longer, getting stronger longer, never weakening, never getting out of shape, not giving in to age by letting it beat you down, beat you up, and beat you around ... the waist. The best way to guarantee that the message will get through.

The battle with fatigue does not start at the end of a workout, or the middle, or the beginning ... it starts before the workout, in the mind. The mind has an open-admission, equal-opportunity policy. No thought is excluded. No thought prohibited. Free will is the bouncer – the muscle that regulates access of thoughts. Depending on how it exercises, free will can block thoughts or let them pass inside. And free will has the authority to toss thoughts out on their ass.

But the mind gets attacked before you step inside the gym. The mind is evil's target. It has a bulls-eye. Evil has sophisticated homing devices, guided missiles that assault the mind 24/365 with impeccable accuracy using unsophisticated, primitive weaponry ... messages. False propaganda. Once locked in on its target, there is no "intercept and destroy" capability.

Evil attacks our mind with false fatigue. SPAM. Bullshit messages. Like trespassers and unruly drunken patrons, evil's messages are uninvited, unwelcomed guests who overstay their visit, scrounge, mooch, refuse to leave and have to be forcibly removed. Evil knows that the mind controls the muscles. The body is under the tyranny of the brain. Muscles are servants to the mind.

Evil has a simple game plan – control the mind to get to the body. Beating down the mind beats down the body. A conquered mind gives evil the win. Evil has a prehistoric but nasty playbook. Self-doubt, worry and the trauma-induced fear-mongering given strength by risk, uncertainty, indecision, negativity, numbness. *What if I fail? What will people think?* Like a trainwreck, distractions attract. Rubbernecking is the farthest that some bystanders and spectators ever stretch.

That's just the start. Evil's advanced strategy is inhumane – bringing assholes into our lives. An endless parade of them slowly marching past, smiling, waving, tossing treats … noisemakers, blocking traffic. Left unchecked, assholes lead us to the worst type of fatigue – the kind that won't fight back. Forced retirement. Leave the game behind, sit in the stands, cheer for winners, laugh at losers, live vicariously through the successful, wear their jerseys, hang their posters, follow them on Twitter … turn on them. Criticize their failures, scorn them … vilify and crucify. Watch life dance by, skate past – eyes glued to the screen, ass glued to the couch. Zoned-out zombies.

Battling evil is a war. The limitless alley-fight – no rounds, no rules, no-holds barred. The weak and unfit get trampled and mercilessly left behind like roadkill. And the strong never go undefeated because evil is susceptible to boredom and loves a challenge … even learned Latin – *nihil temendum est* – and truly fears nothing.

There's no regulation time, overtime … just all the time. The raging battle over mind control is the main event, the tournament with guaranteed re-matches. Good versus evil. Evil lives up to its hype. Even if it can't be knocked out, it can be bruised, cut and bloodied.

You can break some of evil's ribs, make it cough up some blood, spend a night in the hospital. All you have to do is stand up. Let the armor withstand the attack. Here's the problem – good and evil use the same playbook. Both march platoons of assholes into our lives – including the biggest one … ourselves – but for diametrically-opposed reasons. One wants to develop balls, the other wants them to shrivel up.

Asshole proximity has a triple-purpose. Dealing with them is essential in every profession. Asshole-identification gives us perspective by recognizing when we have joined the club. And mission impossible – the assignment: Change the asshole. Changing one asshole changes two assholes – them and us.

Good tries to teach fearlessness; evil tries to teach fearfulness. How do you know who called the play? Answer: The outcome – the feeling. Burst of empowerment means good called the play. Bouts of anything else means the other side did. Rush to the challenge – good was the play-caller. Rush away … .

"... Lift the bar. Don't just re-invent yourself – renovate. Add-on. Re-wire. Challenge yourself. Thinking that leads nowhere is the equivalent of unchallenged reps – wasted reps that lead to no growth. Mental makeover precedes physical makeover. Breaking bad habits starts in the mind. Debate yourself. Oppose your own thoughts. Fight them. Be your own worst enemy. Give your thoughts a contest. Don't forfeit. Uncontested thoughts are a victory for evil."

Chapter 27.1
Partners

American police stations are called "precincts." Canadian police stations are called "detachments" and defined in the dictionary as: A state of separation, isolation, or disconnection.

Honesty in, honesty out. And vice-versa. Dishonesty out, dishonesty in. And vice-versa. The unwillingness and incapacity to be up front is not just a small barrier to successful partnerships, it's a blockade. An embargo that prohibits the movement of the truth. And reciprocates with more of the same until a cold war erupts. An uncivil war. One of the leading causes is unresolved ambition. Narrowly focused ambition. The kind that shrinks our focus to a nanometer of attention, making us oblivious to anything else that's happening anywhere else, including the blessing of a mentor – one who has entered our life to stamp the defining moments where a ladder was slammed down right in front of our face.

Mentors don't cross our path. They're assigned to it. A mission. A secret mission filled with intrigue … that we can easily overlook because of arrogance or ignorance, or both.

"Who's going to tell Jack about the trade?" A trade involves two-sided consent … except when one-side is blind-sided. Dissolving a partnership is a "detachment." Pulling the plug. When it's walking away from a the person who changed your life, it's professional treason, the height of back-stabbing betrayal. Or is it destiny? *Who was going to tell Jack about the trade?*

Nine years as a uniform patrol cop is a potent change agent. A mental makeover. Research has shown us that one decade of doing anything has transformative powers. It can turn the inexperienced into an expert. If "anything" involves domestics, disturbances, drunks and deaths, it can turn that same person into an expert asshole – a giant pain-in-the-ass.

The paradox of getting promoted to detective – the humility of being a rookie all over again mixed with the misguided notion that I did it myself. No help from anyone. All on my own.

"You don't know how lucky you are that Jack chose you as a partner. You'll be getting your PhD in major crime investigations. People would kill their mother

for this chance. Don't blow it." The boss of a detective unit – the inspector – is profoundly insightful, a motivator … an inspirational force.

"Of all the uniform cops he could have chosen, he picked you for some damn reason. He thinks you have potential. He thinks your attitude can change. He's rescuing you. I told him he was making a mistake. I said, 'Jack, look at his fucked-up attitude … he's an asshole. He's a giant pain-in-the-ass.' I warned him. But he didn't listen." … or blunt, i.e., an expert asshole.

Jack never told anyone how, where, or why on Earth he made this controversial choice. He didn't believe in fanfare, public displays, attention of any kind. Jack was not an approval junkie. This Hall of Fame detective believed in old-school – private, business-like, no one else's business, do your work and do it hard. No pretentiousness, no self-importance. No bullshit meetings, no use for his desk – sitting behind it or hiding behind it. The parking lot was as good a place as any.

"You got a minute? I just picked you to be my partner. You'll be on probation for six months. I heard you developed a fucked-up attitude. The inspector called you an asshole. But I remember when you weren't. Don't blow this chance … don't fuck this up."

Giving an asshole a chance is risky but also a challenge. His reasons didn't need words. The message was loud and clear: *"Don't fuck this up like the last guy and you'll stick."*

When we glance in the rearview mirror, we see a trail of opportunities, a connection of ladders that were put up for us. Some are obvious, some are not. But if you stare in the rearview while you're moving, a crash is inevitable.

$$\infty$$

The "one-shot" myth.

If you had one shot, the big chance to become what you wanted, what would you do? Would you pass it, drop it, fumble it … or grab it and hold on tighter and tighter … and tighter?[45] There is no single-shot, all-or-nothing opportunity. Like the gym, policing gives abundant opportunities. There are plenty of sets, even more reps and infinite workouts. Countless investigations, endless calls. 9-1-1–unknown

---

45 A tribute to a masterpiece, *Lose Yourself*. By Eminem.

problem, missing person, unwanted guest – a smorgasbord of calls. And a line-up of people who are willing to give you shot after shot … after shot. Even when you don't think you deserve it anymore. There is no such thing as just one shot. Unless you decide never to take any. One set at a time or megasets is a matter of choice.

Jack believed in the one-set approach to investigations. Focus on one case at a time. Concentrate on solving a single crime – the case at hand. Make one call at a time so that you can eventually see the whole board. Ground and pound. Put the ball in the air only when absolutely necessary. One set, rest, next set. Slow rush … leading to a well-rested 1RM – one-rep max.

The opposite approach is the "informants and interrogation strategies" – the equivalent of a rapid-fire megaset workout, a warp-speed no-huddle. Putting the ball in the air, going deep and deeper … and deeper. The ultimate rush. Solving ten, twenty crimes at a time … or more. Piling up points at lighting speed. No rest, no limits. But lots of partners.

Contrary to the "CSI myth," the most important investigative skill is "informant development" – a product of partnerships … connections. Police-informant is a crime-fighting odd couple. Opponents joining forces. A player from one team crossing the line to the other team – temporarily. Crossing the floor and changing parties – temporarily.

Strange connections that when they lead to solving crimes, the detective gets all the credit for the heavy lifting done by the the silent partner … who goes by the name, "Anonymous."

Sometimes you have to partner up with evil to do good. A network of confidential, anonymous informants – criminals who rat out other criminals – on your team, makes you an all-stardetective. The law enforcement version of social media: *Facelessbook (362 Finks)*.

"Thank you for the invitation."

"Thank you for accepting my invitation."

"Who's been robbing the gas stations during the past month?"

A confession is the product of another crime-fighting odd couple – the criminal's conscience and the detective's interrogation skills. A confession is a voice-activated statement of guilt, with a dual-purpose – a pressure release for the criminal and a big score for the detective.

195

Contrary to the "Psychopath myth," every human has a conscience. Guaranteed, no exception. As long as we have a pulse, we have a conscience. The issue is conscience fitness – is the conscience strong or weak? A strong conscience forces a confession out of any human who has committed a wrong. Forces us to tell someone ... any one. *Why would she tell me that? I barely know her. Why the fuck did I just tell him that???*

The conscience is our connection to the Highest Power. It has one job – judge performance. Pass mark or fail. The grading system is simple. Happy face for pass. Harmony and inner peace. Align with what's right – what's right aligns. Failure is punished with inner conflict that manifests in everything from name-calling and purse-swinging, to all-out war.

The only way to quiet the conscience is to clear it in one of two ways – lift the guilt off the chest or drop the guilt by rationalizing – justify the poor grade. Both have the exact same effect – a guilt-free conscience. But, like missing workouts, rationalizing the wrong has catabolic effects ... on the conscience. It becomes weak, frail and eventually decomposes, rotting away, filling the air with an overpowering, lingering stench.

Confess or rationalize. Truth or bullshit. Self-honesty or self-denial. Admission or delusion. One or the other in a free-will contest. One is the ultimate strength and conditioning program for the conscience. The other causes confusion.

Like an informant, the conscience is a silent partner who does all the heavy lifting behind the scenes but gets absolutely no credit.

∞

Partnerships are works-in-progress.

The word "partner" has an odd family tree. It is derived from the Latin, "partitio" meaning "partition," the act of parting, which led to the 14th century Anglo-French word, "parcener" meaning "joining." Partner and parting have been joined at the hip for centuries.

∞

The "Badge of Moxie" is not a right – it's a privilege. "Tough times" were Jack's classroom. How you handled the pressure of adversity was Jack's scoring system. Pass or fail depended on what you did when reality hit – run away or face it. Get better or stay scared.

Jack's personality test was simple – it boiled down to whether or not you had "Moxie."

The dictionary has five definitions of "Moxie":

i) The ability to face difficulty with spirit and courage.

ii) Aggressive energy; initiative.

iii) Skill; know-how.

iv) Strength of character.

v) Valor.

Jack posted moxie test results in many ways. Some were expressed, some were implied. But graduating was clear, like a shiny badge. *"See that guy? He has no moxie. Never got his hands dirty."*

Failed moxie tests got no rewrite. Permanent score. Jack's strongest statement of contempt – clean hands – a person who rose through the ranks without doing the heavy lifting on the frontline. Those who used career advancement to escape the shadows of the frontline. Those who never walked into an alley ... U-turned before the alley.

Jack believed that promotion through the ranks without earning it was the moxie-less. Jack graduated from the school of meritocracy – selection based on performance, not popularity. That became the criteria for the badge of moxie. No badge of moxie was ever awarded to a graduate of mediocracy – the institute that promoted the unworthy, inept, incompetent, cowardly, back-stabbing, clean-handed products of incestuous nepotism, popularity contests and congeniality pageants.

Unlike the presumption of innocence, there was no presumption of moxie. No Constitutional guarantee of moxie. The candidate had the burden of proof – s/he who asserts must prove. And, the badge of moxie was not a tenured position. Not union-protected. Perform or perish – the plight of untenured moxie.

Dropping the bar never revoked the badge of moxie but not showing up did. Fail to appear meant dishonorable discharge. Cut from the team. So did disloyalty. Any failure of character was grounds for dismissal from the moxie club.

ASSHOLE - **A**ll **S**imple **S**olutions **H**ave **O**ne **L**asting **E**ffect.

A hall-of-fame partner teaches all-star lessons. Don't ignore simplicity. Focus on the basics.

"Jack, some guy named Rego is on the phone. Says he knows who robbed the 7-Eleven two nights ago and who is selling heroin. What should I do?"

"Ask him for the bad guy's name, dammit!!!!!"

∞

The first of anything can be a rush or confusion. Depends on how you view it – challenge or danger. If you fear it, it's danger ... confusion. But, if you see it as a challenge ... rush. A rush changes everything into 3-D HD.

"Quadruple shooting at that shithole ... 24 Diane Street, upstairs ... and Jack's gone home – worked day shift – acting-inspector. You got Jack's phone number??? hehehehehe ... "

Desk sergeants are a pain-in-the-ass. Like parents, they revel in any asshole-management moment – any test that challenges arrogance.

"One. Get the wounded people to the hospital. Two. Don't let anyone touch anything. Three. Ask everyone what happened and take statements. See you tomorrow."

Technically, mentors get time off. Theoretically, they don't. Implied or expressed, "call me anytime" is genuine when a mentor says it because they say what they mean and mean what they say. The secret to life success is a mentor's invitation to, "call me anytime."

Two parts to the secret. A mentor is needed. A mentor is not one of 3,227 confirmed artificial Facebook friends who have lost or have never acquired the wisdom of self-censoring. A mentor is not one of the 27 who "like this" or one of the 362 requests for friendships.

Second, a mentor is not what the rest of our friends are – enablers, coddlers, cheerleaders, accomplices, co-conspirators, aiding and abetting accessories ... after-the-fact parties to all our offences. A mentor is the opposite. A mentor is a life spotter – the workout partner who patiently stands by making sure the heavy weight doesn't crush us, stepping in when we do stupid things that can destroy us, encouraging us to lift the heavy weight alone ... and forcing us to lift the weakness out of us – changing frailties to strength by applying just enough pressure to help push the weight – without doing all the heavy lifting for us.

Mentors teach us play-calling. They make our calls until we are capable of making our own. Not vice-versa. They know exactly how much weight to put on the bar. They will never touch the bar, unless we are stuck or have foolishly put on more weight than we can handle. And even then, they won't lift it – they'll add some pressure but we have to do the bulk of the work. And they will never ignore our laziness when we don't put enough weight on the bar. A true mentor will never commit sins of commission ... or omission – looking away while we feverishly bury talent and hide gifts.

A mentor teaches a system – the basics – so we can learn to do it ourselves. First we watch, then we give it a shot. The key is not to imitate. Be original. We are not meant to be an assembly line of carbon copies that mimic the original. A true mentor has one mission – to help complete our mission. And then leave us to complete the toughest exercise – free will – become a free agent and pick a team – one that shares our philosophy. It isn't easy. Making the right call is a work-in-progress.

A 26-year-old detective as the lead investigator at a homicide is unnatural. "Homicide investigations" are not created equal. Guns, knives, fists, cars ... the playbook is limitless. The ways humans choose to kill each other are infinite. But the reasons don't change. They stay the same, with **3-D** clarity – **D**omestic, **D**rugs, **D**ebt. The 3-Ds of death by homicide. The "3-D homicide" theory development. Love/hate relationships with humans, money, substances. Pain versus pleasure. Find the pain, find the motive. Find the motive find the opportunity. Find the opportunity, find the performance. They're all connected. Find the unresolved conflict, find the killer. Unresolved conflict is the root of all evil.

This was the third visit to this address in the past month. This time without a search warrant for guns and drugs. Four wounded people in one small apartment is Culture Shock. But Culture Shock squared? The sight of a uniform cop doing CPR on a guy with a four-gig prison record ... vomiting.

"... *BIKER WAR, BIKER WAR ...*" A white-shirted, gold-trimmed police administrator at a crime scene is a cross between a tourist, rubbernecker, statue, broken leg and interference taking up air space. Like enabling parents, they'll believe anything.

"*Three are alive ... bikers stormed in and opened fire.*"

"*Did the dead guy's brother tell you this?*"

The first homicide on record remains a training manual. Cain and Abel taught Homicide 001. Starting theory – "next-of-kin did it."

"FUCK YOU PIG" is not a lady-like response to, *"Bullshit,"* in a crowded hospital, about the strangest of conversation topics – the gunshot wound to her ankle. Like ring around the collar, the residue around the wound told the story. Contact wound. She shot herself in the ankle to cover-up the execution of her brother-in-law.

"He was your brother for fuck sakes!!"

"I just wanted to scare him. I didn't think he would start shooting back."

Conscience. The silent partner flipped the switch.

$$\infty$$

Unlike the "presumption of innocence," there is no "presumption of leadership." Not by title, not by rank. Jack believed the title of "leader" was earned, not awarded. He believed leadership was a work-in-progress. Like moxie, a leader was built, not appointed, not anointed, and certainly not born. Moxie and leadership are connected. In Jack's view, the secret was positioning. Know where to stand at the right time and right place – in front, on the side, or behind the scenes. Positioning and situation are connected.

"When things are going bad, get in front. When there's a struggle, stand beside. But when things are going smooth, stand back – give them the ball and get the hell out of the way."

In times of misery, lead from the front. Losing moves leadership up front. Be front and center. Never disappear. Never abdicate leadership responsibility. When it's time to prepare, stand beside them. When heavy work needs to be done and accounted for, get your hands dirty. Get in there and lift with them. And when they're winning – disappear. Get off the stage. Give them the spotlight. Let them call the plays.

Jack never identified himself as the boss or the senior partner. Didn't have to. It was clear. Jack used a primitive way to send messages – actions. But he also sent reminders, using prehistoric text messages without a keyboard. *"It's my second kid's 27th birthday today. What do people your age like anyway?"* Translation: Two of my kids are older than you. So are most of my sweatshirts. Culture Shock cubed.

Jack never carried business cards. He wrote his name on a piece of paper. A personalized note, like an autograph. Not one pretentious bone. But periods of sudden cloud cover could roll in unannounced.

"I'm Inspector Butterhead. I'll be in charge of ... "

"Aw for fuck sakes, I haven't got time for your bullshit ... I have work to do."

∞

"No one has ever turned Enzo. But you're the guy who can do it. I'll make the trade happen. You flip Enzo, we both get promoted." Detective team bosses are like head coaches – recruit talent to boost their own winning record. Dump players, find players ... make a trade – not for the benefit of the team, just to look good.

Flattery can be a blessing or a curse. Who sent the message? Good or evil? Sincere praise is the switch that makes a performance demand a reality. Disingenuous smoke-up-the-ass fuels blind ambition. Time to leave the shadow of a legend or shine in the legend's light?

∞

Pleonasms are repetitions – either wasted reps or valuable reps. Regardless, in the literary world, a pleonasm is a redundancy. Words or phrases that say the same thing but are sometimes valuable reps ... they emphasize, intensify, release pressure, build vivid imagery, or ... serve as therapy. Examples include, but are not limited to: opportunistic sociopath, violent psychopath, great legend, jolting Culture Shock, loud Italian, whining teachers, out-of-shape cops, thieving opportunistic manipulators, strong iron will, guilt-ridden Catholic, a burning fire rages in the soul of a lifter, asshole rookies, IQ-dropping workplace drama, soul-murdering job dissatisfaction, 40-year obsession with working out, anabolic steroids, performance-enhancing growth hormones, acute mind-numbing boredom, cheap scrounger, selfish moocher, incompetent administrator, conventional-thinking lemming, intense passion, extreme exhilaration, dark depression.

Some pleonasms offer no descriptive value whatsoever. In the criminal world, Enzo was a pleonasm. An opportunistic sociopath capable of stealing anything – including emotional and intellectual energy – for the exclusive purpose of converting it to his own use. His ultimate goal in life was fast-tracking – achieve the most with the least. Success without sweat, without sacrifice, without struggle. Reach the destination but by-pass the journey. Path of no resistance.

Enzo was a thought-moocher – had never formed an original thought. A work-scrounger who rode the coattails of the heavy lifters. A scavenging, social parasite who leached off the unsuspecting. Toxic. Radioactive. Public vermin with no redeeming qualities. Wasted reps. Nothing to offer.

Except information.

Infinite information about who was committing crimes. And who was going to commit crimes. Knowing who has committed lots of crime gets you "partner" status on the all-star detective team. But knowing who is going to do it before they did it, gets you in the Fink Hall of Fame. A legend.

∞

Big secrets start with small secrets.

"Enzo, you were scrawny a few weeks ago. What happened? There's no way you got that big working out naturally."

"Test, you know, testosterone. Injectables. I was speeding like a fucker, needles, pills, I was fucking dying, I mean dying, started wasting away, missed two months of working out, thought I was losing my mind. You can't be scrawny out there, so I called that miserable piece of shit Claudio or CJ or whatever the fuck they call him, you know him, thinks he's a tough guy, he's always hanging out at the scum bar on King Street, you know the place, the one where Greg busted up that guy last week, so he hooked me up cuz he owes me for saving his head from getting busted open by that fat fuck Rego. Saw him driving around with that pig last night, in that green SUV, you've seen it, he got rid of that Beemer cuz it was a heat score. I heard he's connected but he's still the same low-life doing the same chickenshit scores and his fat fuck brother is even worse, you know him, he's kinda cock-eyed and has that tattoo on his neck of some fucking flag from wherever the fuck he's from. Where are your parents from, the north or the south? Mine are from some fucking sheep pasture in the south. My bench went through the roof. 300 for reps. How much you benching? My shoulder was fucked up but this batch is unbelievable so I did a few cycles and holy shit, got unfucked up, unfuckulated man, got jacked and couldn't stop but it'll fuck you up. It'll shrivel up your balls and give you tumors. But holy fuck what a pump."

Like rookie detectives, rookie informants need to find the elusive balance between arrogance and confidence. Too far to the left or right is a rookie's worst nightmare – being labeled a pain-in-the-ass. Left-leaning, soft rookies trigger the C-whisperers – chickenshit. Hardcore, right-wing, hard-ass rookies push the needle to the red area – pretentious asshole. Minor attitude adjustments move the rookie to the middle. Like all centrists, they become tolerable and blossom into bi-partisan leaders. "Mental makeovers" are not created equal. Baptisms from truculent belligerence to maturity is painful. The rookie detective/rookie informant hi-lite film rivals *The Best of the Three Stooges.*

∞

Dishonesty in, dishonesty out. And vice-versa.

Who was going to tell Jack?

Betrayal – the cost of opportunity. The language of the opportunistic sociopath.

Chapter 40.16

Chapter 27.2
Forza Italia

Enzo's family was no different than most Italian-North American's with their version of the Holy Trinity prominently displayed in the kitchen – Jesus Christ, the Pope and Pavarotti.

"Those fucking hillbillies, you know, you've seen them. They're all around now. That dumb fucker, Billy Joe, Billy Bob, whatever his fucking name is. You've seen him. He drives that hillbilly truck. He moves guns for that piece of shit on Third Street, Ralph, you know him, that spaced-out speeder, you arrested him, that bean-pole junkie with the tracks up and down his arms, you know him, with those snake tattoos. Dirty fucker. He's connected to that sack of puss Maurizio, or Mo, or whatever that piece of shit of his brother calls him. You've seen him, the guy with the green truck. The cement mixer. Ya, like fuck, cement mixing, he's never worked a day in his life. He came here on the same cattle boat just like the rest of our parents and now he lives on the West side in that mansion with that pill-popper, what's her name, you know, that slut who used to run that whorehouse off Second Street, you've seen her, she got popped for drugs a few years ago. That's how the hillbillies got mixed up with guns, thinking they're tough but that one guy, the slob with the rotting teeth, wears the same flannel shirt everywhere, you've seen him, I smacked him right in the fucking mouth at High-Beam's house, right in front of everybody, and I said, 'Now let's see how tough you are, you piece of shit,' and he ran outta there. He ran and I told him to get the fuck back to hillbillyland. They're all the same, can't take one fucking punch, twice my size, they're always together like cockroaches, scared to be alone, fucker has brown teeth, you've seen him, he's doped up and smacked up all the time. Now they see me and they shut the fuck up, fucking chickenshits. So, the guns were in the truck and Billy Bob says it right out loud like a tough guy. Four of them did the score. Took four of them to do one score. Miserable fuckers, they stole the car

right in front of Mr. Innocenti's store, you know that poor old fucker who shakes, you've seen him, with that fat slob of a kid who thinks he's a bodybuilder. I told him, 'Hey Frankola' that's what I call him. Nicola – that's his middle name. The stupid fucking teachers at St Mary's butchered his name so I started calling him Frankola, so I said 'hey, Frankola, you fat fuck, put a shirt on. You're a disgrace to all of us. Change your fucking name to some fucking mangia-cake name if you're going to compete.' Can you imagine, with the bikini, posing, what the fuck? He's juicing heavy but he's still a fat fucker. He buys from the French guy, the one with that fucked up mustache, the bouncer, Pierre or JP or Jed or whatever the fuck he is, you know at that pit on King Street, with all those losers, you've seen him, he wears those tight t-shirts, thinks he's a tough guy but I smacked him last year right in front of everybody for mouthing off. Now he sees me and shuts the fuck up. My mother buys provolone at his store. They got the best prosciutto, where do you get yours? You should try it there. That poor old fucker talks a lot, he won't shut the fuck up, but they're good people, he's got a good heart. Came on the same boat as my dad. Probably the same boat as your dad. He's a crazy fucker too. Pulled a butcher knife on that fucked-up doper Izzy, you know his brother. Whole family is fucked up. He smacked that chick Diane who OD'd last year, that dying chick, the one with the scabs on her neck, they dropped the charges. Anyway, Mr. Innocenti pulled the butcher knife and swiped it at him. You heard about it. The car was parked in front of his store. That's what they drove to the bank with, four hillbillies in one car. The trunk was filled with heavy artillery. I heard you guys got the car back. Look at one of the tellers. She's got real fucked-up hair and bullet-holes on her face. She's banging one of them. They all got rooms off King Street. They're inbreds. That guy with the brown teeth, he'll roll over. Looks like Jethro. He lives with that scag over the hotel, the bookie owns it, the one with the long winding stairway, the wooden door is broken. They got shitloads of money and can't fix the place up. He keeps a sawed-off shotgun right next to the door. Thinks he's a tough guy. He needs a smack. They all do. Fucking hillbillies think they can come here and fuck around with us."

Like a category on Jeopardy: "Who robbed the bank yesterday?"

∞

Don't blame the circumstances. Blame the failure, unwillingness, or incapacity to change them. Like any sports defensive strategy, Enzo's criminal strategy was simple – full-force press and steal. Knock the shit out of everyone, rob them, run like hell. Mobile, agile, hostile. In a just world, Enzo would have been under 24/365 observation by a team of psychiatrists. An entire clinic devoted to studying only Enzo. A violent, deranged sociopath with no limits. His capacity for causing pain and suffering was infinite. His dark side was his only side and it didn't discriminate. Good people, bad people, he targeted all groups – the weak and the strong. The criminal community feared him. He viciously robbed drug-dealers and thieves, with no mask, no disguise and no retribution. No revenge. Fear causes a predictable reaction – avoidance.

And, he confessed to what he did – eventually. But first, the obligatory lying and denying. The first half of Enzo's interrogations were always one-sided affairs: *"You got the wrong guy."* Then, the second-half comeback. Boredom led to bragging. Not only did he admit the crime, he delighted in explaining the strategy. Like a coach bragging about his/her system, Enzo clearly got a rush from explaining how he made it work. How no one could do what he did. How he was unconventional. How he thought outside the box. An original. But that wasn't enough. *"You cops have no clue what's going on. I know way more than you, way more than any one."*

Motive plus opportunity equals performance. Ratting-out, snitching, whistle-blowing are labels, given by the immature, to those who do the right thing. Telling the truth and exposing wrongdoing shows moral character. Concealing it proves weak-willed cowardice. Moral dilemmas test moral character. They make performance demands on the conscience. Reporting wrongdoing is an intense exercise of free will – a power workout.

The difference between tattle-tailing and ratting-out is the magnitude of the problem and the solution. "You lazy bastard, do your job!!!" Problem solved. If you can solve it yourself, tattle-tailing is wrong. If you can't, ratting out is right. But ignoring is approval, condoning. Tolerance is acceptance. Don't complain about what is condoned. Don't whine about what is tolerated. Don't moan about what is accepted.

Knowing who did yesterday's crimes gets the detective the "First Star" of the game. Knowing who will do tomorrow's crimes is detective, hall-of-fame material. Knowing the past is a shoe-in for, "Employee of the Week." But "Superstars" … they know what was, what is and what will be. Knowing what is about to happen before it happens is next generation detective work. Like with psychics, there's a great demand for knowing the future.

Every crime Enzo committed was planned, straight from his playbook. No random crimes. No exception. A reason for everything. And he scouted the opponent – familiarize and terrorize. A student of the game. And he was connected to a massive network. Buyers, sellers, suppliers, demanders. The human pendulum, playing both sides – a psychological portrait of madness.

And, Enzo was committed to interval training. Working out during his frequent bouts in prison. Iron inside iron. Isolated workouts, ten-week boot camps, good nutrition, lots of sleep. Combined with his infinite source and knowledge of anabolic agents and his uncanny ability to sell them, Enzo was a candidate for hosting late-night magic-fitness infomercials – leanness and meanness on demand.

The paradox of freedom. Enzo's freedom was catabolic. The negative transformation. The lack of free will exercise while free – exercising free will while not free – loss of workout focus. Motive plus opportunity equals performance … the soul of a lifter's golden rule.

∞

"… 20 cc's … don't sleep for days … block of hash cut up … the lab guy fucked up the meth order." Catabolic language. The language of the weak-willed. The language of broken will. Enzo's foreign language needed an interpreter.

"She's dying man, been dying for months … "

"I'm very sorry to hear about that. How long does she have to live?"

"She's not really dying for fuck sakes. She has a major speed problem – advanced meth addiction. Understand?"

But broken will can repair. Weak will can fortify. Soft will can metallicize.

"I'm clean – best shape of my life. Holy fuck been supersetting heavy weight. Real intense, six days a week, heavy bags, speed bags, roadwork. Look at those heroes, you know them, you've seen them, hiding behind tattoos, talking on cell phones, can't shut the fuck up, screaming, throwing weights, smacked that guy Pete for hogging the bench like he was at the beach. Fucking clowns, wearing wife-beaters, posing in the mirrors, you've seen them, they're all over the place, like cockroaches. Fuck me, I don't put up with that shit. I tell 'em, 'Move outta the fucking way or I'll smack you one right in the head.' Fuck'em. I have to get in a

zone or I go crazy. 'Hey, Enzo can I workout with you?' Go fuck yourself, you lazy fuck. You want a friend, go to a bar. Fuck workout partners! They're deadbeats. What a joke. You wanna workout with me, you gotta pass the test. I tell them to shut the fuck up and do what I do. And don't try no motivation shit on me with your bullshit 'one more rep.' Just shut the fuck up and let me get in my zone. Most of these lazy bastards never come back because they can't handle it. I don't need anybody. Fuck 'em all. I got bail. Conditions. You know, curfew, no drugs, can't hang out with losers and low-lifes, the same shit, you've seen it. Ya, my lawyer's a piece of work. He thinks he got me out. I coulda got out without him. The judge, man, you know him, he looked hung over, didn't give a shit, couldn't understand fuck all what he was saying. Musta got wasted last night. I think I seen him at that bar on Main Street, you know the one that Rego owns, that fat fuck, I told him, 'ya you're gonna blow up some day' but he don't care, he's doped up all the time with that tramp, you know her, the one with the eye half shut, she drives that beat up Beamer, you've seen it. Man, you gotta do him for the dope, he can lead you to the top. He's running it, man, all over the place. He's connected to that fat fuck of his cousin, Angelo, you know him, the one that got clobbered last year in that brawl, thinks he's a tough guy, got juiced up, thinks he's something. He's running the pistolas with that strunze vocapiert Cammora, you know him, the guy with the greasy mullet and the porn moustache, holy fuck he's got a whack of guns in his garage, man, he scored big, you gotta hit that place soon. You got a new partner? What happened to the old guy anyway? Who's that fuck sitting outside, man, he's got an attitude. See the way he looked at me? I told him, 'Who you looking at you piece of shit?' You work with him or something? What gym you work out at? Saw Greg at the gym last night, man, he's fucked up, real bad, you know him, he's not all there, remember he cracked open his dad's fucking skull. I'd be dead, holy fuck, I'd been killed. My old man woulda pounded my brains in and sent me to straight to that fucking cemetery, and he'd do it too, almost did a couple times. Fucking Greg, he's a zombie, blown up, he put up three plates eight times and the motherfucker's half dead half the time. How much you do? You can't look at him the wrong way, man, he's fucked up and there's no way to get unfucked up. He just fucking stares, don't talk, you seen it, holy shit, he's walking around, free man, he should be locked up in some mental institution. It ain't right, he's gonna kill someone someday, man, told him to get scrubbed up, those zits are bad, all from the juice, those puss kinds, man, he looks like a zombie. He beat that guy with a motorcycle helmet, hitchhiking with that miserable tramp, you know her, the fucking giant that's about six-three, the one with the head the size of a melon. What the fuck's he doing with her? Ya, he caved the guy's head in for something like forty bucks. That's when I saw that other fuck at the gym, Pete, he was carrying some fucking cannon, stupid fucker makes no sense, tried to tell me he put up four plates, told him to fuck off before I belted him. Hey can you bum a smoke off that guy with the hockey haircut? Is mullet-man your new partner?"

Question … "What's going on Enzo?"

∞

There is no presumption of competence.

"This generation has no moxie. Do they think this is TV? Some guy with four years on the job just told me he was ready for the detective office! He's done fuck all on the road – nothing! Four years! I told him to see me in at least six years and show me some real work, don't come in here and just tell me, show me! No one ever told him that before. I don't pick any one with less than ten years frontline experience. What the hell do they think this is? They're just chickenshit or stupid or both."

Afraid to be in a cruiser or they have no clue what to do, otherwise they wouldn't want to leave it in such a hurry. The inside of a cruiser is the big leagues, the frontline, not the bottom of the barrel. It's the place where you get your hands dirty. No one ever used to think that being a uniform cop was beneath them. They were just happy that someone gave them a job. Now they think they've outgrown the uniform.

"They have to be some fucking big shot wearing a suit. Four-year wonders! They think life owes them. This entitlement attitude disrespects the public and the profession. The frontline is what the public needs and it's where real police work is done, where it's learned. They gotta pay their dues. Getting hired is a privilege, not a right. Being in a patrol car is a privilege, not some nuisance. Four years and they're asking for a promotion! They want to be TV action heroes. They all want to be homicide detectives. They think autopsies are exciting. Morbid curiosity. They stick their faces in the TV set and get excited watching bodies getting carved up. Sick. Parents are the problem. The same people who complain about kids watching TV violence can't get enough of watching dead bodies being ripped open. I told him to stop being a chickenshit – go back on patrol and do your job 'til you grow up."

∞

Warning: Switch confusion can be dangerous to health – public and personal. Switch "on," switch "off." Over and over. Switch reps. Intense switch reps. Supersets. Sooner or later, switch-confusion sets in. Shutting off when it's supposed to be on, staying on when it's supposed to shut off. Both situations can be dangerous.

$$\infty$$

"They wanted information from me. Four of them. Can you believe it? In broad daylight. Didn't they tell you they were coming? He went fucking nuts. You've seen him, my dad's fucking crazy. Fucked right in the head. Look at him the wrong way and he'll lose it. He threw them off the property. In broad daylight. All four of them. Pieces of shit. You know that fat fuck heroin addict across the street, you know Reno, his brother Gutsy, you've seen him, I called him that at St. Mary's, he was a fat fuck then and he's a fatter fuck now. He was on the porch. So he called me and said 'man, you're dad just went fucking crazy, man so you better come here' so I told him 'where'd you get this number you piece of shit, get rid of it, and don't call here again.' Lazy fucker lives in his mother's basement. My father sits on that fucking porch with his expresso and never smiles. He's either working or sitting on the porch staring at the assholes, never talks. He can't speak a word of English and doesn't say shit to no one. Came after me with a bat, swung it, shoulda killed me but missed. That fucking factory is his life. He's a mean, miserable fucker, man, you know what it's like. You've seen it. They got that temper, that fucking streak, holy shit, and you can't fuck around with that. I told these loser low-lifes, man you got it made. Mommy and Daddy giving you everything, holy shit, the only thing we get is a beating. He could put up a few plates right now, right? You know what they're like, they don't back down, they never stop, about anything. Says the same things over and over, 'we didn't come here for nothing. Do something with your life, and don't let them take you for a fool.' That's why I stay away from him. I don't want to remind him and I don't want him to remind me."

Question … *"So, did the drug unit come to your house?"*

$$\infty$$

A calling can be a curse or a blessing.

"That's the way the game is played."

Silence.

"See him? Never got his hands dirty. Look at where he is today. He's running an entire unit and has no clue what he's talking about. None. He thinks he does but he's a coward, can't make a decision, can't think his way out of a wet paper bag. He's got no moxie. But look how far he's climbed. And he's not the only one. Look around. Do you see who's running this place? Those who play the game right. It's not about the kinda work you do. It's about not doing work. It's a popularity contest. The less work you do, the less shit you get in. Doing work doesn't get you ahead. Smile, say the right things, don't rock the boat, party with the right people. I can't play that game. Never could. And neither should you. Don't fall in that trap. Tell people to go fuck themselves when you have to. Don't be afraid to stand up for yourself. If they don't like you, too bad. Work hard, and be yourself so that you can look in the mirror without getting sick. And think about 25 years from now. You'll be 52. Think about the lazy brown-nosers who'll be running this place then. Think about who'll be your boss. Think about how that will feel. Don't let anyone take you for a fool."

$$\infty$$

Heartbreaks are works-in-progress.

"How's the new team?"

"Fine."

Lying to Jack was the same as lying to a parent.

$$\infty$$

Managing failure is harder than managing success.

"He scored big last week, huge score, a deposit bag full of payroll money from his chick's parents. She told him where the money was. That chick he's banging, you've seen her, that speeder from the east side who hangs out at Needle Park with that fat slob Guido. He's going to blow up someday. Been sticking the needle, snorting, you name it. He got dropped by Greg at that bar. Pool cue right across the face, just for mouthing off but really it was about getting ripped off for coke last year."

"So, whose idea was it to break into the apartment? Yours or his?"

"His, he's fucked up. I know I screwed up. He needed the score. I shouldn't have gone. But he's out of control. But listen, I can help you big ... "

"These were old people!! Senior ... citizens. OLD PEOPLE. Can't you guys pick *on someone your own size? You scared the piss right out of them. One's at the doctor right now getting sedated. WHAT THE FUCK'S WRONG WITH YOU?"*

"You got it wrong. It's not like that."

"An 80-year-old lady was murdered during a break-in at her house over six years ago. It's still unsolved. I think you did it."

"You got it wrong. It's not like that."

"Inconclusive." Resorting to a Polygraph test is a sign of defeat – pass the buck. Can't get a confession? Bring in the third wo/man into the fight. Pass, fail, inconclusive. Three possible test scores. "Inconclusive" is the equivalent of marking an essay and saying, *"I have no idea if you passed or failed. Pretend it never happened."* Test over … Enzo 1: Cops 0. My third daughter born 116 minutes later. 116 minutes separating the hell of failing to close a haunting cold case, and the miracle of childbirth. Culture Shock. Comeback needed – failure is not an option. There is a fuzzy line between obsession and passion, winning and losing, challenge and confusion. But the line between hell and a miracle is crooked. Switch "on?" Switch "off?"

∞

We will never know the full extent of our impact. It's impossible to predict how far our words will travel – where they will go, who they will touch … or knock down. Our words can be weapons for evil or messengers for miracles. Every word we say, every word we write has a purpose. Not one sound we make is random.

In *Gift and Mystery,* Pope John Paul II wrote: "Certainly, in God's plan nothing happens by chance." During World War II, a series of events and people shaped and spared the Pope's life. His retrospection forced him to ask, coincidence or connection? He concluded that people had been put on his path for a reason, not "mere chance." By connecting the dots of his past, Pope John Paul II experienced "great clarity." Examining the full picture of his life, he saw, "How all things are connected: Today and yesterday, we find ourselves no less deeply caught up in the same mystery," and saw the individuals and situations that, "God used to make his voice heard."[46] He found his calling. He changed the world.

---

46 A tribute to a masterpiece, *Gift and Mystery* (1996). By His Holiness Pope John Paul II.

But he didn't do it alone. He was led – opportunities mysteriously presented themselves. Example: His ideology was influenced by the writings of Saint John of the Cross – *Dark Night of the Soul* and *Ascent of Mount Carmel* – which were brought to his attention by a clerk, Jan Tyranowski, a mentor whom the Pope called a "saint." Mr. Tyranowski earned his living as a tailor so he could have the resouces to develop his "interior life" – a calling dedicated to the spiritual development of young people ... a calling that, unknown to Mr. Tyranowski, helped shape the soul of a Pope.

Carl Jung, one of the 20th century's brilliant psychologists, wrote about "synchronicity," the concept of connections between people and events as opposed to unrelated coincidences. According to Dr. Jung, careful examination of synchronistic events builds "intuition," the essential knowledge needed to discover the meaning of why things happen.[47]

Solving the mystery of synchronistic moments answers the question of what to do next. What play to call? Two problems can get in the way. Discounting synchronicity as coincidence or rushing past the moment without bothering to examine it.

∞

Sometime in the winter of 1985, the cop that pissed off Enzo ... the one with the mullet, turned on a radio in the detective office just as we were about to leave.

♪*"Time stands ... "*

I turned it off.

"Hey, what are you doing, turn it back on. That's ... "

"I don't care, it's awful. C'mon, hurry up, let's go. I gotta meet an informant. Let's go!"

During the summer of 2009, I was sitting in a barber's chair. The radio was playing quietly.

♪*"I want to look around me now. Time stands still. See more of the people and the places that surround me now."*[48]

An eclectic iPod is deeply connected to iron. Essential to working out. The widest range of music possible.

---

47 Jung, Carl G. (1952). *Synchronicity: An acausal connecting principle.* (Vol. 8).
48 A tribute to a masterpiece, *Time Stands Still*. By Rush.

♪ *"In the grip of a nameless possession. A slave to the drive of obsession."*[49]

I was in too much of a rush, so I forgot to ask the barber about the song so I could add it to my workout selection. Two days later, I called the barber, cited the lyrics and asked him if he remembered what he was was playing the day I was in.

"Geez, are you kidding?? Rush! Greatest Canadian band ever. The CD is RETROSPECTIVE 2: 1981-1987. Did you miss the whole decade?"[50]

∞

Sometimes we can't explain why we are blessed to be in the right place at the right time. Of all the places to be in the world, I had the best seat in the house, the best seat on the planet. A silent lucidity.[51] Living the dream. Not just watching it, playing out the dream. Dream recognition is more important than dream interpretation. Knowing when the dream has turned into a nightmare is the first step in figuring out what it means.

∞

Regret is the starting pistol in the race for redemption. *"Jack died last night."* Pressing delete seemed heartless. But there's no sense in saving a regret.

There is no presumption of moxie.

"Stupid bastard, go do it yourself." That's what Jack's wife should have said after years of hearing, *"Say hi to Jack."* Like a repeat-offender crook at a bail hearing, proving moxie is a reverse onus situation. When we take people for granted, we are unaware of what conversation will be the last.

"You're leaving it behind? Why? Are you sure?"

"Time to move on, Jack."

∞

The badge of moxie is not a tenured position.

Alumni can be pains-in-the-ass. As a Blue Blear grad, Jack never sent mixed messages. *"We never passed when I played. We kept the ball on the ground. Pounded it up the middle."*

---

49   A tribute to a masterpiece, *Mission*. By Rush.
50   A tribute to a masterpiece, a great CD – *Retrospective 2:1981-1987*. By Rush.
51   A tribute to a masterpiece, *Silent Lucidity*. By Queensryche.

The van in the parking lot always sent messages – loud and clear, never mixed either. But I paid no attention while he paid attention. *"That #34 can sure kick and run!"*

Season three of the Niagara X-Men playing in the USA started after Jack's funeral. I had never invited him to a game. Not in season one, not in season two. And no one ever called him to let him know that the team had moxie. A failure of character. Handed in the badge of moxie.

A legacy is the **SUMM** of what is left behind. The amount of **S**ubjectively **U**nique **M**eaning that is left behind – the amount of what is **M**emorable – defines a legend.

Rest in peace, Jack.

Chapter 10/28
The Vicarious Workout

Left unchecked, workout-scrounging will become a pandemic. *"Ya, I worked out with him. Basement gym. Real hardcore. Old-school. Just iron, nothing fancy."* Cops and wannabe cops are the worst workout scroungers. A badge of honor – even though they last just one workout. Or maybe two, or three. But their stories never end – telling people at parties, bars, on Facebook that they're members of "the club." The vicarious workout – living off the reps of others … building a false *reputation*. Scrounge a free workout, get sick, puke, never return, and create your own label – a fantasy. Science fiction. Unlike the post-work bar invitation, the real one-and-run.

One bar breaks the one-and-run rule, the other causes it. *"Aw, man, we puke all over the place."* False advertisement and vicarious workouts are connected. Vomiting – proof of wo/manhood. Myths are the equivalent of steroid-induced muscles – fake. False pretenses. Not real. Bullshit. Both are unchallenged – not passing true tests but accepted as real because of the unwillingness or incapacity of the listener to question the story-teller.

Workout mooching has taken it to a new level. No one asks a golf pro, *"When can I golf with you for some free lessons?"* or *"When can I check out the golf course for a free round of golf."* No one asks for 72 holes for free to "think about whether or not to join." But scrounging workouts and strength coaching is accepted because, "that's the way it is." Conventional thinking. Someone said it, someone followed. Now it's believed to be true. A fact.

Free workout coaching, free gym passes to "check it out." *"When can I work out with you?"* Experts at the "leading-question" technique. The negativeperformance demand. Not, *"May I,"* or *"How much do you charge?"* or *"I'd like to buy one-month's workout coaching."* Just, *"When?"*

The reason why workout moochers scrounge is the same reason why they quit working out – no value, no need. Not needing something makes it dispensable, valueless. They want to be fit. They want to look the part, they want bulging muscles. They want that hulking V-shape that tapers to a tiny, nearly invisible waist. They want the 18-inch pipes. They want to send the message. But … they don't need it.

Working out and fitness in general are not on their radar screen of priorities. Focusing on the natural struggle makes it a pain-in-the-ass. They don't need the grueling work, the exhaustion, the unexplained mystery of emptying the tank, feeling the tank bone dry and the re-filling process. They don't need body construction and reconstruction – tear down rubble, build back up.

Like Star Trek, they want the destination without the turmoil of the journey. Beamed-up to a higher level. Molecular regeneration replacing a generation of toil. Avoid the drive, just arrive. But if they do connect the want to a need, they get plugged in ... for good.

Needs don't just happen. They are works-in-progress. Need is born from a void, an emptiness that chokes the heart and mind and strangles the soul. Absolutely nothing changes until a compelling need develops. The force of compelling need is unstoppable. It guarantees a long-term relationship with working out – one that doesn't condone mooching. It flips the switch and locks it in position.

No switch confusion. Switch "on."

Chapter 27.3
Impact Theory

"To a certain degree man does get lost." — Pope John Paul II.[52]

Guilt by association is a social plague. Sweeping generalizations. Labels. Conclusions based on bad experiences, bad memory, or a dysfunctional memory. Like "dumb Italian," "work-out scrounging cops" and "wannabe cops." Labels stick, until they're broken.

It's impossible to commit the perfect crime. No human can commit a crime without leaving a trackable trace. When two objects meet, an impact happens. A mark is made – guaranteed. The mark may last a long time or a short time – the mark may be superficial or really deep, but a mark is always obvious ... if it's found. If it's recognized. If it's not overlooked – or trampled or erased accidentally.

"Nope, no fingerprints, no shoe prints, no fiber ... nothing." Two theories. The crime didn't happen – fabricated. Or, didn't find it – overlooked the evidence. Didn't see the impact. The search may have been too fast or distracted or not thorough – it's not always easy to see the impact. It takes time, experience, expertise ... and patience. Not finding the traceable evidence does not qualify as "the perfect crime." Unlike television, CSI doesn't always discover the clues. If it did, there'd be a TV program called "CSI Myth." Or "CSI Bullshit."

CSI failure leads to frustration, shouting, insults, dissension, tension ... and a meeting with Enzo.

"That motherfucking low-life Claude did it. Sack of puss ... he told me he did the score. He's been laying low since it hit the papers. Needed dope. He's in bad shape. He tried sliding the basement window at the side of the house and got spooked so he went to the back door and put his shoulder to it, but he's wasting away, he's off the juice, he bounced off it, lazy fucker. His brother's worse, he's moving guns and drugs, man you got to move in on him. So he booted it, took ... the ... fucking ... dead kid's ... camera. Hoooooleeee fuck, lenses and all kindsa shit ... can't get lower, fuuuuuuuck me, dead kid's camera. Tried to move it out but no one'll touch that shit, you've seen him, drives around in that – "

"Where?"

---

52 *Crossing the Threshold of Hope*, By Pope John Paul II.

"Where what?"

"Where did he tell you? Where were you when he told you?"

"Aw fuck, who knows with that guy, he's been all around, I've been avoiding the dumbfuck, man, he's sick, very sick, haven't seen him, fuck him man, he hasn't been at the gym in weeks, lifted three plates the other day for five – "

"When did he tell you?"

"When what?"

"When did he tell you?"

"Coulda been awhile ago, the last time I saw him he was trying to score some speed, man you looked into that fat fuck Fabio? That bastard owes me money. He tried selling a gun last week, keeps it at that asshole's place, you know her, the one with the purple hair, she's got a gut now, man, got wasted with her last year, thought she was dead, for real dead, almost had to take her to – "

Unlike honor, there is dishonor among thieves. There is no code of conduct among thieves. No code of misconduct either.

"Give me a reason. Tell me the reason why you and Claude broke into a dead kid's house?"

"He's a … fucking speeder!!! He did it alone … don't believe him … You can't trust him … Come'on, you, you gonna believe a speeder? He's … a … fucking speeder … you … can't – "

"A DEAD KID"S CAMERA. A DEAD KID'S BLAZER!!!"

Silence.

"FOR FUCK SAKES. WHY? WHAT FUCKING REASON COULD THERE BE TO BREAK IN A DEAD KID'S HOME???"

Staying on message makes it a two-on-one fight. Not even a psychopath can run from a jacked-up conscience. Enzo moved his right hand to his left forearm, pumped his thumb up and down.

"Seriously, you ever think of how fucked up you are? When you're alone, do you ever think how seriously fucked your mind is?"

"Ya I do. All the time."

∞

"The conscience is man's sanctuary and most secret core, where he finds himself alone with God, whose voice resounds within him ... "

— Pope John Paul II.[53]

---

53 *Crossing the Threshold of Hope*, By Pope John Paul II.

Chapter 40.17

"Ora è il tempo di costruire un'enorme forza!!!" Translation: Now is the time to build enormous strength.

Transforming weakness to strength needs a sense of urgency. Life is too short to put it off. And there's only one shot at life. One chance. No practice run. No repeat performance. It makes no sense to accept weakness. None. It makes no sense not to build enormous strength. It makes less sense not to at least try.

The perfect situation is a work-in-progress. Waiting for the perfect situation is a sign of weakness. Make your perfect situation. Lead the movement. Get in front. Show the way. It starts with mindset. What is deposited in our minds, minute by minute, hour after hour, day after day. What we let in is connected to who we let in. How strong are the entrances – to our minds? To our inner circles? How easy is access? Guarded or open-access? The secret is letting in world-changers – those who are or those who have the potential … those that want to be world-changers.

"He who walks with the wise grows wise, but a companion of fools suffers harm." — Proverbs 13:20.

Chapter 33
Breaking Law of Attraction

Answer "yes," or "no," to the following questions:

- Do you crave intense physical activity?
- Do you crave intense intellectual activity?
- Do you have a motor that constantly revs in the high-RPM red zone?
- Do you have an intense need for achievement?
- After you conquer one goal, do you immediately plan the next and the next and the next?
- Do people have a hard time keeping up with you?
- Do you get easily pissed off when people can't, don't or don't want to keep up with you?
- Do you deeply suffer from, and intensely dread boredom?
- Is your boredom immune system weak, making you easily susceptible to boredom?
- Do you crave danger?
- Do you live and die for high-risk situations?
- Do you need a rush every single waking minute?
- Does your mood swing like a wild carnival ride when there is no rush?
- Are you smart and feel an intense need to broadcast your knowledge as often as possible?
- Are you a shit-disturber?
- Do you constantly challenge conventional thinking with wild, not mild, boat-rocking?
- Do you abhor losing?
- Do you think so far outside the box that the box disappears?
- Do you believe in, "I'll do it myself because you'll just screw it up so bad it will be unfixable"?
- Do you despise taking instructions?
- Do you want control over your destiny instead of having someone else call the shots?
- Do you want to call the plays instead of giving someone else the play-calling responsibility?

- Do you insult followers by calling them names like, "lemming" and "sheep"?
- Do you feel a compulsion to let every asshole you meet know they are an asshole, to save any confusion?
- Does it bother you to let asshole behavior go undetected and unrecognized by the victim of it?
- Do you feel intense embarrassment from amateurism and failure?
- Do you feel a compulsion to argue vehemently about every point that you don't agree with, even when the point of the point is pointless?
- Are you supremely confident, strong, iron-willed?
- Do you have high admission standards and armed security for your inner circle?
- Are you suspicious of strangers?
- Are you suspicious of friends?
- After you admit someone to your inner circle, are you fiercely loyal?
- When someone you know does something horribly wrong, do you have the balls to sink their ass?
- Are you unspeakably blunt?
- Do you get morbidly sick and tired of the same old people?
- Do you get morbidly sick and tired of the same old places?
- Do you suffer pain when idle?
- Do you suffer deep pain from mindless, idle conversation?
- Do you suffer even deeper pain from unfulfilled potential?
- Do you suffer gut-wrenching pain from mediocrity – yours or others?
- Do you have to "go in first"?
- Are you impulsive?
- Do you intensely fear and deeply dread being ordinary?

A perfect score – all "yes" answers – means you have potential to be, or you currently are, or you have been, one of two things: A successful, repeat, hardened criminal, or a successful, awesome detective. You are not a "yes" wo/man. You are a high-energy, shockingly blunt, shit-disturbing rebel ... a.k.a., "an asshole."

A perfect "no" score means you are an inept criminal, or you have the potential to be, or are, or have been an administrator – someone on the sidelines, not the frontline. Either way, you are and will likely remain a "yes" wo/man ... a.k.a. "socially acceptable." Lots of friends. Invited to all parties, life of all parties, winner of copious congeniality ribbons.

The *Reming Personality Indicator.*[54] Successful detectives and long-term criminals share eerily similar personality traits. Like attracts like. "Takes one to know one"... and catch one. A former cop, Dr. George Reming, proved what we all knew but were afraid to say – there's a fine, jagged, blurry line between great detectives and sinister criminals. The reason is the arena – it's the same. Cops and robbers perform on the same dark, demented, whacked-out, imbalanced playing field. A culture of violence, immorality and danger, needs outside-the-box survival skills for the wide range of undesirable, controversial personality traits it attracts. The frontline is not for the squeamish, the soft, or the scared. Street survival needs – breeds – street personalities. Same thinking. Different switch.

Frontline policing causes Culture Shock. Every jolt makes a fracture line. Some go deep. The frontline changes people – mental makeover. Identity change – full force, full speed – not subtle, not slow. The "high reality IQ" paradox – a blessing and a curse. The streets dramatically transform personality while sharpening the sixth sense – intuition. Gut feelings move through the mind, heart ... and soul. Rose-colored glasses are replaced with X-Ray vision – the uncanny ability to read better – see through situations, see through people. The frontline hands out scholarships for a PhD in street smarts.

But a price is paid. Street smarts are costly: "The price for heightened awareness often can be pain and disillusionment."[55] Gullibility isn't lost – it's robbed. The natural rate of maturation revs up to warp speed. Innocence gets dumped at an unnaturally fast rate. Everything turns to iron – mind, heart, soul and they in turn, turn to iron for relief and survival.

54　A tribute to a masterpiece. This list was adapted from George Reming's brilliant study published in his 1987 PhD dissertation. Deeply influential research that profoundly impacts public safety. I am indebted to Dr. Reming for graciously sharing his work 20 years ago; I have used it in college lectures, textbooks, and my Master's thesis.
55　A tribute to a masterpiece within a masterpiece. Immortal words by Robert Ladoucer, head coach of De La Salle High School, Concord, California, the most successful high school football team in history. From the masterpiece *When the Game Stands Tall*, by Neil Hayes. Strongly recommend reading the book if you are interested in achieving excellence and understanding the cultural difference that separates American and Canadian high school football.

The arena makes rookie assholes become bigger assholes – both criminals and cops. REPS – **R**epeated **E**xposure to **P**ressure and **S**tress – teaches what cannot possibly be learned anywhere else, on any job site – how to anticipate the worse. How to forecast disaster – and how to prevent it. REPS build the internal antenna – an early-warning radar.

But the antenna can get jammed with overuse, drawing a line on the pavement between self-protection and extreme paranoia. Always anticipating the worst hard-wires the expectation of the worst. The Pygmalion effect takes over – self-fulfilling prophecies. Expect the worst, get the worst.

Cops and criminals. Someone always has their finger on "the button." Switch "on," switch "off." And when the lights go out, it isn't pretty.

Chapter 33, 36, 38, 38.1, 40, 47, 52
Snake-Skin

Friedrich Nietzsche taught us: "The snake which cannot cast its skin has to die. As well, the minds which are prevented from changing their opinions, they cease to be minds."[56]

Shedding one's skin. We were born to grow. But growth has a price. The old skin has to be torn off. A painful process – physically, intellectually, emotionally, spiritually ... the pain of shedding one's skin is connected. But it's essential. Skin-shedding is vital to reaching full potential, vital to preventing the sinister impact of extreme cognitive dissonance, the mind's built-in stress-regulating, stress-inducing, SMS that won't allow running and hiding from destiny.

Like the new unenforceable municipal by-laws to stop carbon emissions, idling is prohibited. Idling contradicts skin-shedding – idling cements old layers of skin. Skin-shedding forces the mind to continually make performance demands. Pushing, pulling, lifting toward new challenges, new places, new people.

Unlike resistance training, resistance to "the calling" is armed and dangerous, relentlessly attacking mind, body and soul. Crime and punishment[57] meets fire-and-brimstone motivation. Pain and pleasure partnering up. Good and evil teaming up to kick ass. Joint forces – suffering the consequences for avoiding destiny. The only difference is the noise. Airport-level applause meter from evil – wild celebrations worse than Montreal riots after any playoff win. But that decibel level doesn't compare to the noise the soul of a lifter makes when pissed off. The soul of a lifter hates losing. Failure to move toward full potential – toward destiny – is not an option for the soul of a lifter.

New skin, new connections. It's impossible to rid skin and replace it without disengaging. Isolation is connected to engagement. The isolation of training, learning, introspection, retrospection – the cost of new skin

---

56 I am indebted to former Blue Bear and graduate of the original X Fitness strength training program, Dr. Jodi DiBartolomeo, philosophy professor, for his teachings of Nietzsche, "shedding one's skin," and "self-overcoming."
57 Tribute to a masterpiece, *Crime and Punishment,* by Fyodor Dostoevsky.

is steep. The heavy price of self-overcoming.[58] Engaging the insider is harder than beating the outsider because of our propensity for labeling – self-labeling.

The strongest labels are attached by the biggest bastard of all – ourselves. We are ruthless to ourselves. The self-labels we manufacture defy imagination: *Not smart enough, not strong enough ... not good enough.* Drilled, hammered, cemented, until they become hard-wired. Overcoming "self" needs training – heavy megaset workouts. Rep after rep, set after set of lifting heavy weight to overcome the obstacles we drop along our path – more and more plates that we willingly slide off the bar.

Self-overcoming is the greatest performance demand imposed by nature and nurture. Contrary to popular myth that there are two guarantees in life, there are actually four: Death, taxes, Toronto Maple Leafs not winning the Stanley Cup and performance demands made by the mind-body partnership. Growth and maturity are not choices. Old skin has to be shed to follow our calling. Change-on-demand is costly. So is not changing on demand.

Resisting the calling is painful. "Callings" are not created equal. Nor are they easily identifiable. Worse than trying to pick a suspect from a lineup of 12 look-alikes. But one thing is certain – it's not our idea. There's no guarantee that our calling is singular or unique or that we'll love it, even though when we do follow, it does actually turn out to be singularly unique. A blessing or a curse. And another thing is certain, "Wearin' the cross of my calling"[59] is a privilege. It's willed on us by the Highest Power. We were recruited. Chosen. Selected. Assigned the starting position. Not a bench-warmer ... a starter.

---

58   I am indebted to former Blue Bear and graduate of the original X Fitness strength training program, Dr. Jodi DiBartolomeo, philosophy professor, for his teachings of Nietzsche, "shedding one's skin," and "self-overcoming."
59   Tribute to a mega-masterpiece, *The Rising*, by Bruce Springsteen.

"To arrive at what now you do not enjoy, you must go where you do not enjoy.

To reach what you do not know, you must go where you do not know.

To go into possession of what you do not have, you must go where you have nothing."

— St. John of the Cross.[60]

We have it ass-backwards – the comfort zone is really the discomfort zone. Life is lived outside the box – inside, it's existed. The rush gets more powerful on the edge of and beyond our prison bars, a.k.a., "comfort zone." We are never truly comfortable in our proverbial comfort zone – we try to break free from it. Consciously or subconsciously, we are attracted away from our comfort zone. Forces unknown try to pull us out of the comfort zone – resisting it causes discomfort. The discomfort zone is the place where we imagine comfort – the place where everything stays the same. The unnatural place. Because absolutely nothing stays the same. No one, no place. Everything gets better or worse but the status quo is impossible. We change every minute – every second.

Even the fight to stay the same is not the same. The force of the rush gets stronger and stronger and stronger the farther and farther and farther we push to shed our skin.

---

60   Tribute to three masterpieces. *Dark Night of the Soul* and *Ascent of Mount Carmel* by St. John of the Cross, as in p. 86 *Crossing the Threshold of Hope*, by His Holiness Pope John Paul II.

Chapter 40.18

X-Fitness Welland "How we deal with uncertainty determines how we deal with stress, pressure, anxiety, which determines how far we go in life. The secret is train for it, using the concepts of 'unknown reps' and 'unknown sets.' Strength and conditioning converts the unknown into a positive force"

— From the 4th & Hell Series.

August 16 at 4:55pm · Like · Comment

👍 15 people like this.

Chapter 34-36
Fourth Quarter

"You think you know misery but you don't. Truly, you don't know what misery is. You've got everything working, all the working parts. You're alive, you have food, you're not fighting in a war, you have hope, you can read, you can write, you have school, you have the gym, you have muscles and you have football. You're the luckiest people in the world."

"Misery" is not created equal. The Sir Winston Churchill Bulldogs were a hopeless, winless program in the lowest class high school league in the entire city – players from the east-side of the tracks.

"You're the new head coach on one condition – don't ask any of us to help you coach. All the teachers have had enough. We have criminals, sons of criminals, soon-to-be criminals ... that kid over there ... no that little guy ... held his family hostage. A SWAT team had to get him out. That one ... the one with the hair covering his face ... his dad is the President of a biker gang. The guy with the tattoos is new ... he's on probation for assault."

"Undefeated seasons" are not created equal.

Weight room, live practices and miracle fat loss – sprints. Fashionably called **HIIT** – **H**igh **I**ntensity **I**nterval **T**raining – reps of sprinting, jogging, sprinting, jogging, cuts through layers of fat like a pathologist at an autopsy. Contrary to popular myth, the fitness industry did not make this post-modern discovery in the 21st century. Football coaches knew the value of sprints and intervals a century ago.

"Can anyone tell me how far were the sprints you ran last year?"

"FORTY YARDS."

"Second question – how many sprints did you run last year?

"Four – at our first pre-season practice."

Guerilla ontology is any practice that radically transforms mindset.[61] It's a way to solve the problem of fixed worldview – set in ways ... stuck in a rut. A deep rut leading to nowhere. The same old thing that leads to the same old failures and frustrations. Nothing changes if nothing changes.

Guerilla ontology is extreme Culture Shock. Radical change with no time to think about it. Bypassing the conventional turtle-like stages of change – meetings, sub-committees, longer meetings, focus groups, more frequent meetings, derision ... attempted murder of the proposed change with cycles of laughter and shaking fists of rage[62] ... advisory boards, endless emails with growing c.c. lists, fear, panic, shorter meetings ... until the idea dies a natural death.

"Here's the new sprint program. It will melt all your fat ... every ounce of blubber shaking on your body. Full-field sprints. Goal-line to goal-line. 100 yards. And, you won't know the number of sprints. It will change every night. And when you hear, 'FOURTH QUARTER,' it means. 'YOU ARE NOT TIRED, RUN FASTER' because the other team will definitely be tired. And AIM FIVE YARDS PAST THE FINISH LINE. That's where you slow down."

"Uncertainty management." How we deal with uncertainty determines how we deal with the crushing stress, pressure and anxiety that try to knock us out of the game. How we manage uncertainty – how we function in the face of the unknown – determines the exact distance traveled in life – and the distance that will be traveled. The secret to uncertainty management is train for it using the concepts of "unknown reps" and "unknown sets." Mental strength and conditioning by dealing with the unknown – converting the unknown into a positive force.

The key is to start without a finish line. Start the workout without knowing where and when it ends. Find out the finish line during the workout – when you get there. Just keep going until there's an announcement: *"Last set."*

---

61 Tribute to Robert Anton Wilson who introduced the concept of "guerilla ontology," in the *The Illuminati Papers*.
62 A Tribute to two masterpieces, *American Pie*, by Don McLean, and Arthur Schopenhauer's *Three Stages of Truth*.

You've got to learn to deal with uncertainty or it will beat you down! The unknown is the greatest source of fear. Everything that's scary is unfamiliar. We fear what we don't know. We fear what we don't understand. We fear confusion.

Conversely, we don't fear what we know. We don't fear what we understand. We are fearless of familiarity. Familiarity breeds contempt of fear. You will not fear what you know. If you do fear it, then you really don't know it as well as you thought you did.

Uncertainty is connected to risk. Danger and uncertainty are joined at the hip. Left unchecked, uncertainty will bombard your brain, rip your heart and shatter your soul until our personality is in pieces ... fragments.[63] Fear of uncertainty will change you into someone you're not, a shell of your former self, an automaton incapable of surviving the relentless pressures of reality – dysfunctional. A puppet tied to the strings of controllers who will steer you in directions of their choice, not yours. A flabby marionette who fails to exercise free will.

"If you think of the big picture, you will quit. Here's the secret to getting through sprints. FOCUS ON TWO THINGS - THE CURRENT REP AND THE BENEFIT. LET ME SAY IT AGAIN – CURRENT REP AND THE BENEFIT. Focus on those two things and you'll never quit, you will stick it out, you will get better, you will get stronger, you will become fearless, and you will win."

Uncertainty is either a challenge that explodes growth ... or confusion that implodes and crumbles. How we handle uncertainty determines the type of force generated – positive or negative. Train for it. Conditioning through intense unknown reps. A training program is needed to change the unknown to known. Uncertainty conversion – familiarity.

Change the focus, change the outcome. Change the focus away from not knowing the finish line to knowing exactly where the finish line is right now, at this moment ... for just this rep. *"You know the finish line for the first sprint. That's all you focus on. You can see it. DO NOT THINK OF NOT KNOWING HOW MANY MORE SPRINTS YOU WILL HAVE TO RUN."*

---

63 Tribute to a research masterpiece by Dr. Carl Rogers who warned us about the shattered personality, the disastrous meltdown that happens when the gap gets too big and becomes recognized.

Focus on finishing the first sprint and the benefits of it – the monster-like strength ... the machine-like stamina. Keep a burning concentration on the rep-in-progress and the rush you're feeling. Focus on the rush. Feel it, thrive on it, crave it. That's how to turn pain to pleasure. When you cross the first finish line, know that you cut it while others cut themselves. Mission accomplished.

"FOURTH QUARTER." Although there is no empirical research that specifically proves it, these two words, yelled during sprints, dramatically slides the asshole needle from high to extremely low. Guerrilla ontology. Two words that radically transform. Misery is a powerful motivator. And a bonding agent. Nothing, absolutely nothing, is a stronger team builder than shared misery. Nothing brings a team closer than shared misery. Nothing makes total strangers want to fight for each other like shared misery does. Not bowling trips, not white water rafting, not pizza nights, not campfire sing-a-longs, not drunkfests, not food fights – nothing will connect the minds, the hearts and the souls of every team member like surviving shared misery. The most powerful commonality on any team, any organization is surviving the natural struggle together. Surviving hell puts everyone on an equal playing field, earns gold card membership into the club and builds the strongest connection known to wo/mankind.

The playoffs that year were a disaster ... for our opponents. Combined score of 100-8. Reached exactly, the "stretch goal" of a "50 points per game." Another move from "C" class to "A" class. Changed seats – voluntarily. To be the strongest, play the strongest.

"Now ... don't ever tell me you can't do something. You're the luckiest people in the world."

Chapter 40.19

X-Fitness Welland "Excuse-making is the manifestation of fear. Rationalization is the language of the fearful. The energy invested in convincing why something isn't possible, why it can't get done, why there's no use in even trying are symptoms of broken will"

— From the 4th & Hell Series.

June 22 ar 2:00pm· Like · Comment

👍 4 people like this.

Chapter 37-39
MMMF – Don't Blink

Witnessing one miracle is the greatest experience. A life-altering blessing. An honor and privilege. Witnessing several miracles is Culture Shock – with a steep admission price. The wrong focus can cost the opportunity of a lifetime. So can blinking. One blink – just one blink – and you can miss out on a miracle-sighting.

Loyalty and challenge are unstoppable forces. Both attract with the strength of magnetic pull – but from which side? Invitation or temptation? Destiny calling or a street-walker beckoning? There's a blurry line between jumping ship to set off on a new mission, and jumping into any bed for a change of scenery.

The entrance at the top of the hill was the only place where a right turn or left turn both ended up at an asylum. One hill, two dysfunctional families. Right turn, Hill Park High School Rams football team – left turn to one of the province's largest psychiatric facilities.

"I'm leaving Churchill to go the Hill Park. They need a new AD. Their football team is worse than Churchill was when you took over three years ago ... wanna turnaround another hopeless program? If you want it, the job's yours."

Good call or bad call? How do you know if it's an attraction or distraction calling? How can you tell them apart – is it a sign to go or a sign to stay? Green light or red light? Who is the messenger – good or evil? Is it your calling or a warning? You can't tell them apart. Not on your own.[64] Consult with your partner. But the soul of a lifter is a mystery – an enigma ... never gives a straight answer.

---

64 A Tribute to a masterpiece, *Sometimes You Can't Make It On Your Own*. By U2.

"When do I start?"

"Why would you take the job? They're misfits."

Your team is exactly like your family. You can complain about them. You can moan about their failings. You are entitled to mouth off about their weaknesses ... but no one else can.

According to Niccolo Machiavelli: "A great leader is one who brings people out of their worst predicament."[65] Misery-busters. But, he neglected to mention how to do it. And neglected to explain the secret – bring people to their worst predicament ... hard-work misery-builders. Bring misery to escape misery – the secret to solving any predicament.

Anyone can thrive and succeed when the situation is perfect. But not vice-versa. The gap between the worst predicament and the perfect situation is the degree of the difficulty on the judges' scorecard. Leaders are measured by how far they close the gap – or how far they split it wide open.

The worst sound a leader can make is excuse-making – the equivalent of a child whining for sympathy. Excuse-making is unbecoming and undignified. The martyr syndrome. Much more is expected from leaders. Although He did not mention coaches and players specifically, Jesus reminded us that the exchange rate is expected to be at par, performance demands are not optional, and the bar is raised for anyone in a leadership role. "From everyone who has been given much, much will be demanded, and from the one who has been entrusted with much, much more will be asked."[66]

Leaders are entrusted with much – the mission. The greatest challenge and the greatest potential reward – the chance to bring other people out of whatever misery they suffer. Doesn't matter if not much is given to work with. Less given is a sign. It's an honour. It means "being chosen" for a reason – chosen to train for the mission, chosen to share the training, chosen to experience the struggle, the infinite lessons-learned, all the insights – you grow the most by helping others grow. You reach higher by helping others reach higher. The chance to make the biggest impact – effecting positive change. The privilege of being recruited for the Goliath-sized battles means you've qualified – must have passed the tests ... so far.

65　Tribute to a masterpiece, *The Prince*. By Niccolo Machiavelli. Written over 500 years ago, *The Prince* is timeless literature, a classic that spans generations and achieves the impossible – it applies to any era in the history of wo/mankind. A leadership book for the ages.
66　Tribute to a super-masterpiece – Luke 12:48.

Leading any team, any group of people, is not a title or an entitlement. It's an assignment, not for the self-gratification of the empty megalomaniac, but for the benefit of others. The leader's reward is a by-product of misery-busting. The struggle and the outcome – not the glory of the rank and status. Not the glamor of the position.

"Excuses" are not created equal. They are classified by tense – past, present, and future. Before, during, and after the assignment. *"We're a young team." "Not much experience." "Don't expect too much." "It's a rebuilding year – five-year plan."* Justifying failure before it happens. The plague of pre-game excuses – littering the road to soften the steps towards an expected failure. Anticipation of pain is worse than the actual pain.

Laying the ground-work for pity is the investment for a return of sympathy instead of scorn and derision. Pre-game excuses start a chain reaction of tireless bitching, moaning and complaining during and after the game, where we separate ourselves from the rest by blaming everyone except ourselves. The blame club. The only place from which we demand exclusion, expect eviction – the only place where we embrace discrimination. *"Not my fault."* Isolation. Disconnection. Coaches blame players, players blame coaches, offense blames defense, defense blames offense, everyone blames the refs. Eventually, excuse-making goes viral – spreading from sport to professional life to personal life, back to … .

The language of the pre-game whiner is a symptom of a deeper problem, developed through rewarded, uncorrected negative reps – continuous problem-aversion. Ducking challenges, dodging risks, detouring around any obstacle that can make us fail – avoiding dilemmas instead of training hard, fighting the problem, and most importantly, beating the shit out of it. Problem-aversion is self-containing – existing inside the box … staying inside the box while the walls keep closing in.[67]

The level of expectation matches the level of training. Where you set the bar determines how you lift it – how heavy, how many times, how often. Training reveals belief. Low expectation, low-level training. Weak expectations, weak training. Strong expectations, strong training. How

---

67 A Tribute to a super-masterpiece, *No Surrender*. By Bruce Springsteen – every version ever recorded – studio and live. The world would have a giant void if it had never been recorded. "….had to get away from those fools" – epic line in a timeless classic. We are lucky to have been alive to hear it first-hand. The equivalent of watching Beethoven live, or on YouTube. If you do not feel a rush or some degree of spiritual blast/connection, even for just a moment, consult with your doctor.

we train exposes what we expect of ourselves, our team, organization … everyone around us. Insider training and outsider training. To train harder, change your expectations … regardless of the hand dealt. When less is given, train harder.

Explosive expectations, explodes performance. Don't lift expectations gradually – raising the bar slowly makes the weight feel heavier. Raise the bar higher by exploding it upward.

The myth of "unrealistic expectation" is not just an excuse, it's a wall – one with a great big "X" on it that screams, *"You're not going anywhere."* Telling someone to lower their expectations is a crime – a tactic used by evil to commit dream robbery. Slowly locking them up. Deception. Misery loves company – lower your expectation so you don't leave me behind.

Misery-building never suffers a recession. Misery-builders are abundant, on the outside: *"Don't put your hopes too high … you're setting yourself up for a fall."* And on the inside: *What If I Fail?* The serial killer of dreams, hopes, trying, adventure, exploring … living every moment to failure – **MMMF. M**aximum **M**ental and **M**uscular **F**ailure. Physical and intellectual exhaustion.

$$\infty$$

It's hard not to stare at a U-shaped scar from ear-to-ear across a shaved head. *"Coach, my name is Greg Schmidt. I want to make a comeback."* The victim of a head-on collision with a drunk driver, thrown through the windshield, impact on pavement, swollen brain, very little chance of surviving, two brain operations – nine hours, one year rehab, fully recovered. Wants to play football. *"I want to live life to the fullest. I want to make every minute count."*

"Impacts" are not created equal. They are measured on the life-altering scale. High or low – depending on how much it changes your life. Some conversations are unforgettable. Usually actions speak louder than words, except when the words are the guts of a miracle narrative – a miracle story told by a miracle survivor. High school football coach is the greatest job in the history of wo/mankind.

"No, absolutely not. You're not playing … unless you bring me evidence that your head injuries are gone. I need evidence from a doctor … no, a specialist. No, two specialists. I need to see written evidence from two brain specialists before I believe you're healthy enough to play."

"Negligence" is not created equal. There is a fine line that separates recklessness from the sequel to a miracle story. Winning is nowhere near the only thing, not in a violent sport where someone's pride and joy can die, end up paralyzed, or carved open on a surgery table – knees, shoulders and any other limbs rewired.

"Coach, here are two letters. Both are from brain surgeons."

A third letter was delivered personally. *"We support our son. He's changed since the accident. He wants to live life to the fullest. He wants to make every minute count. This letter is our consent form."*

High school football coach is the greatest job in the history of wo/mankind.

"Coach, I want to be treated the same as everyone else." Stereotyping is a social plague. *"I think you're too soft on me. You drive everyone else hard. I don't want to be treated differently."* Misery does love company.

"Coach, I know the code of conduct says no punks and we're supposed to be silent warriors but can I make a request?" Written expectations have an immediate impact on the asshole meter. High school football players respond favorably to strict performance demands that separate them from the rest. If the message has purpose and meaning. If bold language is used. High school football players respond to meaning, purpose and bold language because it's part of their expectation – part of the game. They crave order to structure the confusion and chaos that's been built into those special years as they transition from childhood to adulthood – the asshole years.

"I've never played fullback. I know I can do it if you teach me and give me a chance." Stepping outside the discomfort zone starts with one step. *"And I'd like to play both ways – I know I can handle playing the whole game."*

The next step gets easier.

"SCHMIIIIIIIIIDT… SCHMIIIIIIIIIIIDT … GET YOUR ASS LOWER OR YOU'RE FIRED … YOU'LL GO FROM LINEBACKER TO BACKLINER."

Performance demands are not multiple choice exams. They are not suggestions, recommendations, or considerations. High-risk activities demand the strongest performance demands. Survival skills are non-negotiable.

Iron-man football needs iron will. Playing both offense and defense in the same game is a throwback to an ancient time, an era where other social phenomena roamed planet Earth ... kinda like real, in-person social connections. A pre-historic era when stamina and endurance had a different definition. Unlike dinosaurs, the extinct can resurrect through sports.

"SCHMIIIIIIIIDT ... SCHMIIIIIIIIIDT ... GET YOUR KNEES HIGHER."

"SCHMIIIIIIIIDT ... SCHMIIIIIIIIIDT ... DON'T SLOW DOWN."

"SCHMIIIIIIIIDT ... SCHMIIIIIIIIIDT ... FOURTH QUARTER."

"Championship games" are not created equal.

Schmidt made 23 tackles at linebacker. At fullback, he rushed for 202 yards and two touchdowns. Team records on offense and defense. And he got no preferential treatment when the championship trophy was awarded. No mention of his "comeback." A silent warrior.

∞

Don't blink. When opportunity calls, don't blink. Miracles don't have early-warning systems. Miracles don't give prior notice. Miracles are not attention junkies – they do not dress up, stand out, make noise, point to themselves. Miracles don't seek attention, you have to pay attention.

MMMF = MMMF. Maximum muscular and mental failure **M**akes **M**any **M**iracles **F**orever.

Answer the call. Pay attention. Don't blink.

Chapter 34
524-Ps

"You're going back to uniform."

Dr. Henry Overstreet identified originality as a measurement of maturity.[68] Copying others, patterning after heroes is a good starting point for children, but it's not a good sign when you're old enough to decide whether a new PlayStation or mortgage payments is the top priority. Imitation in adults is a sign of stagnation. Original thoughts, original actions – the secret to separating from the rest.

No one ever asks, *"Why did you leave college teaching?"* And no one ever asks, *"What was the highlight of your college teaching career?"* But many ask about my police career. Top questions: **#1** Why did you leave it behind? **#2.** What was the highlight?

#1. The mystery of the ex-cop. Hollywood has taught us that an ex-cop must have baggage. The silver screen is littered with stereotypical ex-cop characters – burned-out, spaced-out drunks running from something instead of running to something. Other people change careers like TV channels – unchallenged … no mystery, no questions. But ex-cops must have a story. The rumor mill works overtime. *"He must have been fired? Did he shoot somebody? I heard he punched out the sergeant."* When the truth doesn't have enough drama, drama needs to be manufactured. When the truth is not known or not experienced, fiction suffices.

Resigning from policing after 15 years was motivated by two dreads – the dread of sameness and the dread of being controlled. Just thinking about, let alone staying, 30-40 years in one place, dealing with endless reps of the **4-Cs** (**c**owardly, **c**hickenshit, **c**hildlike **c**riminals) and the **4-Ps** (**p**ension, **p**romotions, **p**arties, **p**utanas) … in the **3-S** paramilitary organization (**s**aluting **s**uperiors and **s**ubordinates – the ancient art of thought and mind control – institutional caste system) was motivation enough.

"Yes, Ma'am." Rank suddenly gives the mystical ability and license for one alleged adult to control the thoughts and actions of another alleged adult. Rank structure is the acceptable – needed – attitude adjustment

---

68 Tribute to a masterpiece. Dr. Overstreet's research on the maturation process, *The Development of a Measure of Vocational Maturity.*

for asshole 18-year-olds but it's a pain-in-the-ass once your children are old enough to vote. Control is the backbone – and lack thereof – of a paramilitary organization.

Rank can be a blessing or a curse. Followers are blessed to have someone order them around like children: *"Say this, don't say that, go here, don't go there, wear this, don't wear that, talk to him … but stay away from her."* Nonconformists are cursed by the iron-bar confinement that locks up free will – the killing of the spirit. *"Going brain dead,"* is not just a cute answer to, *"How you doing?"* over the watercooler – it's real. Public complaints, internal affairs, having to defend yourself on the street and off the street, to sideliners, bench-warmers who have no clue how the game is played. There's a limit to how many drunks, degenerates, deviants and cock-eyed social misfits you can debate and drag. Cowards who start fights, lose fights, then cry about it. Then there's the criminals … .

Garbage in, garbage out. Environmental disasters – air pollution, mind pollution. Eventually a radioactive sign gets tattooed just above the skull and crossbones on your forehead.

But the soul of a lifter has an unusual tolerance for pain. Extreme tolerance. The blessing and curse of strength. The capacity to withstand tons and tons of bullshit, stops you from moving. The fighter mindset holds you back. The inability to crack under pressure makes you answer bell after bell, round after round, foolishly trying to win the pointless fight. An imaginary fight that is actually not a fight. It's simply evil laughing its ass off, dancing around, bobbing and weaving, ducking every punch but throwing no punches – just enough action to keep you in the ring and away from your destiny.

Mind games leading to the mindless fight, the equivalent of throwing sand, swinging purses, yelling, *"Fuck you!"* and being answered with, *"No, fuck you!!"* – middle-finger waving. The pointless fight rages on until … the eureka moment. The miracle of enlightenment.

The soul of a lifter gets frustrated but will never abandon, no matter how stupid the student is. The soul of a lifter has a limitless playbook. Infinite calls. The soul of a lifter will not rest until the big play is made, the deep bomb that flips the switch, turning on the light and lifting the fog.

The fight is over because there was no fight.

"Fuck you, no I'm not. I quit."

A planned assassination of a police sergeant was investigated twice. The first time by the guy who got his coveted promotion then immediately made the decision that I was, *"… going back to uniform."* The second time by the guy who dared speak the truth about the inept, initial investigation – exposing a malfunctioning, fractured police service – during a multi-million-dollar public inquiry … after which he was told, *"You're going back to uniform."* Everything is connected.

One question remained – who called the play? Good or evil? Time to leave or was I pushed to leave? There are no coincidences, just connections. The play-caller didn't matter. The deep bomb had been thrown.

#2. A thank-you letter from a grieving mother who lost a son only seven years younger than the detective who knocked on her door at 2 a.m., with news that changed her life forever.

The truth is never as sexy as fiction.

Chapter 26.2626
Twenty

"Iron will" is an abstract concept. Multiple interpretations. Plus it's hard to measure. Unlike intellectual IQ, iron will doesn't have a quotient. It's left up to a panel of judges. "How many times can you bench 225?" is part of the football resume. Translation: What is your iron-will IQ? What's the score?

The key to working out for 40 years is mindset. Two of the ingredients in workout longevity are: Make it a basic survival need and, keep score. Competition. Competing with self, age and players half your age. Coach-led team workouts are the secret to rapid natural growth – individual and group – physically, intellectually, emotionally and spiritually. A coach leading the workout on the bench, not on the sidelines. The leadoff lifter. In full workout gear, not holding a clipboard, not with a whistle hanging around the neck.

The lineup is key. The coach always goes first to set the bar. The coach arranges the lineup – the order of lifters – until a moment in time when the lifters claim a lineup spot themselves. Positioning affects performance. The place in a lineup speaks volumes – sends a message.

The coach is the coordinator, making every call without announcing a script – without following a script. 100% uncertainty. No prior knowledge whatsoever of the workout program. *"What are we doing tonight?"* Mystery. It unfolds, call by call. The coach coordinates the workout by judging the situation and making the call – the type of exercise, exactly how it's done, how much weight goes on the bar, how many sets, and most importantly, the "minimum-rep announcement." Setting the bar. The performance demand. Compulsory minimum reps decided by the coach, publicly, in front of everyone. The public performance demand. A level that must be reached by all, even though the maximum is determined by the individual lifter.

MMF. Maximum Muscular Failure. Empty the tank. Rep-calling is a science. The announced minimum reps can never be the maximum. Quick calculations have to establish a known level – the lower level – that the lifter is capable of reaching based on past performance. All prior reps and sets are connected. Not one rep is isolated. Not one set is separated from the rest. They form a chain. Not just today's workout, yesterday's and tomorrow's as well.

The mystery of workout uncertainty forces focus on the current set only. Otherwise, the lifter won't last. S/he'll break. Worrying about the future will break the will. Training for the future and eagerly anticipating it builds iron will, the mental strength and toughness to endure the misery of an intense workout. Full immersion in the current set – going to MMF, looking forward to the next set, not dreading it – is the formula for fearlessness. Burning concentration on this rep – the only one you're about to do, the one you are doing ... with a silent **MMF** attitude: *Bring it as heavy as you can you Miserable-Mother Fucker.*

Love the challenge, need the challenge. Need it deeply. Flip the switch. Then go deep. Go deeper each rep, each set. Dig deep down until the rush gushes and explodes. Feel the rush, need the rush. The miracle of adrenaline and testosterone – AT-blasts. Pure stuff with no side effects. Limitless quantity. No street-corner deals. No conflicts. No diluted rip-offs. Just flip the switch and a blast of hormones flood the system.

"Set #1. 30 reps. 135 pounds. Imagine 225 on the bar. Visualize it."

The myth of the "warm-up set." There is no warm-up set. Warm up before the workout not during it. Every set, every rep has a purpose. Set #1 teaches the science of counting reps – keeping score. No one teaches how to count reps except a coach. The act of counting reps can be a distraction. It has to be converted to an attraction – a way of stimulating more reps, not eliminating them. The solution is not to have someone else count. Self-counting is essential because it unleashes the inner power, the hidden reps, while building mental conditioning – Pavlovian responses. But most importantly, it's preparation for isolation, the time when you have to train alone.

Mental and physical can't just connect. They have to intersect ... slam together. The art of counting reps has to develop, become second-nature and it has to be done silently. And a rep can't be counted at any random moment. Every rep must be counted at a specific time, requiring a split-second decision that makes or breaks the lift. The sticking point, the mid-point of the positive part of the lift – the ascent, just before lock-out. The sticking point is the point where you get stuck or you break-through. The sticking point is like swimming halfway across a lake – keep going or turn back? Both need energy and both can make you sink. And, either one can make you swim harder.

The secret to lifting heavier and heavier weight is facing the sticking point of a lift as often as possible and overcoming it. Making big muscles is directly related to how many sticking points a lifter overcomes. Reaching the sticking point takes effort but not nearly as much as pushing past it. Locking out at the top of the lift is hard but not nearly as hard as pushing through the sticking point.

There are five stages of force to every lift – launch, liftoff, sticking point, coast, lock – sticking point is stuck right in the middle. Five distinct levels of force are needed to lift the weight. All five are governed by Sir Isaac Newton's "Three Laws of Motion," that connect mass, acceleration, momentum and force:

- First Law: Inertia – an object, unobstructed by resistance, will travel at the same speed on a straight line, reaching higher and higher … until a force opposes it. Then, a greater force is needed to match and beat the opposing force.
- Second Law: Momentum – an object, subject to a force, accelerates in the same direction as the force at a magnitude that is directly proportional to the force and inversely proportional to the mass.
- Third Law: Action-Reaction – for every action, there is an equal but opposite reaction. Force #1 vs. Force #2.

Bench Press: The chest is the launch pad. Force #1 – gravity – violently pushes the lifter's shoulders down onto the bench while Force #2 – the lifter – simultaneously pushes upward. The first two inches of travel determines the success or failure of the lift. When the downward force matches the two-inch upward force – sparks fly, like the smoke firing out from under a rocket. This upward force accelerates the bar, driving momentum for liftoff. At the sticking point, boosters kick in to beat the opposing force – forearms and upper arms join the chest and shoulders to push past the sticking point, into the coast stage, where the bar smoothly rides the combined forces to lock-out. Unlike a rocket, the weight doesn't continue flying into orbit. It has to stop and return back to the launch pad to start all over again.

Lowering the weight to the launch pad is not a free ride. Energy is needed to control the speed and to stop the bar at the launch pad instead of allowing it to bounce off the chest like a trampoline. Rockets liftoff once. Two-hundred-and-twenty-five-pound bench press testing is the equivalent of repeated liftoffs and re-entries ... in rapid-fire succession. Load, re-load. Launch, re-launch.

Bodyweight and number of reps at 225 are connected. I'm asked many times to explain, "how?" Simple. The "X Fitness" rule is simple. The first two digits of your body weight are the **Expected Performance – EP** standard – the minimum standard for the "testing" level. For example, at 200 pounds, a lifter should be able to do a minimum of 20 bench press reps of 225 pounds. A 250-pound lifter – 25 reps. A 190-pound lifter – 19 reps. Reaching this level doesn't just happen. A charted course has to be followed, starting with the number of reps that correspond with the first digit of the lifter's bodyweight, then adding one rep at a time until the EP is reached.

No other activity or profession in the history of wo/mankind has been abused like fitness and strength training because of self-directed learning. Very few can reach their EP standard by themselves, without coach-led training. Like body temperature, approximately 98.6% of humans cannot reach a training goal on their own. The 1.4% who can have a special coach – the soul of a lifter.

Competition is not just a force that pits us against each other, it's a joining force. The phenomena of team-training sparks two unstoppable forces – no one wants to be left behind and no one leaves anyone behind. Performance demands go viral. Warp speed impacts reach deeper causing double-digit reps of a 225-pound bench press to become the EP for any bodyweight. A badge of moxie. Less than ten reps is a signed confession of guilt – gutless. Lazy. Suspect work ethic, suspect character, suspect will. Suspect teammate.

"Set #4 ... Test set. No one quits. This one counts. 20!"

Two-hundred-and-twenty-five-pound testing is a race where you set the finish line. A finish line defined by where you decide to stop – when you exercise free will. The key to breaking a personal best – to running up the score – is chunking, grouping reps into two clusters of ten.

Reps #1-10 are automatic, effortless reps. Practice for the grand performance. The key to record-breaking performances is the mindset toward the first ten reps – they must be unchallenging. Never consider the first ten reps a challenge. They have to be boring. Resist the temptation to race, to rev the RPMs into the red zone. At ten reps, convince yourself this is NOT halfway. It's only one-third ... 33%. Nowhere near the finish line. Can't see the finish line – keep pushing it farther back. Keep it out of sight, out of mind.

Rep. #11. The mind starts to play tricks. The unimaginable starts to creep into your mind ... if you let it. A trailer for a horror movie – that sick, twisted demented kind that has no purpose, no meaning except to murder brain cells ... a peek into hell ... the "what-if-I-don't-get-to-20?" preview. Shut it off.

Rep #12. The fight's on. Like a drunken domestic: *"Fuck you"* ... *"No, fuck you"* – evil and good battle for control of your mind.

Reps 13, 14, 15. *"Ya?"* ... *"Ya"* ... *"OH YA?"* – like trying to break up a bar fight between suddenly artificially-courageous drunkards. The brain numbs, forcing you to concentrate while evil attacks it with self-doubt and fatigue. Make a choice – an exercise of free will – drop the bar ... or take the gloves off – 16, 17, 18, 19 ... .

20. Relief can be felt even under pressure. A passage of rites. The indelible performance. Irreversible. Twenty reps can't be deleted. Can't be erased even accidentally. And reps can't be deducted – not for style, not for substance, not for degree of difficulty. No demerit reps. Twenty can't be lowered, not even by one rep.

The hybrid engine – food as fuel, **E-G**ene as alternative fuel. Every meal for three days fueled this moment. And the E-Gene prevented the worst disaster – **E**mbarrassment. The humiliation of not cracking the 20-rep plateau was avoided. "Twenty" presses the secondary switch ... jams the switch, slamming it into high gear. The rush of not being embarrassed, the thrill of NOT stopping at 19 – like a military jet refueling the tank in mid-air.

Rep #21. The stretch run. The brain is a multi-tasker. As the bar lowers, the brain calculates ... still 66% of the way left. Four more to tie the score, five more to break it, nine more to ... .

22. The mind becomes acutely aware that the players watching have positioned the coach in a n*v* place – a place that can't be re-placed ... *My coach is stronger than your coach.*

23. Like evil, lactic acid tries to take you out of the game by breaking your will – but in reverse order. Lactic acid is the sonuvabitch that attacks

the body first to get to the mind. Evil works the other way, making sure there's two-way traffic to block destiny.

24. *Put the bar down. 24's enough. Good job.* Temptations always come along.[69] Rationalization – evil's main weapon. The nonviolent takeover of the mind that justifies laziness, lethargy, losing ... everything we don't believe in, all the negatives that we warn our children about, the evils that we teach them to avoid, to resist, to fight through ... to overcome.

25. *"DON'T TOUCH IT!!"* ... the warning to the spotter – no controversy about the legitimacy of tying the score – no asterisk.

The record-breaking-rep attempt always starts with mixed signals: *What a waste to come all this way and not get it,* combined with: *Absolutely no possible way of stopping me ... none whatsoever.* The dread effect. Fear of anticipated dread versus fighting dread. Winning depends on tolerance. What you can and cannot live with. What you put up with and what you won't.

Less than two seconds to make the choice ... 1.5 to 1.7 seconds. You can't hold up the bar hoping to mull it over. Free will is exercised as the bar lowers. When it touches down on the launch pad, .5 seconds of motionless suspense. If Newton's third law is violated, the bar will crush the chest waiting for the spotter – spotters – the same team who will be on the receiving end of outrageous performance demands, on the field, tomorrow: *"Fourth and long, we go for it ... we don't kick. Show some balls ... ."* Show some balls ... when the time arrives, when you have one moment to practice what you preach, it's time to, "show some balls!!"

After 25 reps, a temporary chest appears. A replacement chest. The new chest is considerably bigger. Its muscles feel like they're ready to explode. Even though the muscles are full to capacity, the tank is nearly empty. The needle is below the "E." The reserve tank kicks in: *Unit to back. 10-78 ... chest needs assistance.* Message to arms: *Get your ass here, bust your ass to help out.* Trying to press the bar with chest strength alone will not work. Something bigger is needed. Drive the shoulders into the bench at the same time as the arms move forward – action and reaction. Again, .5 seconds to decide ... drive the shoulders into the bench and lift!!!

---

69 Tribute to a mega-masterpiece, *Pink Cadillac*. By Bruce Springsteen, who remind-ed us that, ...there's always somebody tempting somebody into doing something they know is wrong ... they can tempt you with all kinds of riches, money and even pleasures ... Any lifter is indebted to the Boss.

The decision to lift another rep, or be satisfied with 25 is based on the willingness and capacity to enter a new place. Need. How badly is the move to the next level needed? Can you accept staying at 25 reps or do you need 26? How hungry are you for one more rep?

Technique is important. Food as fuel is important but nothing is more important than mindset. Nothing is more important than the will to make it happen. "Willing it to happen" is a misnomer. Imposing our will is a myth. It's impossible to will anything to happen. What is possible is exercising iron will – transferring a source of energy to a task that must be completed. Moving a force to force a move.

Iron will doesn't just happen. There is no such thing as "iron will on demand." It has to be developed, repeated, developed some more and repeated ... until flipping the switch makes iron will automatic ... a no-brainer. "On" switch, on demand.

It matches – the force of pressing the shoulders downward matched the force upward. But that guarantees only one thing – the bar will move two inches. The bar goes airborne – two inches. It leaves the launch pad – two inches – toward the sticking point. But if it moves two inches, there's no excuse to not move it to the sticking point – none.

25.5 is always rounded off downward, never upward. The gym will not reward half-reps. The gym does not recognize decimal points, fractions, or partials. The gym rounds off "half" to "zero." Nothing. Like an inconclusive polygraph test, a half-rep "never happened." The gym's dictionary does not include "moral victory." 100% is a pass – nothing less. The gym prohibits re-writes, bumping up marks ... the gym is insensitive, refuses to change and will never submit to sensitivity training. A 50% rep is zero. So is 75%, so is 90%. 100% or zero. One or the other, nothing in between.

Arriving at the sticking point of a record-breaking rep doesn't need a choice. Breaking through or breaking down is not a conscious choice. The outcome is a statement – a bold statement. It paints the big picture, exposes our training, work ethic, mindset ... balls. The result reveals who we are, where we've been, where we're going – completely. Mystery solved ... momentarily.

25.6. Breaking through the sticking point is the equivalent of "last minute to play while protecting a lead." Winning is inevitable, unless a disaster happens. The "coast" phase of a lift got that title for a reason –

once you pass the sticking point, there is no reason not to finish the rep. No excuse not to lock-out and complete 100% of the rep. Failure is not an option. Failing after breaking past the sticking point is inexcusable ... unimaginable. Almost impossible. Dropping the weight would be more than a physical failure. It would be a system meltdown. A total eclipse of the heart, mind ,. and soul.[70]

26!! "Lock-outs" are not created equal. Each one is unique. Some are memorable some are not – depends on the impact. Lockout branding. Rep branding. The first of anything is memorable. Like the first 26th rep. Seven more than the EP. Regardless, no wild celebration. No contentment ... a sign of completion – no more forward progress – which leads to complacency. Four more reps, thirty would be legendary for a 190-pounder.

26 out of 30 is a score of 86.6%. Honor roll. Except the gym prohibits conventional standards.

"How many reps at 225?"

"86.6% of 30 reps."

Silence.

The gym's code of conduct does not recognize traditional academic grades. 100% is the only score. Close proximity to 30 reps doesn't count. No style points. No bonus marks for good effort.

Slight tremor in the left arm – either Culture Shock, a power surge, or power outage. Either way, iron will not reward "off track." Even a half-inch off track is a punishable offence. The bar doesn't lower, it descends. Twenty-six point zero. The only moving finish line in life. One that moves toward you at warp-speed. The only finish line that meets you instead of waiting for you.

∞

Che vergogna (*n.* kay ver goin ya)

"Italian embarrassments" are created equal. And each one reaches higher. Goes deeper. Deeper shame. Double **E-Gene** ...Extreme Embarrassment. Full potential. "Che vergogna" is reserved for any loss suffered by the beloved Azzurri – the Italian national soccer team – or

---

70   Tribute to a masterpiece, *Total Eclipse of the Heart.* By Bonnie Tyler.

another behavior with equally far-reaching consequences, ones that make friends, relatives or neighbors talk and/or shake their heads. *"WHAT AN EMBARRASSMENT."*

"B" on a report card is a vergogna. Cutting the lawn and getting grass on the neighbor's driveway is a vergogna. Failing to plough the garden properly, knocking over a tomato plant is a vergogna. Buying fast food is a vergogna. Missing Mass is a vergogna. Serving as an altar-boy at Mass and loosening the incense jar so the place almost burns down is a serious vergogna. Coming home drunk after a high school dance is a major vergogna. Not having a career at eighteen is an unspeakable vergogna.

Scoring 26 out of 30 is also a vergogna. But the good news is that this vergogna makes an impact on observers. Suffering embarrassment for breaking a record but not shattering it, sends a message that can't be articulated with words. A vergogna is like a picture – worth a thousand words that say: Never settle for second-best, for mediocrity ... even when mediocrity is record-setting. Never be satisfied. Never celebrate wildly. Never act like you are shocked at your success. Act like you've been there before, will be there again, and will go even higher. Never accept underachieving. Never accept falling short of a dream. Never stop chasing dreams. Never stop dreaming up more dreams. Get pissed off when you fail. Very pissed off. Let failure burn your guts ... and soul. But be very careful not to let vergognas make all the joy within you die.[71]

Vergognas should come with a Surgeon General's warning: "E-gene can lead to acedia." St. Thomas Acquinus gets credit for explaining acedia: "A life-robbing dreariness or sadness that leads to a spiritual disconnect." Even though St. Thomas did not mention "vergona" specifically when discussing the inability to find joy in anything, he nailed the definition ... not by coincidence, he was Italian.

---

71 Tribute to a masterpiece, *Somebody to Love*. By Jefferson Airplane, who cautioned us that when we lose "joy" everything within us ... our very self, dies.

Chapter 28
1985

Promise and compromise are connected.

One unknown, amateur athlete making it into *Sports Illustrated* magazine's "Faces in the Crowd" column has lottery-odds chances. Three unknown, amateur Canadian football players making *SI* is a miracle ... miracles. Two of the three players went on to complete nationally-prominent university careers, even though all three started as underdogs – at the bottom of the underdog class.

They didn't just work for success, they believed it. Words aren't enough to describe their effort because many wouldn't understand it. Adults have a tendency to underestimate the will and work ethic of a teenager. What they don't realize is that if the teenager is not working "hard" it's because choosing "hard work" is sometimes like completing a multiple-choice test. If "hard work" is offered as a choice: "D) None of the above," will be chosen by the teenager. It's human nature.

Witnessing just one miracle in a lifetime is the greatest experience – a huge story. A life-altering blessing. An honor and privilege. Witnessing several miracles is Culture Shock.

"Guarantees" are not created equal. Unlike accommodating, enabling coaches who guarantee starting positions, the gym will never guarantee reward without risk. The gym will never guarantee any performance – encore, matching a personal best or breaking it. No promises of record-breaking lifts. No assurances that what was lifted yesterday will be lifted tomorrow. The gym will never violate the first of Ghandi's "seven deadly sins" – wealth without work – a sin that applies to strength and fitness.

Past workouts are connected to future workouts but the connection is not a promise. The gym will not promise that 26 will automatically change to 30 ... or even stay at 26. Because promise leads to compromise. The gym allows for only one certainty – opportunity. A chance to escape a life-sucking sedentary existence. A chance to avoid the devastation of monotony on mind, body and soul. A chance to prevent the ravages of lethargy to attitude, outlook and appearance.

The gym teaches the fundamentals of being different – the basics of bailing out from a life sentence of pressing "replay" ... and "pause." The gym gives a shot at the title, every single day. But, the gym invites – it does not use force. The gym does not take attendance. The gym respects exercise ... of free will. Opportunities are choices. Performance demands are made only after RSVPing.

The unchallenged mind slides downhill. So does the unchallenged body. But the unchallenged soul wastes away – like the gifts buried inside it. The cure for the unchallenged soul is making the biggest impact possible. The kind that stretches and spreads farther and deeper than can be measured. The kind that moves still minds, soft bodies and stuck souls from the miry pit.[72] Culture Shock. The key to making the big impact is injecting purpose into purpose-starved lives.

Purpose is the pulse of performance. Purpose is the driving force that separates extraordinary from ordinary, epic from mediocre, classic from average. Purpose injects adrenaline into the lifeless corpses – the blissfully ignorant who hide from life, pulling shut the curtains, locking the doors, barricading body, mind and soul from any challenge that may disrupt the comfortably numbing routine of programmed, remote-controlled existence. Escape from custody ... breaking from the solitary confinement of the cosmic prison where God-given treasures get buried under piles of toxic waste.

Purpose is not hard to recognize. Some are intended, others are unintended – hidden. Revealed purpose and concealed purpose. But every purpose must to be identified to work it's magic. Sometimes it's as easy as staring away from the mirror instead of at the mirror.

---

72 Tribute to a mega-super-masterpiece, Psalm 40 – "I waited patiently for the LORD; and He inclined to me and heard my cry. He lifted me out of the pit of destruction, out of the miry clay; and He set my feet on a rock, making my footsteps firm . He put a new song in my mouth, a song of praise to our God. Many will see and fear and trust in the LORD."

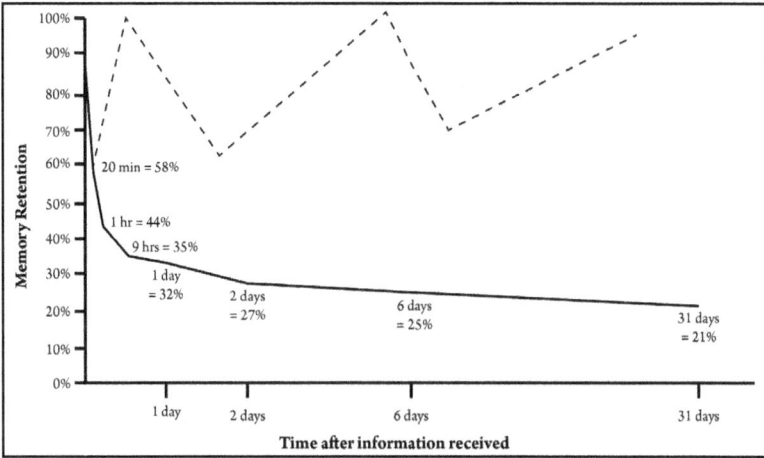

The Ebbinghaus Curve, illustrated in the graph above, demonstrates how weak the unchallenged mind is.[73] That's the intended purpose. The graph can also serve as a visual of how quickly an unchallenged body can become – the unintended purpose.

"Experiences" are not created equal. Like people, only a few experiences are memorable – the majority are forgettable. Depends on the quantity and quality of reps – mental reps. After we hear a sound, see a sight, or meet a person, our memory goes in one of two directions … up or down. The determining factor is the quality of the mental workout, the number of mental reps and their intensity. A single-set of learning or observing does not guarantee a long-term memory. If we never think about it again, we forget at an alarming rate. Almost half of the observation is forgotten in just 20 minutes. After one day, two-thirds is erased. After one month, over three-quarters is dumped in the trash bin. The miracle of the human delete button. By simply not thinking about something, the memory gets erased off the board, one swipe at a time.

The good news is that bad memories can be forgotten. The bad news is that good information is hard to save. Intense reps are needed to upload the information, to store it in the files of the memory banks … and recall it in its original form.

---

73 We are indebted to Hermann Ebbinghaus, a pioneer in memory research, who published the first significant memory study in 1885. The study centrally focused on memory retention and the rate of forgetting. I personally need to give Dr Ebbinghaus double-credit. I have applied the Ebbinghaus Curve in police textbooks and college law enforcement teaching, as part of a Witness Credibility Model. My work would never have been possible without Dr. Ebbinghaus's research.

The secret to stopping the slide down the forgetting curve is hardcore studying, practicing, rehearsing, burning concentration ... mental reps keep the memory file in the 60% to 100% range, peaking memory, saving information in long-term, easily retrievable files. The dotted line on the graph above, shows the miracle of reps – turning the human mind from a cheap one-gigabyte flashdrive to an unlimited terabyte mainframe. The power of reps ... and lack of reps. Delete or save. Change the reps, change the outcome.

The same theory applies to 225-pound bench-press testing. Resting on laurels means a rapid drop in strength, just like memory. Taking extended time off working out starts the quick slide down the steep decline. Strength drops at the same rate as The President's approval ratings immediately after inauguration. Conversely, quality maintenance reps keep the score, the personal-best record, in the 60% - 100% range. But not past it.

∞

Squats are the best exercise ever invented. They make you faster, stronger, leaner, meaner. They peel fat off the body and even more fat off the brain. Squats build unrivaled physical and mental toughness. And squats turn on the T-blast switch.

Testosterone has ordering options. Any kind of arousal ... any kind. Feeling down? Flip the switch, get excited. Testosterone on demand. *Mannaggia la Miseria!* – getting pissed off is the most inexpensive, most potent pre-workout booster ... the secret testosterone secretor, passed down through generations. The workplace, workout T-blast – the hidden benefit of working with assholes and for assholes. Simply do a few mental reps before and during a workout – asshole visualization. Testosterone tsunami. Retrieve bad memories. Turn negatives into positives.

If life is serene, harmonious and asshole-free, try legwork. Legwork arouses legwork. Fighters and lovers can flip the T-blast switch effortlessly. "Arousal" is safe, cheap, works immediately and is created equal. No caffeine, no ephedra. No side-effects. The silent, inner drug deal.

Any exercise that requires both feet planted firmly on the ground automatically qualifies as a quality exercise. Being grounded is the litmus test for ranking exercise efficiency. Squats are top-ranked. The bad news is that squats are not an easy sell. The product being sold is extreme hard work and discomfort ... **HELL** – **H**eavy **E**xtreme **L**aborious **L**ifting. Hating squats is natural. HELL is hard to sell. Squats are risky and filled with uncertainty. Like the dark, they're even scarier when you're alone.

But in a group, fear of squats is managed easier – much easier. The secret is a three-element approach: Appeal to the souls of other lifters – with coordinated, coach-led team training – using **PMS** – **P**ower **M**essage **S**ets. PMS involves the **3-Bs**. Teach the **B**asics, emphasize the **B**enefits, then experience it – feel the legs **B**low-up ... feel the rush! Repeat. Eventually, the discomfort turns into a basic survival need.

The principles of 225-pound squat testing are the same as bench press testing. The first two digits of your bodyweight is the EP standard. But, since legs are stronger than chest, the maximum rep count is expected to exceed maximum bench press. Same minimum, different maximum. The threshold for legendary 225 squat status is simple – the first two digits of bodyweight times two. A 200-pound lifter: 20 x 2 = 40 reps. 190-pound lifter: 19 x 2 = 38 reps. And so on.

The difference between squats and bench press is the feeling deep down in the core of your guts, one that grows in intensity. A spot right above your groin and just below the pit of your stomach that feels like it's been hit with an iron bar, inventing the new sensation of "pausea" – a mixed brew of passing out and nausea.

For testing, the coach goes first, again. The first 19 reps of 225 squat testing are deceiving. The mind and body connect to perpetrate a fraud. They create a false reality that 19 is the half-way mark and the next 19 will be as easy as the first. Pain, anguish, discomfort and suffering do not develop gradually. No early-warning system. Twenty feels like the bar is crushing the shoulder blades. At 24, the left knee involuntarily twitches. At 26, an imaginary hot knife blade slices the lower back. At 30, the testicles feel like they're ripping out of the scrotum. Ball-breaking.

31. Clang. Iron meets iron. The bar smashes against the racks. Emergency landing. The chatter of the inner voice gets louder. *Che vergogna!!* The shame ... seven short of the goal. 31 reps of 225-pound squats is not legendary. Not extraordinary ... not even for a 190-pound football coach. A failure to reach a stretch goal – a lofty minimum maximum – is a sign. A sign to get better. A message to train harder. And it's a symptom of a faulty mindset. Seven reps below a stretch goal sets

off alarm bells. Cause for concern. When the return doesn't match the investment, check out the fund manager.

∞

How do you fight temptation to take steroids? Simple. Proactive strategy – by preventing temptations. And past influences. The right people and right experience at the right time – messages. Powerful messages are needed to prevent steroid temptations from materializing.

Temptation is a variation of evil's "broken focus" play. A play designed to alleviate fear. First, evil pounds fear into our heads – artificial fear. Rams fear, jams fear – stuffing in piles of it, contaminating every space in our brain. All wo/man-made. Then, after fear successfully takes over – establishes control – evil presents a solution ... the easy way out. The painless way. Soul-selling. Evil is an approval junkie – offering a solution to the fear it made us suffer. Evil wants to be our friend by misery-building followed by misery-busting ... the easy way.

The best way to prevent temptation of steroid use is iron-clad character, built by a strong work ethic. It's a team effort. Parents are the coordinators. They shape our base worldview about work – whether it's considered good or evil. A blessing or a curse. Parents coordinate our work-mindset education. Hate it or love it. Fear it or invite it. Flee from it or fight for it. The rest of the teaching staff comes and goes – relatives, friends, educators, coaches, partners, autopsies exposing decayed organs. (Caveat emptor – Buyer beware. Who are they going to call? ... the cops, when they realize they paid obscene sums of money for alleged steroids ... but got ripped off?)

Our attitudes toward steroids depends on the quality of work ethic learned from our parents – the presence or absence of performance demands, made by our parents – enforced by our parents and their support staff. An immigrant work ethic – the machine-like kind that views any form of laziness with contempt ... physical, intellectual, emotional, spiritual – fights any steroid temptation ... long before it even happens.

Poor work ethic builds laziness. Tolerating laziness of any kind is a form of parental neglect. A rip-off. Deprivation of the power that evens out the playing field – real-life education ... practical IQ. Physical laziness, intellectual laziness, emotional laziness, spiritual laziness ... they're all connected. One affects the other. A high tolerance for laziness is giving in to evil – surrendering to the fear of disapproval, the fear of not being liked, the fear that our children, and others who look to us for guidance, won't want to be our best friend. Lowering the threshold for laziness raises the bar.

The gym is the only place that lets you repeat the past – exactly. Equaling a personal best is the equivalent of re-living euphoria. If only life imitated the gym. But, it's also the equivalent of simply tying the score – not scoring higher. Repeatedly tying a score sets off a siren – complacency. Settling into a soft zone – a slimy pit of miry clay … laziness.[74]

The gym does not impress easily. The gym doesn't recognize past performance, doesn't allow living in the past and will not permit staring in the rear view mirror. The gym has the ultimate anti-aging formula: Reaching 31 reps at 225-pound squat every decade for four decades and never letting players half your age pass you, stops the clock and then turns it backwards. Time management. Repeating past-workout performance is the only healthy kind of living-in-the-past. Thirty-one reps make you feel 31.

The personal-best quest has an upside and a downside. Below is the "Incline/Decline" graph. Rapid incline, plateau, slow decline. Spike, same, slide. Its intended purpose is to scientifically illustrate the rise and fall of blood-alcohol concentration (BAC) in potential serial killers, a.k.a., "drunk drivers." The same graph can be used to illustrate the rise and fall of strength.

The spike: BAC/physical strength, rises rapidly – in the beginning. Alcohol consumption and strength are contextual – the effect they have on the body is the big picture. The spike happens in the early stages of both scenarios. It takes only 15 minutes after the last drink to reach a drunk's final BAC. In relation to an entire workout career, reaching big league poundage takes the least amount of time. A novice lifter can make serious gains in the initial stages of a workout career.

---

74   A second tribute to Psalm 40 … not nearl૪   ৬

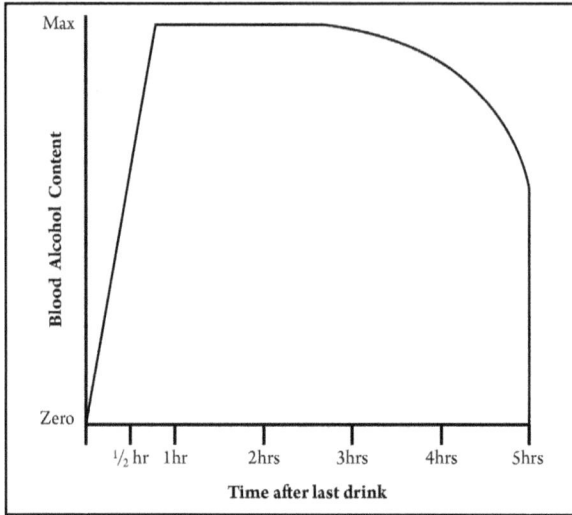

But there are no absolutes – no absolute guarantees, no absolute formula, no absolute positive gain that will absolutely happen. The height and angle of the spike depends on many variables including, but not limited to, nutrition, sleep and who coaches the novice lifter – the environment. How high the initial spike reaches on the graph is an indication of how long the workout career will last ... the height of the spike is connected to the size of the picture.

The bad news for lifters ... once the spike stops, the gains only inch forward. Snail's pace. The thrill of rapid incline doesn't last. The fight starts – for every ounce of iron. Like with BAC, the initial spike is followed by a plateau – a period of no change ... sameness. BAC stays the same for two hours ... lifting performance can stay the same indefinitely. No challenge, no expansion. Then, the plateau starts sliding downwards. Like BAC, unchallenged strength gradually leaves the body. Left unchecked, the slide will make you quit working out, make you soft, change you into someone you won't like. A stranger will replace your true self ... unless you decide to bust your ass.

The good news is that, for lifters, the plateau can rise instead of falling. The decline can be lifted into an new incline. The solution is extreme hard work. Amp up the challenge. Light your inner fire – pour fuel on it. And more and more. Feel the big rush. Get addicted to the thrill. Get addicted to the hard work. If this good news sounds like hard work, change your perception, ASAP, before you lose your fire ... before you have the energy of a neutered dog. If extreme hard work becomes scary, if it instils fear, if it overwhelms you with dread, if you hate hard work ... you have no chance. Game over. You lose. Retirement from working out ... leading to retirement from life.

Retirement is a synonym for "packing it in" ... shutting down the engine. Idling, rusting ... rotting. Contrary to popular myth, retirement does not happen when someone slides you a pension cheque. It happens the moment you lose child-like wonder – the moment you leave behind the fire and dreams and passion and boundless energy that you were born with ... the moment you press the "off" switch.

$$\infty$$

We never know when we're standing on the peak. Standing on the peak can be a rush until the view gets too familiar. If you can't find a higher mountain, at the very least climb the same one again and again, with a greater degree of difficulty.

Twenty-six and 31 were never broken. They became my highest scores, both the product of "1985" – an extraordinary, intense, ball-busting, gut-wrenching unconventional, so-far-outside-the-box-that-the-box-disappeared, team-training system. One that tested the limits of each team member's soul, mind and body.

The conventional way of testing 225 is a rested one-set performance. Do a few light sets with ample rest separating each one. Follow these with the proverbial rage-demonstration – sit, stand, rock, stare, grit teeth, growl, swear, scream. Eventually, the test set. The equivalent of scoring early in the game – when no one is sweaty, dirty or bloody.

Blood, sweat and dirt change the game. When things get messy, dirty ... and fatigue starts creeping in, things start to hurt. The game doesn't look the same – feel the same – when sweat is stinging the eyeballs, when dirt sticks clothes to skin, when the site of blood occupies your attention. Game balls get bigger or smaller but they don't stay the same.

Who can handle pain and discomfort longer? Who can stay strong, get stronger, play harder, when the blood and sweat starts pouring? The test is the rest. How much rest you need to stay strong determines how far you will go in any competition – sports or otherwise.

In 1985, the monotony of conventional, fully-rested, one-set testing led to 19-8-5 megasets. The coach would make the call about how many sets would precede the 225 test – with minimal rest. Infinite megasets could be called. I used, "19-8-5." Long supersets – consecutive multiple exercises: Lightweight high-reps (19 minimum), middleweight mid-reps (eight minimum), and heavyweight low-reps (five minimum). Lots of them ... followed by the 225 test. The purpose of 19-8-5 training was to push the needle close to "E" – then train through it. Build a bigger reserve tank – physically and mentally. Train the mind not to ignore discomfort but change its reaction to it. Instead of hating it, love it.

It made an impact, a huge impact on overall performance – strength, conditioning, on-field, off-field, and most significantly, in the mind. Unmatched physical and mental conditioning built iron will faster and stronger than any other type of workout. Because it was a "fatigue test" designed to manage soul-wrenching discomfort while measuring real 225-pound strength. Realistic strength – the type needed during the pressure of the real game. Life-altering. Transformational. 1985 changed lives forever. Not one Blue Bear remained the same. 1985 challenged conventional work-out wisdom, body, mind and ... soul.

$$\infty$$

Working out is much more than self-admiration, marveling at the aesthetically-pleasing wo/man in the mirror. Working out is the school where we learn the hardest subject in the history of wo/mankind – self. Who we are and more importantly, who we are not.

The real self, the ideal self and the gap between the two. Science has provided compelling evidence that generally, we are clueless about who we actually are. Inflated opinions, deflated opinions – everything but the truth. Like uncommitted college freshman engaged in a year-long celebration of being away from home, parents, siblings, and every other bane of their existence, we are horrifyingly inept students in the course called "Self-Analysis." An honest, credible evaluation of who we truly are and what we have to do to get to where we want to go. Prerequisites to the Masters-level course, "How To Be" and the PhD course, "Street Survival for the Lost and Tortured Soul."

Unlike church and state, the gym is the separation and re-connection of body and brain. The isolation and re-unification of muscle and state of mind. The goal is not to fracture our will but to exercise it. Two choices – fight the resistance and get stronger or run and let it chase you and beat you down. Misery is a change agent. Pain, suffering and all the hurt that the gym dishes out are growth opportunities. Good, not evil.

The gym teaches a hands-on course in self-discovery and growth, teaching how to capitalize on our gifts, maximize each blessing, connect every miracle we are blessed to experience with the bigger network. Stretch and spread. Push limits, break barriers – smash 'em – go past pre-conceived notions, imagine the unimaginable. Achieve the unachievable. Learn to raise the bar … and lift it.

The gym prevents being asked if you'd like to use your senior citizen discount … on your 30th birthday. It keeps the spirit alive and the soul on fire.

Choose "hard work." Break the "off" switch.

Chapter 28.5 – 43
St. Jude

The psychology of working out is more important than the physiology of working out.

In the history of working out, the original X Fitness (1985-2000) arguably, was one of the greatest gyms ever. Who worked out, what was lifted, where they came from, where they went and what was accomplished ... not just physically.

A system that produced the greatest volume of accomplishments – quantity and quality – in the smallest amount of space and time. No system had greater time-space sensitivity – only 150 square feet of indoor gym and 9,750 square feet of outdoor field. Square inch by square inch, pound for pound, age by age, the collective energy – force, mass, momentum – combined with the least amount of natural talent and least amount of expectations. The reason – two words. Two words that high school football players generally don't have the capacity to formulate or communicate – "spiritual event." So when they do, it's real.

The secret behind the experience – the spiritual event – was the absence of fear. What was missing shaped the accomplishments. Fear was conspicuous by its absence. The original X Fitness drove fear into the ground. Teams of lifters hammered fear ... by changing the focus. Training. Gut-wrenching – soul-wrenching – training.

Fear is a product of evil. Fear is a staple of evil's playbook. Fear is not generated by good. Good cannot produce fear. But good supplies the anti-fear artillery. The evidence is clear: "For God has not given us a spirit of fear, but of power and of love and of a sound mind." — 2 Timothy 1:7. The secret to fearlessness in a single sentence.

Evil recruits any one of us to carry out its fearful mission but good has already armed us to fight it. Both sides can make us dangerous, but only one arms us.

St. Jude, the saint of hopeless causes, was the patron saint of the original X Fitness – the second-chance gym where the only admission standard was a free-will exercise. Hope for the hopeless.

Athletic Darwinism. Survival of the fittest. A system that's measured by it's natural-selection capacity. The value of a program is connected to the degree of difficulty. The extent of challenges. The system, not human opinion must select the fittest. Progression by merit – the fundamental principle of meritocracy. Athletic Darwinism intensely exercises free will. Reps after reps of decisions. Choices. Tough calls. Quit or continue. Stay or leave it behind. The choice to get better or get worse.

Athletic Darwinism and meritocracy are connected – the choice is made by the student, not the teacher. By the player, not the coach. By the worker, not the boss. Players cut themselves, coaches don't do it. Employees promote themselves, not management. The natural struggle is connected to natural selection. Performance is the universal language of meritocracy, understood globally. No translation needed.

Athletic Darwinism, misery and memory are connected. The value of Athletic Darwinism is measured by surviving. Misery-busting is memorable. And memories of the original X Fitness are described in six words: *"Toughest practices ever. Toughest workouts ever."*

Badges of moxie. X Fitness, a culture of accomplishment. A culture of unprecedented growth – academically and athletically, professionally, personally. The psychology, philosophy and sociology of the X Fitness System connected with the physical set-calling system. One-of-a-kind. Unique. Memorable. Nothing like it.

All-American and All-Canadian football players, full contact light-heavyweight Jiu-Jitsu World champion, two-time Canadian university football MVP, record-breaking Jr. B hockey scorer, three *Sports Illustrated*-recognized single-game performances, two-time Hec Crighton award winner – pro signings – athletes and cops. No system has made a greater combined impact on sports and front-line law enforcement … for free. No one paid. No one got paid … with money.

Athletic Darwinism. Don't be part of the elimination, be part of the selection.

Chapter 40.24

Chapter 34
Culture Shock

"What's it like going from policing to college teaching?"

Silence.

"Culture Shock. He's going through Culture Shock."

Dysfunctionalism never goes away completely. Like an unused muscle or brain, dyfunctionalism atrophies. But it never really disappears. Dysfunctionalism causes confuck-tions – warping of judgment, twisting of reality and blurring the line between right and wrong, sanity and madness.

When a simple question can't be answered, the soul of a lifter goes to work. It opens the playbook, uses every resource available to solve the mystery. She was not even listening to the conversation. Engaged in some latest-gossip contest with her friends and husband. Two decades later, she can't remember saying it – my sister-in-law turned her head and shouted in my direction, *"Culture Shock. He's going through Culture Shock."* Diagnosis, cure, caution. The equivalent of a Surgeon General's warning on a pack of cigarettes.

The soul of a lifter uses innovative messaging, straight-forward stuff. But unlike Travis Bickle, there's no confusion, no need to ask, *"Are you talking to me?"* let alone listening. Disconnection blinds us to the oblivious obvious. The cost of being unplugged. *"Culture Shock. He's going through Culture Shock."*

The soul of a lifter is not nasty … at first. The message was a gentle-wo/manly one – not with the force of: *"Hey you dumbass wake up, grow a pair of balls and get out if you hate it so much and go do what makes you happy"* – not yet.

- Never ever become really good at what you hate to do.
- Never never ever become the expert misery-buster in a profession you despise.
- Never never ever ever get addicted to the praise, flattery and approval of opportunistic manipulators who want to ride your coattails.
- Never enjoy the most accolades from the job you least like doing.
- Never ever become a pain-reliever for pains-in-the-ass who want to circumvent the natural struggle.
- Never ever never let people become addicted to your pain-and-suffering absorption capacity.
- Never ever ever work in an environment deeply entrenched in anguish, hostility and hatred, spread by those afflicted by the post-modern disease called, "unfulfilled career," a.k.a., "unreached potential."
- Never become a victim of professional scrounging.
- Never let sensitivity replace sensibility.
- Never never butcher, compromise, or otherwise carve up your deep-rooted beliefs.
- Never hack the core of your spirit.
- Never ever never ever become a snake-oil salesman.
- Never commit soulicide. Do not attack, mutilate, or massacre the essence of your being – your soul, your spiritual connection. Never pull the plug on who you are – and who you were meant to be.

The soul of a lifter never sends a neat list of simple "never" rules to follow. No step-by-step Tweet, Facebook message, text message, or even the primitive communication called face-to-face verbal dialogue. No, the soul of a lifter is the mystery messenger, we're the interpreter. Like a complicated game of charades, we're expected to translate, "sounds-like" into rapid-fire calls that have to be made in the blink of an eye.

"Culture Shock. He's going through Culture Shock." The soul of a lifter is relentless. Never gives up, ever. Is driven. Passionate. Borderline

obsessive. The soul of a lifter won't stop until the message gets across. Even if takes 20 years. Even when you thought for sure you had committed the unthinkable.

The attempted murder of the soul of a lifter should be a crime. The government should criminalize any self-inflicted harm to your soul. Mangling the soul – leaving it to rot – is unconscionable. The suspect should be charged with negligence.

The attempted assassination of the soul of a lifter is the only crime where the victim is also the suspect. And, it's the only crime where it takes forever to identify the victim. Like ignorance of the law, failure to recognize a dying soul could not be used as a defence. Neither could dysfunctionalism. Like any crime victim, a mortally wounded soul of a lifter needs justice.

The symptoms of a soul of a lifter on life-support include, but are not limited to:

- The belief that you're indispensable in a dispensable organization.
- Self-importance becomes the biggest growth you experience.
- Being identified exclusively by your day job.
- Confusing the bush leagues with the big leagues.
- Fighting the non-fight, and /or fighting no opponent.
- Failing to recognize your descent into workplace prostitution.
- The delusion that inferior quality is not.
- Distracted attention … not hearing the soul's pleas for help, or seeing the soul on life support.

The worst symptom is what St. Paul warned the Ephesians about: "Futility of the mind."[75] The wireless disconnection that isolates mind from soul when the lights go out: "Being darkened … because of the hardness in their hearts."

GET UP!!! I'll help. LIFT.

Silence.

The soul of a lifter never takes time off … don't confuse silence with absence. The soul of a lifter takes from a limitless playbook to challenge

---

75 Tribute to a masterpiece of masterpieces, The Letter of Paul to the Ephesians. Ephesians 4:17-18

physically, challenge intellectually, challenge emotionally, challenge spiritually. The soul of a lifter never turns its back and never ever turns over play-calling responsibility until we're ready. Not too soon, not too late – just the right time.

Chapter 37
2% – Bush League

If you're willing to give it your all, all will be given.

Wanting to get to the next level, and paying the price to get there, are two separate concepts. Not many are willing to pay the full price. Half price isn't enough. Only a full investment nets a full return.

I've coached and taught thousands who want to be – "wannabes." Wannabe pro athletes. Wannabe scholarship athletes. Wannabe cops. Thousands want to get paid for performance. But most of the thousands do not want to pay the price. Not the price needed to eventually get paid. In 35 years of working with young people, I'd estimate 98.6% didn't, don't – and won't. Many pay partial price – physical or intellectual, but most will not pay both. Some pay the price in the weight room, some pay the price in the classroom … and some pay the price outside both, in the real world with currency called, "character."

2% get there. Not 50%. 2%. Thousands want to get to the next level but 100% will not invest fully. The desire to perform at the highest level is rarely matched by the desire to train for it. Intention and action, when matched up, light a fire. Mismatches don't.

The good news is that 2% of thousands is hundreds. For those who were fully committed to the journey, there's light traffic at the top. And of those traveling, many seem to have come from nowhere. Professional Darwinism – selection of the fittest.

The bush league paradox – miracle or misery.

The bush leagues are not on the map … or any map. The bush leagues are not on anyone's radar screen. You've got to go deep to find the bush leagues. And you can't see the big leagues from the bush leagues. The road is long. An ordinary drive won't make it. But an extraordinary drive … .

The Hamilton Wildcats were a brand-new, first-year, Canadian semi-pro football team that couldn't be found even on the bush league map. The bush league GPS did not recognize their name, city, and especially country. Born in July 1994, their pre-season ended in disaster – head coach fired, more than half the team quit one week before the first game – seven days before the their first game ever.

"I'm offering you the job. But there's only 13 players ... and only four days left." "Job" usually implies wages and resources. "Owner" usually implies the existence of an organization. At least some structure. Not in semi-pro football. They use a foreign language.

There's a fine line – a blurry line – between accepting another St. Jude challenge and accepting an invitation from a street-walker. Either way, addicted to the thrill. Using a museum artifact called a "land-line telephone," eighteen phone calls can change destiny – nine calls to former players to fill out the roster to the bare minimum of 22, and nine calls to successful American semi-pro teams, including the best – the Brooklyn Mariners, the Goliath of American semi-pro football. The most wins since 1957, the Mariners were 42-2 during the last four years. The Wildcats, new schedule, new challenge – new performance demand – a road map out of the bush leagues – playing the best. A primitive, untested GPS to the big leagues.

To be the best, play the best. Research shows that the two greatest blockers of growth and potential are coddling and protecting. Soft training and soft opponents make soft bodies and even softer minds. Athletic UnDarwinism – the weak getting weaker ... and disappearing from the game. Shielding young athletes, adult athletes, or anyone in general from Goliaths, prevents Davids from stepping up. David fighting David has no allure – and absolutely no benefit. No one gets better – in fact, they get worse.

Strength is connected to strength. Facing strength builds strength. To get strong, compete against the strongest. Ducking the strong weakens. Challenge and future are connected – predict the future by looking at today's challenges. And yesterday's. The degree of difficulty in our past and present challenges determines our future. Our past and current misery-busting determines the drive – where we go ... and where we won't go. The struggles we beat, set us up to beat the next struggle. Challenge yourself against the toughest, the smartest, the brightest ... the winners. The champs. We are the sum of who we compete against – what we struggle with. Our competition shapes our personality – defines us. What we fight builds our will – either a solid or shaky structure.

Athletic Darwinism. Academic Darwinism. Professional Darwinism. Business Darwinism. Raising the natural-struggle bar raises the lessons learned – lifts the reality IQ. Or drops it. Depends on the reaction to it – how we respond matters.

"Canada, eh? Hahahehe. How close are you to Toronto?"

"Less than an hour drive."

"Sure, we'll come there. It'll be a good vacation. The guys can bring their wives shopping."

∞

"Gauntlet-droppings" are not created equal. Some are soft, barely audible, sand-throwing insults. Others echo in the brain, soaring off the *Ebbinghuas Curve*, jamming two switches – the replay button and the rush button – the control lever to the blast-furnace inside the guts that lights the fire and miraculously keeps pouring an infinite supply of fuel … splashing buckets and buckets and buckets … .

Being an outlier in one's own mind in not enough. An outlier separates from the rest. Breaks from the pack. Can't find the "follow" button, can't see it … can't even bear looking for it. Follow-phobia. Fear of following, fear of box-confinement.

Thinking outside the box is not enough to qualify as an outlier.[76] There are two more steps. Living it and convincing others to follow. Anyone can think outside the box because thinking it and living there are not the same – different pain. Outside the box is a lonely place. Isolated. Thinking outside the box is private. Living there is public. Public opinion and private opinion are connected – and isolated. Public opinion sways private opinion much easier than vice-versa.

Thinking and living outside the box are easier than the third step, because the soul of a lifter has an audience of one. Convincing others to follow is the greatest challenge listed in the leader's "job description" because the outlier him/herself produces Culture Shock – the hardest impact of all to handle. An outlier is hard to handle.

Unconventional ideas are the hardest product to sell. But there is a secret sales plan – evidence. S/he who asserts must prove. Build a case. Charge the jury. Over and over. Same message, stay on message. Overwhelm

---

76 Tribute to a masterpiece, *Outliers*. By Malcolm Gladwell. Any book written by Gladwell *(Tipping Point, Blink)* is a masterpiece but Outliers is the best. Gladwell, a Canadian, pays tribute to the wild successes of those who thought and lived so far outside the box that the box disappears. And he showed that wild success does not just happen. It doesn't mysteriously grow out of nowhere. Successful people, by whatever definition, are not born, they are made.

them with "Exhibit A" all the way to Triple-A. An outlier relies on three secrets to prove his/her case beyond a reasonable doubt – track record, benefit and the 66% rule.

Track record: Proving the outlier's credibility is the first step in buy-in. Track record and buy-in are connected. The past is an indicator of the future. Prove that outside the box has worked in the past ... and will work again. Habits are hard to break. And their volume level is much higher than words.

Benefit. What's in it for them? How will they improve? What's the profit? Benefit and buy-in are connected. No benefit, no buy-in. Show them that Culture Shock works ... by proving how it worked in the past ... and present. Evidence of who benefited in the past. And point out their daily improvement. Remind them of what they are experiencing, seeing – feeling.

66% rule. It's human nature to buy-in. Compelling research proves that at least two-thirds will conform to the thoughts and actions of others even if it contradicts personal beliefs. The majority are followers – for no reason. So, when reasons are proved ... the numbers explode – the pack grows.

Convincing any team to follow an outlier needs a role model – someone who lives it, someone who makes outlierism a lifestyle. And, most importantly, someone who doesn't blink. Failure to blink is a pre-requisite for the title of "outlier." Live by outlierism, never ever die an inlier. Say what you mean, mean what you say. Don't blink.

∞

Do the math – 19 plus three does not always equal 22. A football roster of 22 is puny. Suspect. But when three of the players are kickers, the roster is actually only 19. Only if the three kickers re-define "commitment," do the numbers add up.

"We do things different. Way different. No one else does it this way. The reason they don't is fear. The reason we do things different is because it has worked for years – my system scores lots of points, we win and players get recruited. I'm on a ten-year streak of never kicking. No punts, no field goals. No PATs. We go for it anywhere, anytime. So you will never be a conventional kicker. You will never get to score any points, never get to punt. You will only

ever get to kick off – because we have to – and when you do kick off, you aren't the safety loafing around mid-field. You have to fly to the ball – make some hits, go after the ball … get your hands dirty. And we never kick off deep unless we have a big lead. Short kicks – onside kicks over and over and over again until we get a big lead. When we kick deep, you sprint your ass downfield and make tackles. If you don't, you're fired. I've done it before and I'll do it again. And during practice, don't think you're going to stand around kicking. Get reps at real positions. We go live all the time. Find a real position and learn it. You will be the official back-up to a real position. That's your official title. Back-up to a real position. If your girlfriend asks you what position you play, you say, 'Back-up to a real position who works overtime as an onside kicker.' If you mother asks what position you play, do not say, 'Kicker.' Tell your mother you are a back-up to a real position who works overtime as an onside kicker. When the media interviews you and asks you what it's like to be a kicker on a non-kicking team, correct them immediately. Tell them you are not a kicker. You are a back-up to a real position who works overtime as an onside kicker. Now, if you want to quit, go ahead. I won't call you names. No one here will call you names for quitting. Guaranteed. People who can't cut it and cut themselves are never mocked. Mocking quitters is not allowed. That's a promise. If you quit and we see you in the supermarket, no one will call you a chickenshit coward. That's a promise. Calling people chickenshit and coward is not allowed. But, if you're going to quit, do it now. Don't steal reps. Rep-robbing is a crime. Don't be a thief and then quit a few weeks from now. Quit today. Save yourself grief and spare the team aggravation."

All three stayed. Perfect attendance. Not one of the ex-kickers missed one practice or game. And never missed a weight room workout. One of them, Dan Giancola, a former Blue Bear opponent, got a shot at the pros – signed by the Toronto Argonauts of the CFL as an undrafted free agent, enjoyed a long, prosperous CFL career and earned a Grey Cup ring … without ever scoring one point during his Hamilton Wildcat career. An outlier. Connection, not coincidence.

"My career is in your hands." The key to attracting is inviting, not guaranteeing. Sandy Annunziata was a monster lineman, a prominent university football player, top CFL draft pick … and cut by the Calgary Stampeders. Unemployed. Career over … apparently. Needed a second chance.

Stopping dreams from turning into nightmares has a price. Driving one hour each way to practice on a cow pasture masquerading as a football field. Ragged uniform, and working overtime – played both offense and defense ... for the first time since the end of his high school career ... the day the Blue Bears reached their next-level beating of their Catholic school, cross-town nemesis. Sandy was the opposing tight end who was shut down with a newly-designed, flawlessly-executed SWAT defense. Connection, not coincidence.

Sandy never missed a Wildcat practice. Worked out in the weight room like a hungry animal. Never acted like he was above the bush league. He did the time and was rewarded with a ten-year professional career in the CFL, earning two Grey Cup rings. Current business owner, radio/TV personality and politician. An outlier.

#34 Blue Bears got his pro shot after an illustrious All-American university career – drafted by the Edmonton Eskimos of the CFL. And cut during his first pre-season. Career over ... apparently. Needed a second chance. He paid the same price but the fall from the big leagues to the bush leagues was a little steeper than Sandy's – two hour drive, hand-me-down uniform, no change rooms ... just bushes. Forced to go deep to escape. But he never missed a practice. Or a workout. Never acted like he was too good for the bush leagues. He ran for hundreds of yards behind his former high school opponent. Connection, not coincidence. He did the time and got a second chance at the pros – signed as a free agent by the Montreal Alouettes of the CFL. An outlier.

Sandy Annunziata, Dan Giancola, #34 Blue Bears – St. Jude is a tireless saint.

The Hamilton Wildcats formed an intersection, the crossing of paths, where potential was revved up and rose to the next level, where destinies took turns but did not play out – yet.

Three souls of lifters saw barriers, saw opportunities and made soul-performance demands. The uncommon type. The type that has to go deep. The type that says, *"You knocked me down, but not out!"* All three made the investment. Paid the price – full price. A deep price. Deep in the bushes. And they went deeper – had to be seen to be believed. Words can't explain it – or the good fortune to have been an eyewitness. Front row seat.

"Hope you had a nice vacation!" Post-game hand-shaking is an opportunity – a chance to be an asshole to the opposing coaches. 28-25. Miracle comeback – scored with six seconds left in the game. Brooklyn Mariners lost only their third game in four years. Wildcats went undefeated.

Email become popular a year after our 9-0 season. A miracle undefeated season – 22 foreigners. The only Canadian team, at the time, playing against American competition. People had said it was crazy – David and Goliath. No hope.

Iron will not let fear in. Iron will shuts out fear. The iron will to fight, surfaces when you go deep enough.

When the first chance doesn't work out, work out, work through it and fight your way back … or lay down, quit and retire – be sure to ask for your seniors' discount.

∞

The gym has a good heart … and a good soul. The gym will never call you names if you reject it. Because you will do enough of it on your own when muscle turns to mush, when hardness softens, when the flab mounts.

Chapter 40.27

"Leave the presence of a fool, or you will not discern the words of knowledge."   — Proverbs 14:7.

Chapter 33-38
Silent Warrior

Female lifters score much lower on the asshole scale than males – except in team training. Two or more have the asshole equivalent of one male. Female lifters have a higher tolerance for pain. One alone – never complains, brags, annoys, narrates, reminisces, socializes, provides expert commentary after every set, and never-ever does the unthinkable – tries to motivate herself or her coach with conventional feeble-minded, obscenity-laced, conjured, unimaginative primal screams. If she is going to do it, it had better be real – creative, original ... genuine profanity straight from the heart ... and soul. And it better be clever. Moving. Inspiring. 98.6% of people are clueless about how to lead by example. Stunned amateurs. Disconnected souls.

Vince Valvano knew the connection to the soul of a lifter. Actions ... not words. Silent warrior – **SUAL** – **S**hut **U**p **A**nd **L**ift. A secret that is not a secret. Used to turn around six losing football programs and two losing college law-enforcement programs. The secret to building powerhouses – strong, harmonious teams, organizations, or any meaningful relationships – is having no secrets about expectations and philosophy.

Leadership change in an organization is the equivalent of responding to a 9-1-1 call. An "unknown problem." Uncertainty and risk. No one on either side of the problem has a clue what's going on or what to expect. The solution is replacing uncertainty with certainty. Remove risk by removing doubt. Teams/organizations deserve clear expectations and philosophy to remove the natural ambiguity and confusion brought on by new leadership.

I've been given many opportunities to respond to a 9-1-1 call as well as provide a leadership change. Throughout, I've been blessed with thousands of memorable players, memorable games, memorable performances. It's impossible to single out one player who stands out, but, it's easy to identify the one player who is the soul of the my system. The Vince Valvano Award represents a program and personal mission statement that has never failed to turnaround a broken program. Batting 1,000. Also known as the "Silent Warrior Code of Conduct," a statement that has worked miracles – repeated, warp-speed transformation of big league assholes.

The Silent Warrior Code of Conduct is far more than a team mission statement – it is a GPS for strength of character. Maturity. It has made a profound impact on thousands of student athletes and college students who have heard the story behind the **Vince Valvano Award.**

"Our program will continue the annual tradition of recognizing strength of character with the Vince Valvano award. It will be given to the student-athlete who demonstrates all the personality traits and qualities that will guarantee success in the gym, on the field, in his/her professional career, and his/her personal life. The award will be given out after every game, season and semester to the people who perform like Vince Valvano."

Vince was a defensive tackle that I coached at both junior and senior/semi-pro between 1989 and 1995. Vince achieved what no other player has ever done. In 1995, he was voted semi-pro all-star, on both offense and defense in the same year, by the people who would know best – opposing players. In 1994-95, Vince played for the legendary Hamilton Wildcats semi-pro/senior team, a juggernaut that went 20-2 during those two years. In 1994, as an expansion team, the Wildcats recorded an undefeated 9-0 season playing in the USA. In 1995, the Wildcats joined the Northern Football Conference. As an expansion team, the Wildcats demolished the record book. They still hold 13 NFC offensive records.

During those two years, Vince played 60 minutes of every game – defense, offense and all special teams. He was the smallest (height-wise) lineman on the field but the strongest and toughest. He led the team in tackles both years, an unheard of achievement for a defensive tackle. At 5'11" he was David playing in a valley of Goliaths.

This is Vince's profile:

- He never missed a practice – ever. And he had to work as a manual laborer, laying bricks, during the day.
- He never missed one live rep during any practice.
- He never came off the field for even one second during any game.
- During two years, he never stood on the sidelines during practices or games. And practices were live, every play, not the walk-through-aimlessly type.
- He never complained or made excuses.
- He never caused one second of grief for his teammates.
- He was feared and fearless.
- He was relentless.
- POUND-FOR-POUND, HE WAS THE STRONGEST PLAYER IN THE WEIGHT ROOM.
- POUND-FOR-POUND, THE STRONGEST ON-FIELD PLAYER IN THE LEAGUE.
- When he was told he had to play both ways, he said, *"Great. All I want to do is play."*
- He never said a word to anyone on the field. No swearing, no theatrics, no punk behavior ever.
- He had an unrivaled work ethic.
- He was beloved by his teammates.
- Not one recruiter ever looked at him – because of his height, but he never resented those who moved on to the CFL. He enjoyed the success of others.
- He always put the team first.
- He never cared about his stats. He never bugged anyone about how many tackles, sacks, etc.
- Covered in cement dust, he ran from his car to the change room so he would not be late for practice.
- He respected the game.
- He respected his team.

- He never embarrassed himself or the team.
- He was intensely loyal.
- He truly loved the game – his actions proved it, not his words.

In summary, Vince Valvano was a silent warrior – relentlessly committed to reaching full potential and making an impact. He is the reason that sports exist. He is the motivation that personally drives me to develop more Vince Valvanos. There is no guarantee that the Vince Valvano Award will be given out. No entitlement, just earn it. The criteria: **S**ize, **S**peed, **S**tamina, **S**kill, **S**trength and the sixth "**S**" to make it complete – **C**haracter.

Tracy Hart, the first (original) X Fitness female graduate, was the first female recipient of the Vince Valvano Award. In six months, she transformed her body and mindset into iron will. Like with Vince Valvano, the reason was a molten-lava soul of a lifter. Not a miracle pill. Not a miracle diet. Not a miracle workout program. Just a blast-furnace force soul.

$$\infty$$

The gym is a place where you can't be let down, disappointed, or frustrated by uncommitted teammates or mail-it-in co-workers. The gym is a place where you depend on self ... where you stand on your own. Independence replaces dependence.

Chapter 40.28

X-Fitness Welland "The gym will not recognize the age of entitlement. You can't add the gym as a friend. Iron will not lower itself to conform with the social pressures to transform into a divided self – a fragmented personality that rewards laziness, tolerates incompetence and accepts mediocrity for the sole purpose of not losing friends"

— From the 4th & Hell Series.

August 15 at 5:36pm · Like · Comment

👍 14 people like this.

Chapter 33.5 – 38.5
2010 A.D.

Soul erosion corrodes the spirit.

Imagine parenting over 600, 18-25-year-olds. In your sightline every day. All day. Now, imagine parenting over 600, 18-25-year-olds who want to play with guns.

Teaching and coordinating two community college law-enforcement programs for two decades rots the soul. Decays the spirit. Intellectual, emotional and spiritual putrefication. Social isolation. No profession attracts a wider range of personalities. College law-enforcement programs are a unique kind of Academic Darwinism – survival of the misfits, unfit and a few fit. Everyone survives.

Policing attracts extremes, a sad fact corroborated by empirical evidence. The mentally healthy to the mentally deeply unhealthy, functional and dysfunctional, the dedicated, the degenerate, the upbeat and the deadbeat. An accomplished student with a Master's degree in theology, and a potential Unabomber in the same 200-plus lecture hall, on any given day.

One reason for the bizarre dynamics is the scope of the police playing field – light and dark, good and evil. The world of crime-fighting is a limitless arena that attracts limitless participants – and limitless personalities.

The other reason is "open admission." Open admission to Ontario's colleges is legislated by the government. A combined make-work project and boot camp/inmate rehab/open-detention facility for those who have not yet been caught – the undetected. Open-admission is supposed to replicate life – equal opportunity, exercise of free will, decision to take the shot or not, along with a natural struggle to fortify the weak, all for the grand purpose of strengthening the team called "planet Earth" – the global society. Wo/mankind. No one is left behind in the academics race. Everyone's a winner.

But in reality, a campus full of those who have slipped through the investigative cracks. Minimum entry standards, high school diploma, or not. Ability to read and write, or not. Mandated soft curriculum – the equivalent of steroids – academic performance-enhancers – hard work not required. Delusion.

Open-admission teaching should come with a Surgeon General's warning: "Teaching open-admission community college, police wannabes will rot the mind," – beneath a color photo of a decomposing brain. Performance limits, intellectual restrictions. A ceiling to what you can teach. Intense reps – teaching the same material over and over to the same people, over and over. A cultural phenomena – seemingly the exact same 600-plus every year. No change.

There is some merit in the philosophy – open admission leads to open graduation – but neither opens doors. A college diploma does not guarantee a gun, bullets and salary. Turnstile academics.

When you and your employer don't share the same philosophy, you have three choices – assimilate, leave, or fight for change. I chose the obvious, which led to the inevitable.

Blending into a crowd, packed in tight, tied to the pack leader is actually not a choice. Assimilation is the kidnapping of the soul. The divided soul of a lifter, a few real parts mixed with strangers. *"Let it go. Relax. Have a beer. Ignore him. He's just a giant asshole."* We have been duped into believing that "letting it go "is the answer to internal peace and harmony in the workplace and in life. Letting it go is bullshit. Misleading. And letting it go at the wrong time softens, weakens – mushifying body, mind and soul.

Assimilating was never an option. Instead, I became the anabolic agent of academics, a volatile mixture of street-level prostitution, snake-oil salesman and miracle marketer. Quadrupling enrolment from 150 to over 600. Depending on perspective, explosive growth or explosive decomposition.

The secret to recruiting is delivering on the promise of life-altering experiences. Attracting anyone – customers, students, players, friends, spouses ... any relationship – is the promise of fireworks. And a track record for detonation. Explosive experience, explosive growth.

SUMM – **S**ubjectively, **U**nique **M**eaning equals **M**emorable. Guaranteeing and delivering memories packs them in. Anywhere. Business, school, sports – professionally and personally. Good memories go viral. Great memories attract.

"WHO WANTS TO SEE AN AUTOPSY?!?!?!"

Shameless self-promotion. Shameless audience-arousal.

Getting a crowd reaction to rival the Shea Stadium hysteria that welcomed the Beatles to America is simple – exploit the suffering of others. Fixation with autopsies is a disease – an incurable morbid curiosity. A sinister mindset that ignores the fact that someone's life ended, usually prematurely, violently and senselessly.

"WHO WANTS TO BE ON THE SWAT TEAM?!?!?"

Obsession with guns and uniforms stems from the inner abyss – the psyche beneath the "vacant" sign. The psychological void that cannot be filled with self-security. The deep emptiness that can only be filled with artificial identity and synthetic layers of false protection.

2010 **A.D.** – **A**rmed and **D**angerous. **A**ge of **D**elusion. Not just age of entitlement, age of skewed reality. Misguided souls who have never been led. Misled. Students wasting opportunities, hiding their talents, littering classrooms with crumpled gifts and shredded blessings. The greatest intellectual energy invested into figuring out how to get the most by doing the least, how to circumvent the process, how to detour around the natural struggle. A culture of apathy – lethargy lingering in the hallways like the stench of dead bodies in the morgue.

Mothers and fathers calling me, shielding their 20-year-olds from reality.

"Johnny says you played SWAT team again and he didn't get picked. Again!"

"Is Johnny there? Put him on the phone."

"He's in the middle of a computer game."

Leadership has been replaced by friendship. Leaders abdicating their responsibilities and demoting themselves to "friends." Parents are friends with their children. Teachers are friends with students. Coaches are friends with players. Bosses are friends with their employees. Everyone refusing to grow up. Parents want to act like children, teachers want to act like students, coaches want to act like players. The role-reversing self-demotion has led to social chaos – children raise children, students teach students, players coach players, employees manage employees.

History will write a sad commentary on the early 21st century, the era where alleged mature, fully-functioning adults turned into approval junkies, counting cyber-friends as a legacy-measurement.

Arken Smith Just reached 5,000 friends. I had to start dumping a few hundred today.

October 15 at 4:13pm · Like · Comment

21 people like this.

Then 25 more "adults" pleaded not to be dumped.

Twitter. Lowering IQ with less than 140 characters. Adults following adults like sheep, breathlessly announcing their real-time beer-commercial existence.

HYPOCRITE !!!

The street-fight between the morally right and wrong. Packing and cramming students into lecture halls, knowing that the selection process for the big leagues is a filter through which only a chosen few will creep.

Contrary to popular belief, the soul of a lifter is not always a congenial, jovial, chuckling, back-slapper. The soul of a lifter can be a miserable bastard. A name-caller. Like a referee-induced coaching rage, the inner voice can raise the decibels to iPod max, ear-bleeding volume – reminding the victim of the perils when the only career growth is hypocrisy.

"Do you still work here?"

The soul of a lifter is a **SMS** expert – **S**hort **M**essages, **S**oul-driven.

"Still." Not, *"How's work?"* Uses short jabs, just enough impact to remind ... fight or flight. The soul of a lifter chooses every word for a reason. Purpose-driven SMS. *"Still"* – a caution – beware of the motionless life.

One, lone college teacher, fighting for change, trying to slow the rotation of the academic turnstile is the equivalent of stepping in the ring and fighting yourself. No opponent. Shadow boxing. Throwing bombs at an imaginary opponent. Fighting the non-fight. Knowing and believing that the minor leagues are an essential farm system ... but also knowing it only matters when there is legitimate hope. Otherwise it becomes bush league, a place that has a parking limit. Overtime parking in the bush leagues has a price that can't be calculated in dollars and sense.

There's a crooked line between real hope and false hope, between empowering and enabling. Positioning is the key. Which side to take? The answer is not hard to see. Recognize when the fight is over. Look for signs – darkness ... lights turned off. Emptiness ... no one left in the stands.

Soft leadership is an oxymoron. Misleadership. The softening of social will through misguided, artificial connections. Meaningless connections. Purposeless connections. Social UnDarwinism – building a culture where the weak will not only survive where they will be led to deeper weakness.

Soft training is an oxymoron. Athletic UnDarwinism. Survival and artificial progression of the weak. Building a culture that embraces mediocrity, rewards ineptitude and doesn't just ignore incompetence ... celebrates it.

Soft education is an oxymoron. Academic UnDarwinism, survival and advancement of the intellectually weak and emotionally fragile. Setting them up for failure ... bush leaguers practicing in the big leagues – without a hope of ever playing.

Exhaustion. Fatigue worse than heavy megasets without rest. Trying to figure out whether I was an accomplice in pushing the unsuitable and unfit across the stage ... or an eyewitness to miracles.

∞

The gym has off-the-chart self-expectations. The gym sets the highest bar for itself. And for others. An equal exchange of expectations. No one is exempt from the gym's lofty standards.

The gym is fearless. It will not settle, compromise, surrender, or give in to the pressures of heavy weight. It does not celebrate mediocrity, apathy, lethargy.

Chapter 40.29

Chapter 40
Raging Soul Of A Lifter

The myth of "positive thinking."

Positive thinking is isolated. It has to be connected to set the soul of a lifter on fire. By itself, positive thinking is a match that hasn't been struck. There has to be something to strike the match. A problem. A need ... a compelling need. Misery. The deeper the need, the harder the strike. And when the match strikes ... .

"It won't work out."

The great energy-drain. There is no greater waste of energy than arguing why something won't work without proof of it – evidence. The same four words infiltrate the world of cops, coaches and college: It won't work out. The power of fear and conformity manifests in the "won't work out" argument. Usually, it's conveniently based on history – distorting the past to predict the future. Or romantic reminiscing of what should have been as opposed to what really was. "It's always been done this way," ultimately becomes the rationale for why, "it won't work out." The magnet that pulls us inside the box.

A summer, Canadian, 19-and-under football league is a quadruple oxymoron – a contradiction of season, sport, age-group, and culture ... in today's culture. In 1997, a group of six teams built a league without one penny of public funding. Fundraising and personal pockets. All with one mission – help high school student-athletes move to the next level. More reps, stronger competition, greater opportunity to get recruited by universities. It "worked out." The league is still thriving.

"He won't work out."

Too short, too slow, too fat, too skinny, too unconventional. Like drunk drivers who blow "Over 80" but think they are entitled to drive, the 1997 Niagara Colts summer football team started its first season with over 80 players who were used to star-status on their high school teams. **BMOC** – **B**ig **M**en **O**n **C**ampus. Guaranteed first-stringers not used to competing for their jobs. Entitled.

The over 80 crew included nine quarterbacks and 14 wide receivers. Eight quarterbacks were pretty – the prototype, statuesque, stud quarterbacks. The ninth one wasn't. Tom Denison was lumpier and frumpier ... but he struck the match. Raging soul – and kept throwing fuel on the fire.

The problem with a soul of a lifter on fire is "appearance" – at first glance. Can't see it. Hidden. Concealed. Buried deep down waiting to escape. Waiting to unleash. But get out of the way when the door is kicked in.

Eleven of the 14 receivers were pretty – the prototype, statuesque, stud receivers. The bottom three were not. Steve Smith, John Spencer and Dave Staples were skinnier, minnier ... but they struck the match. Raging souls – and kept throwing fuel on the fire.

Athletic Darwinism cut down the over 80 to 26. The good and the bad left. The ugly stayed, including Tom and the three receivers. They all worked out. And flourished. Two record-breaking seasons. More fireworks than July 1st and 4th combined. Fuel was thrown on the fires by throwing fire – the most extreme amount of passes thrown in single games. A warp-speed no-huddle offense system designed to execute over 80 plays per game – the equivalent of a double-header. With one mission – go deep. Over and over ... go deep.

Tom Denison moved to the next level, winning the Canadian university Player of the Year – twice – becoming the most prolific passer in Canadian university history. Steve Smith played four years at the same Pennsylvania university where Blue Bear #34 graduated from only a few years earlier. St. Jude is a tireless saint.

A soul on fire doesn't have to be pretty. It doesn't have to be attractive. But it will burn up the competition.

Chapter 32/44
Business Darwinism

"X" is symbol of strength and endurance, a lifelong dedication to athletics and fitness, and a commitment to never quit.

Ideas don't just happen. They are planted. *"I'm opening a gym. I'm calling it X Fitness, like my basement."*

Ideas either die a natural death or are given life. Life-and-death decision. The secret to keeping an idea alive is announcing it. Push the idea from the mind out into the world. Let at least one other person hear it. Once it flies through the air waves, it becomes a public announcement. And a personal mission. An assignment.

"You're fucking crazy. Gyms are high-risk. It won't work out."

Test #1. Endure intense external negativity. Fight the bombardment of fear and doubt from the outside. This is the first set of the first business workout – the first test. There's a secret to passing the first test – invite it, fight it and knock it on its ass. Let it come at you. Don't avoid it. Never side-step. Face it head-on. Bring it heavy. Stare it down, don't blink. Then swing. Body shot or head shot, just stop it in its tracks. External negativity is necessary to build strength. Just like loading heavy plates on the bar. The one-punch knock down is important not to show off, but to intimidate the biggest bastard of all.

Maybe I am crazy. Who needs the aggravation? Maybe he's right. What if I fail?

Test #2. Recognize the biggest bastard is the one inside yourself. Self-doubt and inner fear. Tag-team partners. Another attack, this time from the opposite direction. Inside. When you fight, they will try to reciprocate – try to knock you on your ass … for the count. The secret to passing the second test is past training. Trust your training. We are the sum of our training and the **SUMM** of our training. Add up every physical and mental workout. Then, add every **S**ubjectively **U**nique, **M**eaningful, **M**emory. Every set, every rep that has been invested into your body, intellect, emotions and spirit. Use flash cards – replay the memory slideshow of each investor who sacrificed to make deposits in your inner bank's vault. For good measure, press "replay" again. Commit to never wasting past sacrifices – theirs and yours. Then block the punches. And start swinging back.

"They accepted your offer."

Test #3. Don't blink. My "public announcement" was quickly followed by purchasing a building, followed by another assignment: *"We open in three weeks."* A vacant building stood silent, staring. The secret to not blinking is to stare back and go deep.

"Twenty-one days won't work out."

A 21-day makeover. A three-story building – 7,000 square feet gutted and renovated, showers and washrooms built, equipment bought and moved ... transformed into a gym. A three-month job reduced to three weeks. Twenty-one days "worked out." Stretch goals stretch performance. Sixty, full-year memberships sold a week before opening day – while the gym looked like a war zone. Action attracts action.

The secret to opening a business is making the strongest performance demand possible. Like a home-opener, schedule an opening date – April 1, 2001 ... and show up. Train, practice, work your ass off, find some stones ... and show up. Five weeks after the idea was born – X Fitness opened its doors. Failure to appear was not an option. Alternatives invite procrastination. Performance demands demand performance. No excuses, no complaining ... just get the job done. A sense of urgency builds urgency-senses ... survival instincts.

$$\infty$$

Business Darwinism 101: Learning what not to do – how to survive in business – cannot be discovered by researching what-to-do in endless streams of "how to" business books.

The reason businesses fail – the reason any organization or team fails – is no iron will. The unwillingness and incapacity to participate in the natural struggle. Not wanting to fight and not knowing how to fight. Weak will or broken will. No stones ... or lost stones. Bad fighter – not in shape physically and mentally to handle the misery of the natural struggle inherent to every business. Predictable and unpredictable misery, the kind that can buckle the knees or make you a wo/man of steel if you last – when you get through it, when you don't cave in.

Like with any business, gym business survival starts at the top – iron-will mindset. Fearlessness. The real kind, not the artificial kind printed on tattoos and T-shirts. The mind drives the gym; body and soul are its teammates.

All three are connected. All three have to be in top shape to survive – lean and mean. Because when the soul is not in top shape, the other two cannot rebound, they deteriorate and eventually collapse.

The soul of a business is not artificial and not superficial. The soul of a business is neither nourished nor undernourished, fit or unfit, healthy or unhealthy. But it can become dysfunctional. A lost soul of a business will always be searching. A tortured soul of a business will always be crying for help. A divided soul of a business will always be picking up pieces and trying to paste them back together. A pre-occupied soul of a business will not grow properly. The broken soul of a business will eventually die.

∞

Business expertise will never be fully learned and understood unless you invest your own money in your own business. It is impossible to fully understand business until you feel the gut-wrenching knots-in-your-stomach stress of trying not to lose every dollar – every penny – you own. I have studied business formally and informally. I earned a Master's degree with a major in organizational studies and leadership. I have read volumes of business books. I have made organizations that I did not own, very successful. But nothing – nothing prepared me for owning a gym. I have never lived the emotions I've felt owning a business that risked every penny of my family's money. Armed robbers, 9-1-1 calls, 4th and 10 on our own one-yard line, parenting 600 college students, trying to make muscles … raising three daughters. Nothing caused the same choking stress as being in business. Not even close.

Spare me the bullshit of MBAs and titles earned in other people's organizations. When it's not your money on the line, you're getting a half-assed business education. Sure you're learning – but not the deep stuff.

Starting a business from scratch, with your own money, keeping it open, and making it grow are three separate concepts, but they're connected by one secret – Business Darwinism. Survival of the fittest. Surviving the natural struggle and thriving from it. Business strategy is a survival manual. The key is understanding the natural struggle. Knowing what it is, what it does, how to rise above it before it beats you mercilessly.

Endless lessons-learned, the deep insights from dumb-ass mistakes and half-assed thinking. Blunders and business IQ are directly proportionate …

business IQ skyrockets if the fumbling and bungling set up an internal **RADAR** – **R**ational, **A**nti-**D**umb-**A**ss **R**easoning.

To keep the entity alive, a survival manual describing what to do, and more importantly what not to do, has to be followed. A code of conduct that sets the stage. Like with working out and athletics, performance demands make or break a business. They build you up or bust you up. You get what you expect.

Starting a business, leading an investigative team, coaching a team sport, coordinating a college program are connected. In fact, they are identical. System, training, performance. Playbook, make the call, execute – line-up and repeat. Teach, learn, workout, practice, workout, make the cut. Kick-off.

My business manual:

- Face of the program: One head coach, not two.
- A system: One playbook, not drawing up plays in the dirt.
- Training: Practice, simulation ... workout.
- Play-calling: Informed decision-making not ass-grabbing seat-of-the-pants winging it.
- Functional team: Tireless, intellectual, workmanlike staff. Not sluggards with the competence of Curly, Larry and Moe.

All five principles are connected. Deeply connected. A manual that develops human resources to full potential, that reaches higher and makes the biggest impact possible. Because if a business fails to make an impact, it will feel the full impact of Business Darwinism.

∞

The secret to staffing a business is to replicate a sports team – try-out, workout, game-day. Practice, prepare, perform. Repeat. The process has to be tough enough to separate the strong from the weak yet give the weak a chance to get stronger. Growth opportunities. Employee efficiency is directly proportionate to the quality and quantity of available growth opportunities. Organizations that offer none will atrophy like sagging unused muscle.

"Have respect, earn respect, get respect."

When the business is in its infancy, giving choices invites the wrong calls. The wrong choices will be taken. Guaranteed. Because wrong choices are easier. Much easier. Like a head coach, the owner has to call the plays until the players are trained and prove they can call their own plays.

An audible is an "in-the-blink-of-the-eye play-calling change." A play is called, then you check to see if it's smart or stupid. Keep the call – or change it … audible. The first audible at X Fitness was to take down the, "Have respect…" sign – one of the traditional gym signs that builds walls between business and customers. The respect sign wasn't just imbecilic customer service, it was a sign of things to come – a message to the play-caller to smarten-up … fast. It was a sign that said: Be serious. Are you out of your mind handing over business play-calling to a rookie play-caller? Have you lost all your judgment? Take back play-calling immediately!!

Gyms haven't changed much in 40 years. A grumpy bodybuilder posing as a customer service rep standing behind a counter, eating chicken, barking rules and pointing to signs listing approved and prohibited conduct. The warmth and inspiration of a prison camp. Never hire anyone who treats humans as chain gang members. Protocols and code of conduct have to correspond directly to the level of customer maturity. Posting orders is for the military.

The insulting sign was taken down 30 minutes after it was posted – but it took a while longer before the real message sunk in. Experimentation is the cornerstone of innovation. But never experiment with play-calling. Play-calling in sports or real life is an art – a science. It doesn't just happen. Takes a lot of experience – decision-making under fire. Play-calling responsibility is relinquished and delegated only after you teach it and the quarterback learns it – after mastering the pressure of his/her own job. Never pass the play-calling ball because you want free time to do something else.

Even though messages travel at the speed of sound, sinking in happens slower. The key is to speed it up. The miracle of word-speed – word that breaks the sound barrier – news that travels at warp-speed. Good and bad, news travels faster that the speed of sound. Sonic blasts resonate each time the sound barrier breaks. News that lacks meaning fades away into oblivion – good or bad, meaningless news is erased. But meaningful news is stored – and keeps vibrating.

Customers have limitless gigabyte capacity for gym selection. Choices lead to random selection. The secret to increasing gym membership is reduce the choice. Make it a no-brainer – only one gym to choose. Then, word-of-mouth connects to the 66% conformity rule. Say something loud enough and long enough ... **BS** Reps – make a **B**old **S**tatement ... and repeat it.

The best way to reduce choice is by branding. Business brand starts with personal brand. A gym needs a business narrative, BS that says: You can trust us – you will get better performance here, and your performance will get better. The fastest way to build a compelling business narrative is to transfer a human being's compelling personal narrative to the business. The face of the program is the human connected to the image of the business. The secret to selecting the best human to be the face of the program is track record – the most extensive bio wins. Choose the bio that speaks the loudest. Then make a bio-transfer – the person's history to the business. Transferring extensive experience and expertise to the new entity results in a business narrative that screams, "CREDIBILITY and INTEGRITY." Successful bio-transfer is the evidence that proves the case: Our gym is the only one you must select.

S/he who asserts must prove. Customers are expert lie detectors. Businesses have to keep passing the Business Polygraph Test. Bio-transfer is the key to passing each test – make a BS ... and stick to the story. Bio-transfer builds trust.

The most powerful brand, and the one that spreads quickest in the fitness industry, is a combination of street smarts and book smarts. No combination makes a more potent, more viral brand. No other brand stamps harder, moves faster, and makes a bigger impact. Reality IQ – evidence of professionalism, presence and performance.

Performance is the track record used by customers to analyze the Business Polygraph Test results. Customer mindset. Iron-will customers.

Professionalism is an opinion formed by customers based on the absence of negatives – bungling amateurism. The absence of Three Stooges and Keystone Cops antics.

Presence is the capacity to captivate. Prolonged passionate attention. The ability to hold an audience's attention – one person or a mob. The science of not boring another to death. Being memorable. Being different. The key is relevance. Being interesting doesn't just happen. Interest has to fill a void in the listener's mind.

A high score in reality IQ eventually leads to an MBA – Mended Business Asshole. Learning from having been an asshole and/or making the infinite half-assed, ass-backward, dumb-ass mistakes.

"How much asshole experience do you have?" should be the lead-off job interview question because no one is immune from assholism. The key is not becoming an assholaholic. What matters is what you learn from being an asshole. Lesson-learned insights start with asshole recognition. Identify it. Admit it. Confess it. Correct it. Graduate with an MBA.

Confession heals the soul, restoring peace and harmony – temporarily. Until the next screw up.

Is the customer always right? No. If you believe that, you will go broke. "Unruly customer" is an oxymoron. Customers who act like barbarians are not customers. They are liabilities. They are poisonous. Malignancies who spread toxins with force and equal distribution. They are unwanted guests. Prohibit entry of assholes. Regulating access regulates income.

$$\infty$$

Life-altering experiences attract. To survive, a gym has to be a benefit-driven business. Don't sell memberships, build an experience – a life-altering experience – and they will come. Same as any type of recruiting – college, sports, any place that needs to attracts members. How you look in tight clothes, minimal clothes, or no clothes will not guarantee gym success. No one gives a shit what you look like. If they do, be suspicious – LOSER ALERT. What customers care about is what they want to look like and what they want to feel like.

Me-first flex-texts – those self-absorbed, narcissistic Facebook posts that expose skin alongside breathless announcements that oatmeal was replaced with a high-fiber drink, attract a small population to your gym – a subculture … not enough business to survive. A successful marketing campaign starts with giving evidence of developing others. Selling your altruistic track record – your coaching resume … your professional experience in mentoring, coaching, teaching – prodding others to unlock their potential. Your past commitment to putting up ladders. The quantity and quality of dreams you've helped to materialize. The size of the impact? What has your impact registered on the world – outside yourself?

Selling fitness is not easy. The key is sell reality and never lie. Never ever distort, fabricate, exaggerate the truth because deceptions make unfriendly ghosts that will relentlessly haunt and torment. Like a grueling workout, just one failed Business Polygraph Test is hard to recover from. The label of business bullshitter is indelible. An unerasable negative brand. Selling fitness is selling work. Selling hardcore fitness is selling HELL – all of which requires a paradigm shift in the mindset of the potential customer. A change of thinking.

Respect the fitness profession by not making false claims. The best message is the simplest: Hard work is needed to start your fitness program and even harder work is needed to stick with it but we will coach you. Sell the connection, not the isolation.

A customer giving your business money is a symbol of deep trust. Accepting their money is a contract. Giving your word that you will deliver. The essence of Business Darwinism – surviving and thriving. The exchange rate – trust and delivery. Intense reps are needed to replicate the exchange rate over and over again and keep it off-balance. Always give more than you receive, more than expected.

Customer development and management is the science of recruiting and retention – the art of customer attraction. The key is the level of **IMOC** – **I**mpact **M**ade **O**n **C**ustomer. Big impacts attract – the benefit, the experience, the rush but the biggest impact any business can make on a customer is giving positive value – more value than they paid for. Makes customers return and talk – a network of business informants.

The golden rule – treat a customer's money as if it were your own. Because that's the objective – to change ownership of money. The exchange must be voluntary. By consent. Willingly given. Otherwise it's a crime. Never mistreat a customer's money. Everyone knows that money is not "the root of all evil." The temptation of the negative exchange rate is – to give less value than what was paid for. The temptation of unearned money, to rip-off, to avoid the natural struggle of attracting customer investment – the temptation of wealth without work. Mistreating customer money is a crime – distrust. Unconscionable breach of trust.

The key to Business Darwinism – never quit.

Build armor and wear it – the secret to surviving in the fitness industry ... any business. Balls of steel. Novocaine in the blood. Ice water in the veins. Willpower. Otherwise, you will collapse – physically, mentally, emotionally, and spiritually. If you don't have the stomach to handle intense pressure, disappointment, agony, horror, anxiety, don't go into business. Keep working for someone else. Stay under the control of someone who is living their dream.

But if you have the capacity and willingness to fight, become your own boss. Start your business. Control your life. Be the driver, not a tailgater. Be a player, not some loud-mouth fan in the stands living vicariously through the lives of the people you are paying to watch. Don't wear a jersey with a millionaire's surname stitched on the back. Make your own jersey – print your own name on it. Don't sit on the couch watching others experience miracles. Live your own miracles.

Business and Fitness Darwinism. Don't be part of the elimination, be part of the selection.

Chapter 44
Culture Shock

Imagine.

You get your dream job while in a nightmare job. The dream job pays only $3,000 annually, the nightmare job pays $100,000. You are 44 years old; you've spent 26 years in professions that never once made you jump out of bed and shout with joy. Make the call.

Part 2.

Both jobs have the potential to make incalculable impact on countless lives. Both jobs put you in-place, where you belong. On fire. Not just moving people, pushing and pulling people uphill. The only difference is that the $3,000 job makes the soul burn with passion. The $100,000 job burns up the soul. Tortures it. Cuts it up into puzzle pieces. Make the call.

Part 3.

Imagine never having made a decision based on money – but knowing the cost of following your passion ... taking pay cuts with every career change, never accepting any job or any challenge knowing what the starting salary was, working for free at jobs that paid others doing the same job hundreds of thousands. A habit of following passion, not compensation ... not pension. Fearless of financial risk. Now make the call.

Part 4.

The dream job and the nightmare job are located the same distance from your front door. Just opposite directions. No moving. No transplanting. Now make the call.

Offensive coordinator at an American university is a dream job for a Canadian football coach who's used to working for free in a nightmare reality – a culture that invests a fraction of its resources into a sport that, in the United States, is synomomous with religion. The odds of a Canadian beating out eight competitors who didn't need a passport to get from home to job every day, were lottery-type. Changing a culture of thinking doesn't just happen.

According to the university head coach, in an interview with the Buffalo media over his new hire: *"The fight wasn't even."* He, *"has hired a guru."* The job offer was a no-brainer. But Culture Shock makes you blink. I didn't ask about salary.

Two months later ... two months of alternating between dream job and nightmare job ... Culture Shock. The annual salary was announced – $3,000 per year. Not month ... year. And the job required full-time commitment. Culture Shock squared. Blink.

"Blinks" are not created equal. $3,000 for a full-time university coaching position is the equivalent of taking advantage of immigrant labour. Foreign work, foreign pay. Here are the lessons learned:

i) "Dream job" is contextual – relative. Wake up from your nightmare before you define anything as a "dream job."

ii) Never ever never act desperate. Never! Desperation doesn't just cloud judgment, it bombs it to pieces.

iii) Read the signs carefully. If something doesn't make sense, it's senseless. It's not meant to be. It only takes a blink of an eye to see senselessness.

But Culture Shock blurs vision. Build up an immunity to Culture Shock or never ever make any calls until you're cured. Recognize the symptoms – confusion, irrationality, sudden personality change, confusion ... and hoping to work magic by trying to turn insanity into sanity through nonsensical rationalization and illogical self-justification.

Stop imagining.

Chapter 52
Soul-Searching

< Back to Messages | Mark as Unread | Report Spam | Delete

Henry Tourden June 25 at 4:16 pm
Hi Gino. My brother want to train but he dont know how to do it !! I want to know how he can gain for to grow. He 75 kg now. What is best routine for week??? What about creatine he needs to grow? You know great product for to obtain better results?? We live in (3,154 miles away.) Thanks for helping.

There is no off-season. Not for working out. Not for getting better. Not for making others better. Not for scrounging. And especially not for soul-searching.

Soul-searching doesn't just happen. Soul-searching is a mysterious mission – an enigmatic work-in-progress. Finding where to go, how to get there, the calls to make, who we really are, what we really want to be, what's holding us back … deciding whether we want to know – need to know – and whether we're giving it our all. Why bother at all? And what happens when – if – the questions are answered?

Soul-searching is an attempt to find the sidelines of the playing field, the boundary that separates right and wrong – the line of demarcation between what we're supposed to do and not supposed to do.

A search warrant would be helpful but it's impossible to get one for soul-searching because one of the requirements is that you know exactly what you're looking for beforehand. No fishing expeditions. Soul-searching needs more than authorization, more than force – you can't just kick in a door and look around. It needs … a lift.

∞

> 40 years of working out **x** 52 weeks
>
> +
>
> 40 seasons of coaching football **x** 30 players per season
>
> +
>
> 15 years of policing **x** 50 co-workers per year
>
> +
>
> 20 years of college teaching **x** 600 out-of-shape wannabe cops per year
>
> +
>
> 10 years in the gym business **x** 6,000 gym members
>
> +
>
> 8,000 Facebook friends ...
>
> _____
>
> **Total**   **INFINITY**

The number of free performance demands add up. And up. And up. Infinity. Endless. And they multiply and spread out of control because I sprinkle on them the strongest fertilizer of all – the unwillingness and incapacity to say, *"No."*

"Can you write a workout program for me?"

"Can you write a diet for me?"

"How can I make (insert body part) bigger?"

"How can I make (insert body part) smaller?"

The equivalent of asking a doctor to: *"Give me a prescription, anything at all ... for free, without doing any tests."*

The myth of "prescribing a workout by distance" – no tests, no evaluation ... no history. Blind, uninformed decisions. A form of madness promoting more madness. It's impossible to just write out a workout program without testing the person – without conducting an investigation. Every solution is a customized cure. Tailor-made. A match that fits the situation. Prescribing a workout blindly has the same outcome as any blind decision – a crapshoot. Donkeys pinning tails – or tales – on other asses. Lotto-workouts – take your chances. Try to beat the odds.

And yet, I don't say, *"No."* Instead, *"How long have you been lifting? What's your max bench for one rep? If I send you a workout, is there someone who can translate for you?"*

There's a crooked line between being a blessing or curse for others and to yourself. There's a blurry line between the reward of helping your fellow wo/man and devaluing what you do to minus-zero. There's a squiggly line between exchange rates – balanced or unbalanced ... the difference between a tank perpetually filled by a reciprocal exchange ... and a tank drained the last drop by a tilted, twisted, lopsided exchange.

A workout prescription without instruction – without coaching – isn't worth the paper it's written on. Real coaching is the greatest gift we can give a person. Turn on a light, flip someone's switch. Bring someone out of darkness and confinement. Release someone's energy – physical, intellectual, emotional, spiritual ... unlock it and free someone of their inner inmate.

The miracle of the gift exchange – giving the gift of iron will automatically returns it. On one condition – it has to be unconditional.

"It's too hard to do. It's never been done." Nine words that instill fear. We've been programmed since entering planet Earth to believe two detaining myths – powers of arrest – that lock up who we are, what we have to offer and what we were intended to do.

Myth #1: Opinions are fact.

Myth #2: Conditions must be attached ... to everything.

We have had definitions drilled into our minds that are nothing more that opinions – speculation ... baseless conjecture that somehow manages to enter "The Rulebook." The life manual that dictates how we are supposed to live. The book written by the misinformed – the agents of social control. The Mind Police. The regimentation that drills how to march in lock-step formation ... to the orders of self-appointed, self-anointed who have trouble running their own lives but have somehow solved the mystery of how everyone else should run theirs.

Definitions of what's "too hard to do" and what "can't be done" are generational – sprouting up, multiplying throughout the ancestor tree ... until someone breaks a branch. The conditional conditioning is a programming nightmare – can't do this unless that happens and if that happens then this must follow. All of which leads to an intricate web of rules that are interpreted by thought-controllers according to need and situation – theirs. Their call is final – no challenge, no instant replay review.

Teach, coach unconditionally. Dispel fear. Share what you know. What is released rebounds. The miracle of the rebound effect – we become what we teach. We develop what we coach. We get shares of what we share.

Searching troubles souls. Troubled souls search.

Chapter 36/48
The Valley of Elah

The secret to winning is "No Secrets."

Send a message to your competition – this is what to expect. Don't keep secrets from the opponent. Never hide your strengths. Show them what you've got. Everything. All your strengths. Showcase your power. Never conceal. Today's performance determines tomorrow's. Don't just win – win big. Steam-rolling solidifies the message: Did it once, will do it again. Communicate the expectations – don't beat around the bush. Show them you will go deep ... and go deeper. The expectation of the knock-down capacity of "powerful" is scarier than the actual force. Intimidates. Causes fear. And the opponent's worst enemy is fear.

Fearing competition is a symptom of insecurity, low self-esteem, broken will ... and evidence that evil is winning the game. Evil has scored more points. Miracle comeback needed. Never fear competition, no matter what the source – embrace it. The stronger the better. Instead of fearing stronger competition, rise up to it ... and pass it. Pass a lot and pass quickly. The solution to facing and beating strong competition is simple – just do it better. Get better, keep getting better, become the best at it. Train, train harder, train the hardest. Then out-score 'em. Pile up the points ... run up the score. Play your game, not theirs. Facing the strongest and beating the strongest sends a message.

No one cheers for Goliath. But very few have the stones to throw them at him. Goliath was an asshole of Biblical proportions. Unchallenged ... and untested. He had been awarded the presumption of "unbeatable" without earning it – title of the toughest by default. No one had ever given him a fight. Until David found some stones.

In 2004, X Fitness started a movement to form a community college football league in Ontario ... without any tax-payer money. With the blessing of the local college, a pilot project began. The Niagara X-Men were born. A non-profit organization to help community college athletes get university scholarships. The pilot project started with two teams in season one, expanding to three in season two. The first season ended unceremoniously ... no approval from the college athletic directors to make the league official. Then three games into season two ... silence. Unlike a criminal's right to silence, no response to a proposal is a statement of denial. A non-verbal message – rejection.

Rejection is not a crisis – it's an opportunity.

By conventional measures of success, the Niagara X-Men were models of achievement in season two. Undefeated, three wins, no losses, combined score of 117-14 – in Canada. A monster. But the team was not improving, they were decaying. Mistakes, wild celebrations, trash-talking. The needle was moving up the asshole-meter. Goliath was acting out, bored of the non-competition. I knew the cure – Culture Shock.

Sometimes you have to cross a bridge to get to the next level ... to get stronger, fight someone stronger. Don't pick on someone your own size, pick on someone bigger. Cross a border. Find a Valley of Elah. Find an unruly monster looking for a fight. Look into an abyss. Google "Goliath," send a message ... and lay down the gauntlet.

A simple search can find not just one Goliath – five. Five American university football teams lined up to fight my monster Canadian football team – happily sending directions to their homes, in the valley. Season two became season one of Niagara X-Men in the USA.

Miracles have two main ingredients – hopelessness and help ... the jaw-dropping divine intervention kind. But the real trick is the **2-Ps** – **P**ositioning and **P**assion. Listen, then move. Get hungry – deeply hungry ... receive the message – catch it. Then go in motion. But before you piss off Goliath, get in the weight room. Lift heavier. Get bigger, faster, stronger ... especially in the mind.

The irony of the post-modern Goliath – sympathy. And advice. After Goliath beat the piss out of us, free consultation – without scrounging: *"Man ... you're not just coaching football, you've got to change a whole culture of thinking."* The equivalent of: Man ... David. You've got to get bigger stones.

∞

"The sad part is that 99% of life is unremarkable." Guy, mid-20s, sitting in a booth at a coffee shop – talking to his friends, also in their mid-20s, loud enough for me to hear – two booths over. The real sad part will be if he doesn't change – doesn't turn the percentage around.

Darkness is a failure to turn on the switch. Broken switch.

Fix the switch. Change the dialogue – inside and out.

Never say you can't do something. Don't listen to anyone who says you can't. Never say something is too hard. Tune out anyone who says it is. Never convince yourself that a challenge is unconquerable. It's not.

Never accept roles imposed on you. Make your own. Control your destiny. Don't let others control it.

Never accept bad news. Change it. Never accept losing. Let it burn a fire. Get up and fight when you have to. Stop fighting when the fight is over.

And never get soft. Build strength. Build armor. Otherwise, life will pound the piss out of you.

It's impossible to stay the same. We get stronger or weaker, better or worse, but we don't stay the same. It's impossible because every experience changes us. Every thought, every action, every reaction … every inaction changes us. Reinvent by adding-on. Shed your skin. Build an addition. Change. Get better. Get stronger. Reinvention is painful. So is the failure to reinvent.

Be a warrior.

$$\infty$$

The gym is enlightening. It lets you shine, wants you to shine. But the gym is demanding. It expects you to go deep, reach higher, break limits, fight Goliath, beat Goliath. The gym is not an enabler. It empowers.

Chapter 52/26
Guilt

The secret to winning is to outlast them. Make them fear fatigue. Nothing intimidates more than a motor with no "off" switch. Make them blink and winning is guaranteed.

The gym is a pain-in-the-ass. So is iron. So is the soul of a lifter. Stubborn, insistent, extreme. Uncompromising, unforgiving. Unrelenting expectations. Never allowing a free pass. Having to earn every ounce of muscle and every drip of fat melted. Not once can they make it easy. Not once can they tolerate sloth and laziness.

Leon Festinger is not a household name but he solved the mystery of the soul – by defining the miracle of "cognitive dissonance" – burning internal conflict brought on by acting contrary to personal beliefs. Gut wrenching guilt fueled by personal betrayal. The raging internal war between what should be, but is not, and what should have been, but wasn't. Self-disservice. Kicking oneself in the ass. The price for not investing in the moral bank.

Although Festinger did not mention Italians and Roman Catholics by name, some people are prone to extreme bouts of cognitive dissonance, without cause. Habitual guilt – cruel and unusual punishment. Neural pathways of shame formed by intense reps of, *"Che Vergogna!"* A punishment far exceeding the crime and with no constitutional appeal.

The myth of the "tortured soul." The soul does not torture – the lifter is the torturer. The myth of the "lost soul." The soul knows the direction … is never lost. The lifter gets lost. The intended receiver of messages gets lost when messages are dropped, fumbled, batted down, or blocked by interference. Or erased, marked unread, or never finished being read because the eyes were taken off the message. Evil plays dirty.

Lifelong battles are exhausting. Lifelong battles versus fat, functionalism, inner peace … all take a toll on the soul. Senseless wars need peace treaties. Someone has to intervene to bring the parties together and draw up an accord. A settlement. Armistice. Shake hands.

It's impossible to work out for 40 years uninterrupted, without steroids, without a stage, without a conventional prize. It's not possible to lift heavy and heavier for 40 years. It's not possible to reverse the digital age – to get leaner and meaner at 52 than you were at 25 … unless something deeper than passion is at play.

The literal, formal Italian translation for "bullshit" is, "merda di toro," but the informal translation makes the biggest impact – "porcheria." With the right tone of voice and body language, and weight transfer, the impact grows. Impacts accumulate.

Impacts go deep. A challenge makes us bigger or smaller. A challenge makes us shrink or stretch. It depends on mindset. Mindset is the difference between doers and watchers, players and spectators, strong and weak. Mindset separates ordinary from extraordinary. Attitude separates pack leaders from the pack.

Mindset determines how we handle the three toughest tests – failure, pressure and isolation. How do we handle bad news? What is our reaction to disappointment? And can we work alone, especially when we have too much time to think?

Iron addicts blend religion and iron. The gym is a sanctuary of light and hope and spirit for the soul of a lifter.

Chapter 40.38

Chapter 18-52
A-Game

"Just when I think I'm out … they pull me back in."

Michael Corleone and Silvio Dante both understood evil's tireless, workman-like capacity. Endurance, stamina. Evil never retires. No pension, no buy-out, no 15% seniors' discount. Evil defies age. Knock evil down, knock evil out, evil gets back up … right back into the dark alley. Knife fight, gun fight, fist fight, pursue swinging, sand throwing, name calling … any conflict to break your focus, to divert your attention, crush your spirit, crack your concentration. Evil's intended purpose is simple – to stop yours.

"Hey buddy, it's been a long time … you still working here? I'm retiring soon. Can you get me a part-time teaching job?"

"Life-saving" is not created equal.

"Teaching job???? You've ripped off the taxpayers by staring at the clock waiting for quitting time for almost 30 years. Now you want to rip off their money AND their minds? What have you done to better yourself? Have you ever even stopped by a university? Don't bullshit me … all you want is summers off, weekends off, statutory holidays off, take the easy road, pay some taxes and then drop dead without having done a fucking hard thing in your life. Is this all you want out of life? Malingering? The soft life? You were lazy when you were a rookie cop now you expect me to believe you've changed? You were smarter than any rookie I ever trained but you pissed it away. Flushed it down the toilet. Is this what you teach your kids? How many kids do you have one, four, five … "

"Two."

"What if they became like you? Would you be happy? Path of least resistance. Barely get by. Coast through life. You're a zombie for fuck sakes. You want your kids to kill their dreams like you killed yours? Retire then die? Have you picked out your casket yet? Ever wonder what happened? Zombied-out at 46. What year did you die? 1984, 85. Now you rot in an office staring at the clock, counting days to retirement, wishing your life away. YOU RETIRED 30 YEARS AGO.

"Only 26 ... I've been on the job 26 years."

"How old are you? 45, 55 ... "

"49."

"Now you want me to put you in front of 200 college kids so you can rot their brains? Make a life while you still can! Dream bigger for once in your life. Tell yourself you have wasted one career and use that to inspire your ass to not waste the rest of your life. You have no passion for teaching. You have no passion period. You just want an income to supplement your pension. Be honest with yourself for the first time in your life. Stop bullshitting yourself. Stop being a pathetic liar. Do what you really want to do. There ... I just saved your life."

"No argument. You're right. Was that your A-game?"

"No. B-minus."

Recidivists. Repeat offenders.

Coward is not an insult ... not name-calling. Cowardice is a disease ... a habit that no one corrected, learned behavior. Cowardice: The habitual sprinting at warp-speed away from challenges, struggle, and/or honesty. Cowardice is a failure of character but not a character fatality because it is changeable. Cowards can transform. Miracle comebacks happen every day. Courage is not a DNA molecule. Courage does not just happen. It's taught, learned, practiced, processed, internalized. Infinite cycles of failed tests and passed tests. Courage is the habit of standing up to what needs to be stood up to and fighting what needs to be fought. The difference between courage and cowardice is free-will fitness – how free will is exercised. But it's impossible to exercise free will without getting your hands dirty. Artificial, insular, pin-bubble worlds will not flex free will.

Underachiever is a special kind of coward. A term invented by an excuse-maker to cover up the truth, darken it. An expert whiner. The model martyr. Inventing the word was the biggest achievement of an attention-seeker drowning in self-pity, unwilling and incapable of accountability and responsibility.

Iron is the best pain-reliever. Here's a remedy for darkness – innovate. Be creative and design an off-the-chart workout. Put down the book, do not go by the book, and challenge yourself to the most agonizing physical workout that you can handle – not what you think you can take ... what you really can take.

Start with self-dialogue – the myth that talking to yourself is bad, is bullshit. Reminding yourself to, *"GET OFF YOUR ASS!!!"* is not only acceptable, it's a survival mechanism. Then get pissed off ... at whatever is killing your body with unused, overflowing cortisol. Then grab a bar. Turn on the iPod. Use your imagination. Design the world's longest dropset. And set a world-record for the longest megaset ever. Tell people to get the hell out of the way. Shut off the damn cell phone. Log off social media. Stare at the iron – think positive thoughts ... *Fuck you!!!* – then lift. And keep lifting. Hold on until your arms are ready to explode. Snap a death grip on the bar – do not let go. Do what you have never done before. Pass it!!

Beat the piss out of pain. Push it – drag it ... lock it up. Then repeat. Count to ten, or five. Or just lift with no rest – set after set after set ... set a record. Do the hardest thing that your mind can dream up. Empty ... the ... tank – for real. Not the bullshit kind – the lie ... the half-tank deception. The one where you act like you're in agony – but you're not. Just lift. Shut up and lift. No theatrics. When you cannot lift another ounce, go hit the bags. Heavy bags, speed bags – just pound them. Soak your clothes in sweat. Then lace up your running shoes. Turn up the iPod volume ... and run. Shut off the TV. Turn off "Dancing with the Stars" and look up – at the real stars. Run and stare at the stars. Looking at the stars – that's when soul-searching starts. Then move faster. Longer strides. Run harder. Don't leave a dry spot on your clothes. Let sweat burn your eyes. Don't dry it off. Convince yourself that sweat can't burn your eyes. Feel exhausted. Not empty. Exhausted.

At that point, you will have searched your soul. Not just looked around – dug deep and investigated. You'll have discovered evidence of three conclusions: That you really knew very little about yourself, that you can be a real tough bastard when you make your mind up to be a tough bastard, and that you have lots more to learn about yourself.

Chapter 40.39

Chapter 51.51
Guardian Angel

If evil wants a fight, give it one. Call evil out. Go in the alley ... but fight hard. Don't just dance around. Don't back down. Don't blink. Move forward. Charge forward. But don't blink. Make the performance demand of all performance demands.

Repeated exposure to death and destruction on the policing frontline turns your soul into iron. A blessing or a curse? Will that won't bend or a bent will? Either way, the usual Culture Shocks have no effect on the infrastructure. None. Complacency. Until, caught off-guard by one that slipped through the cracks. A different kind – one with the ability to take me somewhere in my head where I had been only once before. It fell on me in four parts – like a scary movie. A 116-second horror flick.

Scene 1: Conventional mail delivered to my house.

Scene 2: "Jail Inmate" printed under the return address – a federal penitentiary in Virginia.

Scene 3: *"... and in 1985 a Guardian Angel appeared in my life ..."* written on page one of the six-page hand-written letter.

Scene 4: Signature – #34 Blue Bears.

The End.

"Fuck 'em all. Fuck their dreams."

Congratulations, Satan ... you motherfucker. You did what couldn't be done. You penetrated the hardened soul. Like a sledgehammer crashing a boulder, smashing it to pieces. The type of shattering that can't be re-built overnight. It's only the second time you did it – the second time you got through. You know the secret – information that the human mind can't process. Like the death of a father. No, not the death … the way a father died. The unexpected. The no-way-humanly-possible-to-forecast way. The unimaginable.

Unthinkable. #34 was dead. Wasting away in the Pen while the soul of a lifter uses a pencil and paper to bare his tortured soul.

Being helpless to take away someone's pain does strange things, like a fictitious choking feeling. For a moment I felt that something was strangling me. Squeezing my throat. My mind was looking for someone – something – to fight with. Then it stopped almost as quickly as it started, replaced by a darkness. Not the kind you're engulfed in while running on pavement at midnight, imagining the power of the stars and letting out a silent primal scream: *"THANK YOU GOD ALMIGHTY FOR LETTING ME DO THIS EVERY DAY!"* Words of gratitude that mix with a Zombie set to provide a few seconds of peaceful rush.

No. This darkness is a place that your mind drags you to – a place that won't let itself be explained, dealt with, or reconciled. It's a place that forces you to do one thing – fight the biggest fight you've ever faced. Fight like hell. Anger and regret combined cause the soul of a lifter to mobilize the troops, pound the shit out of evil until it's bleeding so bad that the fight has to be stopped.

High-impact moments – the kind that bares one soul and touches another – are not always an emotional pump. Or an intellectual pump. Or a spiritual pump. Like the positive high-impact moments, the dreaded ones are life-altering. Transformational. A branding event, indelibly etched not only in memory but in psyche. Eye-witnessing a powerful lesson that can never be taught in any classroom – it has to be experienced … being mentored on the science of being human. The greatest challenge of all – trying to feel someone else's pain over yours. Trying to absorb someone else's pain while you desperately search for anything on Earth to absorb yours.

When you fail miserably, a painful lesson is replayed in your brain – you can't absorb someone's pain at the moment of infliction. As much as you try, it can't be done. Pain can be bounced, passed around, handed off, intercepted, fumbled, picked up – but pain can't be taken away right after it's inflicted. The best we can do is ease the pain, the equivalent of ice or heat on a physical injury.

Shared misery, whether it's in the gym, on the field, or in the field makes a powerful connection – a bond, chained together with links of soul-wrenching pain. Pain is a powerful motivator. The pain of this hand-delivered Culture Shock prompted two powerful performance demands – LIVE IT. Live your life! And live it hard!! "Life is too short," was re-defined. Again. The gas pedal was slammed to the floor and riveted down. Second – forgiveness. Forgiveness is, and should be, automatic when shared miseries go deep. But forgiveness is not always strong enough to turn down the volume … .

"Let someone else coach these motherfuckers."

Right after the moment of infliction, we tend to fight for the #1 ranking: My pain is greater than yours. A Guardian Angel would understand.

Chapter 41

Do we mend our soul or does the soul mend us? Three rapid-fire Facebook messages begged the question.

"Who sent them?" Was it evil with its age-old trick, "flattery?" The defensive formation that keeps us in one place, stopping us from moving toward our calling, our full potential ... our destiny? The kind intended to kick the shit out of us when we're down and hurt? Or, was it the soul of a lifter's first therapy session? The first reminder that the assignment is not done yet? Mission incomplete.

| < Back to Messages | Mark as Unread | Report Spam | Delete |

Leon Robinson June 8 at 6:44 pm
Coach. How are you? I was explaining to my wife how much you did for our team and how much you pushed me to be the best on and off the field. AAAAAAWWWWWW Man. Good to connect with you again!

Gino Arcaro June 8 at 10:07 pm
Leon. You, Carlton, everybody at Churchill remind me why I coach. Very proud of what you've accomplished off the field. You guys came from a different era. I miss you guys and the whole Churchill era... bad. It was a great era. You guys were a GREAT team.

Leon Robinson June 9 at 5:45 pm
I've added on to my arts skill set. I remember you worked with me on putting together that textbook cover for McGraw Hill, and it was one of my first published gigs. And years later I'm setting up to release my first art book. I'd like to see your gym and let you meet my boys.

Gino Arcaro June 9 at 11:12 pm
I'll never forget. That book became very special, for many reasons. I have to see your art book. Really want to meet your family.

Chapter 41

< Back to Messages | Mark as Unread | Report Spam | Delete

Kevin Ling June 12 at 9:24 pm
Hi Coach, thanks for getting back to me. You were the reason I played. Can't wait to visit your gym.

Chapter 41

< Back to Messages | Mark as Unread | Report Spam | Delete

Ann Carballo June 14 at 10:51 pm
Thank you for your input into Annel's life at Hill Park High School. It came at a time when a young man needed to be taught fortitude, endurance and commitment. Every practice session has left its mark in Annel's life ... no one knew then that your training and discipline would be transferred through him into the military, all the way to the Afghanistan warzone. May God bless you and your family for every minute that you have invested in my son's life. A very proud and grateful mother. Thank you very much.

Gino Arcaro June 15 at 12:47 am
Mrs. Carballo:
I am deeply honored and deeply touched by your message. I am privileged to have been Annel's coach. Thank you for this message. I will frame it and prominently display it. This came at a time in my life when I questioned why I invested so much into coaching football. Thank you for answering the question.

Chapter 2010.05.31
Exorcism

Isolation, separation ... revelation.

Inner demons are not terminal. They are good news. Bad-ass demons are a sign – a good sign – that something big is in the plans. That's why the opponent becomes vicious ... trying desperately to win a big fight – trying to stop something big from happening. Like change.

When is it time to leave it behind? A soul-searching informant will tell you ... rat out your conscience. When growth stops. Growth opportunities – present or absent. If they let you grow, don't go. If you don't grow, go. Leaving too soon builds regret. Leaving too late builds rage. Not leaving at all builds both.

"Exorcism," derived from the Latin word "exorcismus," is much more than a street-level alley fight between good and evil. It's spiritual warfare. The second letter, X, is the Greek letter for "Chi," the first letter of the word "Χριστός," translated as "Christ." Modern-day exorcism invokes the same Higher Power as in the dark ages when demon-casting was thought to be the last hope of change.

May 31, 2010. A.D. Armed with knowledge ... that shedding skin means to leave everything behind, temporarily, and dangerously pissed off at the demons, the gloves came off – three demons cast out in the span of five hours.

"Demon-casting" is not created equal. Nor does it just happen. It needs an iron-will leader. One that will fight the mob-mentality when it gangs up ... when condemnation becomes the national pastime ... when the 66% rule kicks in. It needs the soul of a lifter who will ensure that demons don't just lose, they get vanquished. Winning is not enough. The score gets run up. Merciless beating. When the soul of a lifter gets pissed off ... total annihilation – bury the opponent and then back in the gym to train for the next fight.

Now ... don't ever say we can't get it done.

Shedding skin. Training in seclusion. Soul-searching ... alone. Peeling and scraping off the old. Connecting to the next level by disconnecting. Controlling the rush by concentrating on the rush, without being in the rush.

Destiny is a work-in-progress.

Isolation, separation … revelation.

Enlightenment doesn't just happen.

The curtain doesn't just lift on its own.

An investigation is needed to discover the clues – answer the soul of a lifter's question, even though asking, *"What did you learn so far?"* is the equivalent of asking an informant, *"What happened?"* Holes and gaps in the story. Order mixed with chaos. Way too much information.

Informants have an intended purpose – make life easier for the investigator … any investigator, any soul-searcher. The unintended purpose – heal the soul.

But the first interview barely touched the surface. Didn't go deep enough. A lot of clarification needed. The next interrogation will get down to business.

$$\infty$$

The gym lives up to the expectation of others – without exception – but never lives up to self-expectations.

The gym is never satisfied. No wild celebrations. The gym shows it has done it before and will do it again – even better.

About the Author

Gino Arcaro is a Canadian football coach and former police officer. During his unique 35-year professional career, Gino has worked as a patrol officer, SWAT officer, detective, college professor and program coordinator.

He is a best-selling policing textbook writer, strength training coach and business owner – founder of X Fitness Welland Incorporated.

Enjoy the book?
We would like to hear from you.

Post a review on Amazon, Goodreads or let us know directly at
reviews@ginoarcaro.com.

Follow Gino on Social Media

GinoArcaro

@Gino_Arcaro

+GinoArcaro

GinoArcaro

Gino's Blog

Follow Jordan Publications Inc. on Social Media
for up-to-the-minute information on Gino and his books

GinoArcaro.Author

@JordanPubInc

+GinoArcaroBooks

More Books by Gino Arcaro

4th & Hell Season 1

"We were David with a Canadian passport, failing miserably at winning just one football game against stars-and-stripes-draped Goliaths." It came down to fourth and hell – a face-to-face showdown. No disguises, no masks, no secret weapons. No one huddled on the sideline. No one huddled on the field. Both sides knew what to expect. No surprises, no guess-work, no mind games. Making the call was a formality. All that mattered was running the play to see what would pass. Someone would execute; someone would be executed.

Selling H.E.L.L. in Hell
from the series Soul of an Entrepreneur

You may be starting out in business or just contemplating making the big decision. Gino Arcaro knows what you're thinking and wants to make sure you know what you're not thinking. His thought-bending tales, while entertaining and steeped in reality, will make the would-be business owner take a second and third look at the situation before jumping in. And, for those already "self-employed," Arcaro offers a unique slant on dealing with day-to-day customer and employee challenges.

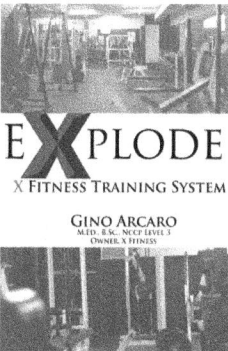

eXplode: X Fitness Training System

Sought after his entire adult life to help others achieve their workout goals, Arcaro put his weight lifting theories and routines into this manual. His "Case Studies," true stories from his 40+ years of working out (completely natural) bring a sense of reality to the average gym-goer who just wants to get in shape, stay in shape, and most-importantly, not quit. No gimmicks, just discussion and formulas that can be tailored to any situation regardless of how long or how intensely one has been working out.

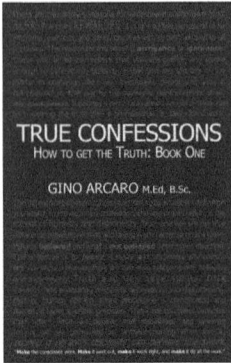

True Confessions

Gino Arcaro relates and upholds a simple fact: "Everyone has a conscience. No exceptions. If you're alive, you have a conscience. The myth of 'no conscience' actually means 'weak or dysfunctional' conscience." Therefore, a truth-seeker must appeal to the conscience, meaning, "make the conscience work out, make it work right, and make it do all the work." True Confessions is a manual for anyone whose job it is to get the truth. For example, Human Resources personnel during the job interview process or Law Enforcement interviewers who can use Arcaro's theories to open a window into the psyche of a suspect under interrogation.

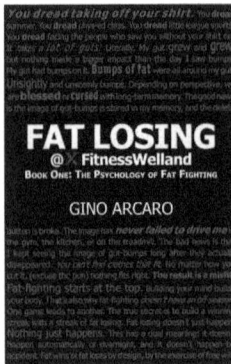

Fat Losing: The psychology of fat fighting

"Waste Mis-management leads to Waist Mis-management"

This is not a diet book. This 40-page eBook explains the most important truth about fighting fat: it begins at the top – literally. Without a proper mindset, no amount of dieting or counting calories will workout. Digesting Fat Losing is the first step to understanding how to change your habits and thinking for once and for all. It contains practical discussions that engage the reader in re-thinking the obstacles that stand in the way of becoming a healthier person. Gino Arcaro, a self-proclaimed "dysfunctional 12-year-old, trying to overcome my obesity," is an expert on the subject. He's written Fat Losing to share what he has learned and practiced for over 40 years.

Be Fit Don't Quit

Full of exercise ideas young children can try on their own or with a parent, this book will rekindle in any adult a love for the simple act of playing. Gino Arcaro has spent his life working out and teaching young adults about the importance of "being fit." He wrote Be Fit Don't Quit to express a tried-and-true message: Exercising is natural and fun. Never quit!

SWAT Offense

By connecting partial concepts that can build any formation, any pass play and any running play to fit the situation, at the line of scrimmage, Arcaro has designed a system that eliminates the need for a conventional playbook that has to be memorized. Memorization is replaced by translation of a simple language. He designed the SWAT offense as a solution to a nightmarish reality of limitations – poor talent and poor resources, a one-man coaching staff, open-admission players, and on top of it all, out-matched opponents…willingly sought out! David constantly calling out Goliath. Arcaro's SWAT offense is the most unique offensive system you'll ever see because it has limitless offense capacity but no playbook. A unique feature of the SWAT Offense is its ties to SWAT Defense.

SWAT Defense

Making the defensive call has never been harder. Coordinators have the greatest challenges in football history. Spread no-huddle offenses, extreme passing, clock-changing rules. More to defend, less time to think. Arcaro's SWAT Defense shows how to beat the spread by forcing the offense to go deep and crack under pressure. "A stress-filled workplace for quarterbacks and receivers leads to an explosion." Central to Arcaro's system is his decision-making model that teaches defensive coordinators and players to make the right calls – those split-second decisions that have to be made about 60 times per game. Making the right call is not easy. Like any skill, defensive decision-makers need guidelines and experience to develop into full potential. A unique feature of the SWAT Defense is its ties to Arcaro's SWAT Offense.

For more free book previews or to purchase Gino's books go to
WWW.GINOARCARO.COM